STEPHEN WARD
SCAPEGOAT

DOUGLAS THOMPSON

STEPHEN WARD

SCAPEGOAT

THEY ALL LOVED HIM... BUT WHEN IT
WENT WRONG THEY KILLED HIM

JOHN BLAKE

Published by John Blake Publishing Ltd,
3 Bramber Court, 2 Bramber Road,
London W14 9PB, England

www.johnblakepublishing.co.uk

www.facebook.com/Johnblakepub **facebook**
twitter.com/johnblakepub **twitter**

This edition published in 2014

ISBN: 978 1 78219 760 7

British Library Cataloguing-in-Publication Data:

A catalogue record for this book is available from the British Library.

Design by www.envydesign.co.uk

Printed and bound in Great Britain by CPI Group (UK) Ltd, Croydon, CR0 4YY

1 3 5 7 9 10 8 6 4 2

Papers used by John Blake Publishing are natural, recyclable products
made from wood grown in sustainable forests. The manufacturing processes
conform to the environmental regulations of the country of origin.

Every attempt has been made to contact the relevant copyright-holders,
but some were unobtainable. We would be grateful if the appropriate
people could contact us.

For Bobby McKew, God bless him

'LET US DRAW AN ARROW ARBITRARILY. IF AS WE FOLLOW
THE ARROW WE FIND MORE AND MORE OF THE RANDOM
ELEMENT IN THE STATE OF THE WORLD, THEN THE ARROW IS
POINTING TOWARDS THE FUTURE; IF THE RANDOM ELEMENT
DECREASES THE ARROW POINTS TOWARDS THE PAST.'

Arthur Eddington, *The Nature of the Physical World*, 1928

CONTENTS

BOOK THREE: DEATH BY SNOBBERY

TIME'S ARROW

'TO BETRAY, YOU MUST FIRST BELONG.'

Harold 'Kim' Philby, 1967

July 1926: Cranford Magna, Dorset, England

It was an hour or more into lights out at the start of the summer term at Cranford School and in the spartan dormitory the teenager's heavy snoring rumbled like tectonic plates before an earthquake. Sleeping to order and timetable isn't easy and the adenoidal pupil was an irritating nuisance.

The murmur of annoyance began from the end of the dormitory and by the time it reached Stephen Ward the order was to slap the snoring boy in the bed beside him: he didn't. Instead, another pupil clambered over his bed and whacked the culprit on the head. It was a dull thump, yet enough to fracture the boy's skull. The injury was discovered before breakfast. It was a serious business and someone had to pay the price. If no confession, the dormitory would be punished en masse.

Only open for three years in Cranford Magna, near Wimborne Minister, the school (motto, prescient for one young pupil: *Nisi dominus frustra*: 'unless the Lord is with us, it is in vain') prided itself on being run as one of Britain's most esteemed public schools. So, with an intent at grandeur as misconceived as its illusion, the game had to be played that way. Justice had nothing to do with it.

Needs must; discipline had to be seen to be done. Like the other pupils, the 13-year-old Stephen Ward feared being considered a sneak. He knew who was responsible but stayed quiet. He was in the bed next to the injured boy. He was selected as the guilty party. He was caned, eight of the very, very best, in front of the entire school.

Some long time after, a housemaster told him: 'We knew you hadn't done it. Someone had to get whacked, it just happened to be you...'

Stephen Ward hadn't told, he'd done the *right* thing and played the established English game. In the dormitory he was, he said, a famous fellow.

ON SCHOOL TIES

'WE LOOK ON PAST AGES WITH CONDESCENSION,
AS A MERE PREPARATION FOR US... BUT WHAT IF WE'RE
ONLY AN AFTERGLOW OF *THEM*?'

J.G. Farrell, *The Siege of Krishnapur*, 1973

London, 1963

It was, of course, after events had become public that the truth, unlike the grief it caused, became a private matter. Yet truth, always tricky to detect in the moment, can be remarkably less elusive over time. The passion and desperation to guard secrets has diminished and the entropy around them finds some order; there's a chance to discover what's hiding in other people's memories.

Few enable malicious misunderstandings without purpose. At a time when you caught paranoia like a head cold, there were many keen to see Dr Stephen Ward out of the way. They won. They brushed him off as they would a flaking of dandruff.

'Slow' is too fast an adjective for the way life was squeezed from Ward. What frenzy there was happened in the method, a frantic gathering and notation of whisper and innuendo arranged in manila envelopes, neatly numbered in magenta ink, and placed in filing cabinets of hearsay, a busybody of evidence.

The scaffolding around the case was shaky but a stiff collar of determination held it together, as did the lies and the circumstantial evidence looping the noose hanging from it. The demise of awkward people is always convenient. The manner of Ward's passing, whether solely by his own hand or with the help of another, was a tortuous business. Yet instead of his death deflecting interest in the great political and judicial and society-changing scandal of the twentieth century, it ensured an everlasting headline. It is a case which public interest dictates has no statute of limitations. No mythomane can ignore it. In the natural order, right will always aim to correct wrong, and so the story of the persecution, trial and death of Stephen Ward more than half a century ago lives on, as do many of those who surrounded him and his times.

Ward was a social and sexual cavalier. He knew everyone who mattered, and a lot more who mattered only to themselves. He knew their likes and dislikes, their little peccadilloes. In turn, naturally, they knew not him, but only the confection of the person he gathered around himself.

Stephen Ward was never a character, anything but.

To many of his London companions of the early post-war years, he was a man looking for love and – the novelty – he was always happy to help others find it. He had the amused manner of a confident man but apprehension prevented him from being patronising. He held his head back as he talked to you, a cigarette a constant between long, pumice-scrubbed fingers; it made him appear intrigued, eager for information. He looked at you like a menu.

'I didn't like him at first,' confessed Bobby McKew, 'but I realised that was jealousy – he got all the good-looking birds.'

If Stephen Ward had not been totally indoctrinated in the old boys' political and social world, Bobby McKew might have saved him from trial and, possibly, death and in turn the British taxpayer considerable sums.

At that time, McKew, because of his keen (and sometimes larcenous) charm and close friendship with World War II double-agent Eddie 'Zigzag' Chapman, moved in extraordinary Intelligence, social and gangland circles. One friend was Horace Marsden ('one of the "funny people" from MI5') who advised McKew: 'You might want to tell your friend Stephen Ward he's about to be arrested.'

It was on a warmer than usual evening in London that Bobby McKew drove north from Marylebone to Regent's Park for a meeting with Stephen Ward, untold until now, like much of this book. The two men were on friendly terms – they shared a social circle and Ward's former wife was a close friend of McKew's longtime girlfriend.

The location to the south-east of the park opposite the London Zoo was convenient for them both, the park somewhere McKew used to have private conversations – 'If you didn't want to advertise, you took a walk in the park. If there was untoward interest, then you could see anyone watching you.'

It was hot and Ward talked about it being stifling weather and not even officially summer – 'He was relaxed, he wasn't anxious to know why I'd asked to see him.'

'It's a lovely evening, Bobby. Just lovely,' he said, grinning at McKew.

Irritated in the circumstances by Ward's joviality, McKew gave him Horace Marsden's message without any dressing: he, Stephen Ward, was to be arrested at any moment. There was no surprise in Ward's eyes, no shock or loss of demeanour. McKew remembered: 'He wasn't bothered, he was calm. I repeated that as I understood it from Horace things were about to become very difficult for him if he was arrested. It seemed someone believed he should shove off, get out of the firing line.'

Ward smiled. 'My dear Bobby, I do so much appreciate what you are saying, but there is another picture within the frame.

'I know certain people – they are friends, they will look after me. Nothing will happen to me. But, Bobby, I do so very much appreciate you telling me this, but please don't be concerned about me.

'It will be fine. I've done nothing wrong, nothing is going to happen to me.'

Stephen Ward did say he hadn't learned much at Cranford.

BBC Radio Home Service, 8 June 1963

A key figure in the Profumo Affair has been charged with living on immoral earnings.

Dr Stephen Ward, a London osteopath and friend of Christine Keeler, was arrested in Watford and taken to Marylebone Lane police station.

The arrest comes three days after the resignation of the Secretary of State for War, John Profumo. He admitted he had lied to parliament after MPs accused him of having a relationship with Miss Keeler, a 21-year-old call girl. MPs also allege that Miss Keeler had relations with a Russian naval attaché and that the affair posed a risk to national security.

Prime Minister Harold Macmillan described the resignation as a 'great tragedy'.

Dr Ward has not been allowed bail but his literary agent, Pelham Pound, said he was 'confident' he would be freed after his court appearance scheduled for Monday June 13. Mr Pound visited Dr Ward at the police station and described him as 'extremely cheerful'. He had earlier collected some of Dr Ward's belongings from his Bryanston Mews home in Marylebone.

Last night detectives searched his former flat at Wimpole Mews and took away some items in a brown paper parcel. Dr Ward has been charged with living on the 'earnings of prostitution' at 17 Wimpole Mews since January 1, 1961.

The son of the late Canon Arthur Evelyn Ward, Canon of Rochester Cathedral, Dr Ward has treated such illustrious names as Sir Winston Churchill, Paul Getty, Douglas Fairbanks and Elizabeth Taylor.

He is also an artist and has had members of the Royal Family and politicians sit for him.

BOOK ONE
TARTS, TOFFS AND TROUBLE

'WE'RE BRANDED ON THE TONGUE. THERE'S NO OTHER NATION LIKE THIS WHERE SOMEONE CAN PICK UP THE PHONE AND THINK: "AH, HE'S ONE OF US." AND TO THAT STRANGE BACKGROUND, THIS TRIBALISM WRITTEN INTO OUR SOCIETY, THERE BELONGS A HUGE AMOUNT OF DUPLICITY. WE'RE A NATION THAT IS GIVEN TO SUCH EXTRAORDINARY SUBTEXT IN ITS COMMUNICATIONS WITH ITSELF THAT DUPLICITY IS ALMOST WRITTEN IN. WE HAVE NEVER LACKED IN THIS COUNTRY FOR PEOPLE WITH LARCENOUS INSTINCTS AND CHARMING MANNERS.'

John le Carré, interview with Jake Kerridge for the *Daily Telegraph*, London, 25 March 2013

CHAPTER ONE

DOCTOR IN LOVE

'YOU CAN DO ANYTHING YOU PLEASE HERE,
SO LONG AS YOU DON'T DO IT ON THE STREET AND
FRIGHTEN THE HORSES.'

Mrs Patrick Campbell, George Bernard Shaw's choice
as the original Eliza Doolittle in *Pygmalion*, 1910

'Don't you ever *fuck*?!'

Startled, Dr Stephen Ward looked over as more questions were launched towards him on the chilly late-evening London air.

'Just like to look? Window shopping? *Bastard!*'

The quizmistress, a Miss Bloody Mary, was gesturing towards Ward, marking him out to her three friends standing companionably with her outside The Dorchester hotel in Mayfair in 1952. These were ladies, girls really, but aged by Max Factor panstick and boredom, to whom Mrs Patrick Campbell's axiom was altogether alien.

Only moments earlier, Stephen Ward and Michael 'Dandy Kim' Caborn-Waterfield had left Princess Margaret and her regal entourage at The Milroy nightclub atop Les Ambassadeurs at 5, Hamilton Place. Now, different ladies were in waiting.

At first, it was all a little embarrassing. The two men were taking a couple of enthusiastic Rank Cinema starlets back to Caborn-Waterfield's apartment for romantic improvisation. The interruption made it clear the working girls had recognised Dr

Ward. Though the incident might have been shrugged off as unpleasant at most, it turned nastier, potentially deadly.

The street girls, like most throughout Mayfair and Soho, were controlled by the Messina Brothers who ran vice in London's most lucrative patch with ruthless efficiency, big cars, loud voices and suits to match. Sharp razors, jangling bicycle chains, noisy street battles, quiet police pay-offs and silenced witnesses. Salvatore, Carmelo, Alfredo, Attilio and Eugene Messina saw their work as simply a corporate extension of the white slavery enterprise pursued by their Sicilian-born father Giuseppe at the turn of the century. They were hands-on, personally patrolling their street network, in turn paternal and intimidating. Work was their life and, appropriately in their case, vice versa. They took it extremely seriously; anything or anyone who threatened their game, their profit, was ferociously dealt with. No one complained, especially not the police, who were extremely well rewarded in cash and kind.

The pitch outside The Dorchester was 24-hour prime. The 'mugs' were upmarket, usually safe and generous. The girls, who were on a flat rate, fought for it, not for the money but for their comfort, especially in the winter months when their outfits were only good for temptation.

There was space for four, maybe five, ladies making evening offers along the stretch of wall by the banqueting doors to The Dorchester. Below were the hotel kitchens, the hot air drifting up and escaping through metal grilles, agreeably warming the goods.

There were some screeching cat fights and also confrontations between the Messina brothers or their thugs from the Tottenham gang with other ponces trying to move their girls into the spots. Young man-about-town Michael Caborn-Waterfield witnessed much of it: 'I'd taken a flat at 60, Park Lane, which is on the same block as The Dorchester; if you're coming down from Marble Arch it's the last turning on the left and then it's The Dorchester. It was two-way traffic and just a walk up and down, and it's where Stephen got himself into a stupid little fix with the Messina brothers.

'My flat was on the first floor and the sitting room overlooked Park Lane and my bedroom window was out onto Aldford Street; along with Shepherd Market, it was a treasured pitch.

'Before I met Stephen at the bar of "Les A" [Les Ambassadeurs] in 1952, I'd noticed from time to time, usually between 10pm and midnight, a XK120 grey drophead Jaguar sailing by down Park Lane and the driver was slowing. He was kerb-crawling these girls.

'His car was very chic, people didn't have them. It was only seven years after the war. The girls all thought he was a very monied man and also he was a very attractive man. But he was just looking at them – he never stopped and never did business. I knew all the girls – they had a key to my flat and they never took any liberties. They used to hide my money because they were afraid the "dirty debutantes" I mixed with would take it.'

Caborn-Waterfield, who talks the way Cary Grant looked as though he should – slow, soft and suavely – set the scene: 'I'd met Stephen with Paul Adam, who was the bandleader at The Milroy, and we'd become good chums. London was truly a village, the same faces everywhere. Paul was one of Princess Margaret's favourites – he always had a special number for her – and it was a lively place. The starlets used to have dinner with the producers and then make excuses and escape upstairs to us in The Milroy. One night there were two new girls and I said to Stephen: "Let's take them back to my place, chat them up." As we were walking up with these two, Bloody Mary stepped out from her pitch and the other girls and started screaming at Stephen. There was a hell of a row. I said: "Come on, girls, he's a friend of mine."

'I had little influence. They screamed: "He's a dirty fucking bastard!"

'It all became nasty and one of the ponces came along, a young one who grafted for the Messinas. He got into it and he'd taken Stephen's car number and was going to make trouble.

'Stephen was kerb-crawling – he was voyeuristic and he wasn't performing. He wasn't short of money. He didn't have a back up of money but he had a bloody good income. The Messinas would have roughed him up – they murdered without conscience. We had galvanised dustbins and the lids became weapons in the fights, being swung around like the bicycle chains. But if they wanted to send a message they would cut someone, scar their face. It was the Messinas' sort of advertising. Invariably, when there's money and villains around, there's always problems. Stephen was fearful of that sort of thing, any sort of physical confrontation.

'To help Stephen, I got a message to the Messina brothers to tell them Stephen was a friend of the Duke of Edinburgh. The Messina brothers didn't want that level of aggravation; there were some people they couldn't pay off.'

It was a solid connection and timely. On 8 February 1952, the Duke's wife, the Princess Elizabeth, formally proclaimed herself Queen following the death two days earlier of her father, King George VI. Despite the viral nastiness of the Messina brothers, that fact, said Caborn-Waterfield, constituted 'enough clout to make them back off'.

Stephen Ward's 40th birthday was on 19 October 1952, and by then he himself was a prominent character in London's high society, albeit a waste of a good time for Bloody Mary. He was also fortunate that the much-liked and connected socialite Kim Waterfield knew the 'crusading' newspaper reporter Tommy 'Duncan' Webb, who was tapped into all that happened in London: 'I told Tommy one of the girls had a thing for Stephen and felt rejected, and that's how it happened.'

He was a conflicted man, this vicar's son, but also a man of determination and conviction: a devout believer, not in God, but in whichever road he travelled. Yesterday was never an option. By then, he'd gone a long way. As a boy, Stephen Ward always felt that 'somewhere life must surely be exciting'. His father, the Reverend Arthur Evelyn Ward, was a scholar, a man who dwelled on history (he had a First in Modern History from Balliol College, Oxford) and was happiest locked in his thoughts and his library. He suffered from the spinal disease ankylosing spondylitis, which had bent him over 'like a mole creeping among his books', a neighbour recalled. When Stephen Ward was born in 1912, his father was the vicar of Lemsford, near Hatfield in Hertfordshire, and the family – Stephen, John and Raymond, twins Bridget and Patty – moved with the job: first, Holy Trinity Church in Twickenham, then St Matthias in Torquay, with his father eventually becoming Prebendary of Exeter Cathedral in 1934.

The Reverend Ward's second son rebelled against the formality and conformity of not just religion, but also the pecking order of life. However, through his father, he learned and always believed that all humans are equal, irrespective 'of their creed, colour, race or gender'. For Stephen Ward, everything was open to all. He was never keen on the Tenth Commandment.

His mother was, by all accounts, a delight, an engaging flibbertigibbet. Eileen (Vigors) Ward was from County Carlow, Ireland, and a family who had aspirations and achieved them in Law, the Church and the Army. She simply expected her son Stephen to follow the family tradition. From a young age, he grew tall and was slim and fit. Attractive in manner and look, he had a feline agility. Yet he was a disappointment to his academic father who could not understand his son's failure to study. Ward first learned to deploy charm as a protective weapon in the family home.

His academic mind was never questioned but his application of it always was, first by private tutors, next at a Middlesex preparatory school and then at Cranford School, the former Dorset home of Viscount Wimborne, the English politician Ivor Churchill Guest, who had been Lord Lieutenant of Ireland at the

Easter Rising in 1916. At Cranford, they knew more about Wimborne than about Stephen Ward. He was only remembered for being punished for fracturing a fellow boarder's skull. He didn't do that, and he never forgot it either but nor did he succeed at his lessons or on the playing fields. But he wanted to achieve and was sufficiently self-aware to acknowledge a distorted self-image to his friend Warwick Charlton: 'I used to live in a sort of dream. I wanted to be good at everything. I wanted to pass exams brilliantly, to be noticed for my fine mind. I also wanted to be good at games. Alas, none of this happened. When it came to the point, an inbuilt and fatal laziness stopped me from putting everything I had into the effort. I never had any real idea of what I wanted to be, but I knew what I didn't want: I most certainly did not want to follow in father's footsteps.'

And he didn't.

'I wanted to travel and to meet people. I told my father that I wanted to leave school and get a job. He was puzzled. He never did understand me and now I had that all-alone feeling again, for I knew very clearly that I could never make him understand. To my surprise he overcame his doubts and agreed to my leaving school. I was an awkward nuisance and, after all, the Lord was always on hand to help out if things got too difficult. Now the cuckoo (I'm sure he thought of me as such) was really leaving the nest, and, although I sensed his alarm at my obvious lack of purpose, there was, I felt, almost a relief in getting me off his hands. I can't say I greatly blame him for this.'

It was remarkable equanimity in a 17-year-old whose bespoke charm fitted perfectly. That calm demeanour never lost discretion at the jumps. Ward leaned towards a medical career but failed to secure a suitable college. Instead, he found himself rolling out rainbows of carpets in the City of London. He stayed with family friends and took a job (for 27 shillings a week) at the Houndsditch Carpet Warehouse, where he was to display what was for sale to wholesale buyers. He did that with some panache but his patience wore thinner than the carpets. After the seasonal rush, he suddenly announced that he was leaving to work abroad.

It was the winter of 1929 when he went to Germany. It was a shaky moment of European history, with Adolf Hitler becoming a whispered name and his party, the National Socialist German Workers' Party, invading right-wing politics. Ward arrived in Hamburg shortly before Christmas, and the new Nazi Party HQ, with a job as a translator for Shell Oil. He was not fluent in German but 'an uncle used his influence'. His connections were impeccable, like his plausibility. He was part of the British Club in the city and mixed with the foreign embassy crowd, fondly with the daughter of the Swedish Consul. He played club tennis and attended cocktail parties. He learned fluency in diplomacy, how to be in exactly the right place in the room at the perfect time to light the cigarettes being held by the influential or attractive.

He looked older, naturally dressing the part, and his frame and features carried it off. Hamburg was a perfect place for him to further and develop his interests in the 'ladies of the night' unabashedly on parade along the Reeperbahn, the mile-long street of sex-on-offer in the St Paul's district of Hamburg. There was no innuendo. It was all on show, held together by corsets and necessity.

Ward gossiped to his friends that his sex life kink started with the girls of the Reeperbahn. It was good fun – and good economics. He could pay for sex or get his thrills for free, looking at the girls pouting and posing and inviting in the windows of the red-light district: sex by window shopping. Ward adored Hamburg but there was a problem – he claimed a practical joke with his boss at Shell backfired – and he moved to France. His mother helped (behind his father's back) by sending funds to Paris, which allowed him to study at the Sorbonne, at the university's Cours de Civilisation. He found a job in the kitchens of a club, Chez Florence, but did more sketches of waitresses than dishes; he also mixed with those who arrived for the nightlife rather than the food. This led to more income as, between student classes, he escorted tourists – 'It didn't take long for me to realise that many of them were more interested in real girls than the Mona Lisa.' He received more requests for visits to The Sphinx, a highly mannered brothel, than Notre Dame Cathedral. The Sphinx, renowned for its glamorous flexibility, with girls, naked bar necklaces or other carefully placed pearls, dancing with the customers, was known in Paris as 'an expensive place to fuck'. And guests were expected to tip, most delighted to do so. If Ward had any surviving illusions about the ways of the flesh, they were abandoned by then: he'd gone all the way from basic farmyard to fantasy.

With winning understatement, he confided to a friend: 'I often wondered what they'd think of me back in Torquay, if the parishioners could see the vicar's son in a rather novel situation.'

They very nearly did, for Ward tired, as he did of so much, of Paris life subsisting on crushed packets of Gauloise and a budget. Always broke, waiting for money from home, he followed the money back to Torquay. Meanwhile, he had established a look that would remain with him: a white shirt with a collar a half-size more than he needed, grey slacks or dark suit trousers with a double pleat that accentuated his narrow waist but kept the cloth away from his body. Maybe he sprayed on affability for he reeked of it. Certainly, he was a leading attraction in 1932 for the younger set of Torquay. His mother's indulgence of her favourite son, the cash and the MG sports car, a racy red number she bought him, got him top billing on the eligibility marquee.

There was a moment when he stumbled into possible stability. He became involved in a serious relationship with 18-year-old Mary Glover, daughter of a local businessman. She fell in love with him, but her parents were not so besotted. Ward had everything a girl could want except prospects. He called Mary 'his Maggie' – he always had to personalise girls, mark them out with his extravagant giftwrapping, and she would tell a friend: 'I was absolutely fascinated by Stephen. He had enormous charm and all the girls were captivated by him but I knew he was faithful to me. One day, he asked me: "Maggie, when are we going to get married?" He never gave me an engagement ring but we both understood that, when he made good, we'd get married.'

But the 'making good' option was not leaping into Ward's life, which, professionally, was going nowhere. His mother brought family connections into play. Her brother Edward Vigors, an Examiner of Standing Orders at Parliament in Westminster, introduced his nephew to his fellow Irishman Jocelyn Proby. Renowned for his kindness, Proby had a degree from the Kirksville College of Osteopathy and Surgery in Missouri. An enthusiast of osteopathic medicine, he persuaded Ward that he would be a success as a practitioner: 'There is no doubt that Stephen had a very good brain – but no direction. Edward Vigors and I really hijacked him and sent him off to Kirksville. But we were so confident he'd do well that we agreed to pay his fees.'

Ward proved an instant convert: 'The more I thought about it, the more excited I became. I saw fame and fortune opening up overnight. I would be the most brilliant osteopath in the world. After all, orthodox doctors tended to be a stuffy lot. This was a new world. I would conquer it. Kirksville was the best place to study; in England the word was scarcely respectable.'

As the end of 1934 approached, Stephen Ward looked out towards the Statue of Liberty as Cunard's Edwardian enterprise, the RMS *Mauretania*, sailed for New York. He took a Greyhound bus (with little more room than his third-class berth on the *Mauretania*) from New York to St Louis and then a local Missouri yellow-painted bus connection for the long, often bumpy 185 miles on to Kirksville, and a new beginning.

The speciality at Kirksville was osteopathy but general medical studies were considered vital. As the students trained, they were put into practice around the town. Ward might deliver a baby in the afternoon and in the evening be helping with emergency surgery following a farm accident. While he was in Missouri, 'Maggie' Glover met an eminently suitable future husband, the stockbroker Bernard Bartlett. She wrote to tell Ward that their romance was over and he confided in a friend: 'I was desperately upset but at least this taught me one thing, something we all have to learn: love won't stand much separation, of distance or time. I decided that I would never again become so seriously involved with anyone. It hurt like hell for a bit.'

Yet, not too long: a university friend reported that Ward's *'pinga grande'* was an attraction at a Mexican brothel when his chosen girl wanted all her colleagues to steal a glance. In turn, Stephen Ward was just as curious about America, an avid adventurer.

During university breaks, he visited one state after another, from California across and down to the Florida Keys. The athletic Ward put himself about and was much-more physically capable than he'd ever displayed in England. He spent time by lakes and in national parks (Nevada, Wyoming and Arizona), intrigued by native American life, tales of the Wild West and the Red Indian hereafter of the *Happy Hunting Ground*; he panned for gold and went fishing, worked as a mortician, in cafes and bars – anywhere to get extra cash to fund his travels – but always, always, he visited the red-light districts. In Hollywood, he went to a movie studio and to a 'slipper club' on La Cienega Boulevard, above the Sunset Strip. In Chicago, the brothels still retained the speakeasy accoutrements of Prohibition, secret doors and rooms where all kinds of nonsense could take place out of sight. He was enchanted.

It was free and easy; no one made judgements, you just had your fun. What was good for one was often good for another. America offered the Great Outdoors and no inhibitions indoors. He'd become more serious about his painting and sketching, bought books on line drawing, and found he had a true talent. It was also a babe magnet – women really did want to see his etchings, and they adored being visually imagined. He'd mastered anatomical drawing but faces fascinated him. He never caricatured, he drew as he saw. For Stephen Ward, all women were beautiful – some just needed his help to complete their potential. His English accent, broadcasting baritone melodies, coupled with the facility to relax his companions had the American girls swooning. They may have wanted more than they got. The young Ward enjoyed the palaver of American 'petting'. He relished describing the teasing code, the ritual to friends.

'You touch the girl's hand. She must make a sign of withdrawal. Never take this seriously. From the hand you move to the lips. You kiss. The lips, of course, are closed. Once you have kissed, then you caress more expertly, more lingeringly. You may touch the body but petting must be staggered over a period. There's an art in this sort of stimulation. I found it an exciting emotional experience. You could spend hours and hours with them and in the end you did achieve a sort of orgasm. But direct consummation would have quite spoiled the effect. It was a sort of delicious sigh.'

Another pleasure, one that came almost as a surprise, was that he had great skill as an osteopath: he could manipulate joints and pain with much the same dexterity as he applied to people. After six years, he graduated from Kirksville College and, after successfully sitting the Missouri State Medical Board examination, he became Dr Stephen Ward.

He was about to get his finely trained hands on some extraordinary people.

CHAPTER TWO

DOCTOR AT SEA

'PITY YOU DIDN'T TWIST IT RIGHT OFF.'

Winston Churchill to Stephen Ward, after Ward told him
he had treated Gandhi for a stiff neck.

Winston Churchill was naked from the waist down a
moment after Stephen Ward met him. The leader of Her
Majesty's Opposition stood before Ward wearing only a blue and
white striped pyjama jacket, holding his habitual smoking cigar.
The Conservative champion was suffering from severe back pains
of which he had been complaining loudly to his family.

His daughter Diana and her husband, the politician Duncan
Sandys (who, wounded in action in 1941, had a permanent limp),
had been pain-free following osteopathic sessions with Dr Ward.
Diana Sandys recommended him to her mother, Clementine
Churchill. She, in turn, warned Ward on arrival with his portable
treatment table at their London home in Hyde Park Gate not to
take any nonsense from her husband. Churchill was sitting in bed,
smoking one of his chubby cigars, which he waved in Ward's
direction. As he set up the treatment table, Churchill huffed and
puffed, murmuring about doctors. Business-like, Ward asked him
to sit on the treatment table. Churchill pushed himself out of bed

minus pyjama trousers and got in position. Dr Ward said he would ask him medical questions.

Impishly, Churchill said he could ask them while he was in bed, which he promptly popped back into. Ward countered that it saved precious time if he did his questionnaire while treating patients. Churchill duly obliged and moved face down on the table, still smoking his cigar.

They were to have a dozen more treatment sessions in 1946 and Stephen Ward learned much from Churchill about painting and how world politics were played similarly to chess, with compromise and sacrifice, and about Churchill and wartime debt-heavy Britain's attitude to America, to Russia and to Stalin. Only a little more than a handful of years since his American adventures, he was taking political classes from the very top, where he always wanted to be, and for once paying attention to his lessons.

It had been a more assured and debonair Dr Stephen Ward who returned by ocean liner to England in 1938 with one suitcase. There was no luggage to follow – the baggage would arrive a little later. Like all who ventured to America, he had seen the prospects but, despite the opportunities, socially as well as professionally, his dreams were of being something in British medicine and society, with each strand of that life complementing the other. If there was one thing he totally desired, it was to be somebody.

He was most certainly that in Torquay, where many saw their aspirations through net curtains. He opened an osteopathy clinic on The Strand, across from the seaside town's harbour, and his skill and manner brought him many patients. Word circulated, and for a time, to be a qualified member of the county set, one 'just had to have an appointment' with Dr Stephen Ward. He was good fun for the girls, too. A careful listener and storyteller, he had tales to tell of his adventures in America. Life was going his way. Then, as it did for millions of others, war rudely interrupted plans and dreams and futures.

Dr Ward felt especially affronted. He couldn't even get into the war. His US medical qualification was not recognised by the British Medical Association or by the Royal Army Medical Corps; he volunteered the moment war with Germany was announced but had to wait until 23 January 1941. He was conscripted as a private in the Royal Armoured Corps stationed at Bovington, next to the Dorset village of Wool, about ten miles west of Poole. With the 58th Training Regiment, he learned to drive a tank and was taught how to shoot and operate a two-way radio. He delighted in learning these new skills and rather liked the idea of being Private Ward, all-rounder. Though he said rank did not concern him, his Commanding Officer's power seriously improved his circumstances.

He cured the Colonel of the 58th's bad knee, following which the CO relieved him of all duties and established him in a clinic on base. All his clinical equipment was collected from Torquay and set up in a Nissen hut, which for more than two years became Dr Ward's surgery. There he treated everything from headaches to heartache, bad backs, swollen toes, inflamed muscles and a miscellany of training injuries. He did a superb job, and being appointed Lance Corporal was his small reward. Patients came from other bases and Services. He was happily, but unofficially, approved. Ward enjoyed telling the story and did so often: 'More people were coming to me for treatment than to the Medical Officer (MO), who was also called Ward. At a regimental boxing match one of the fighters was badly hurt and the Colonel shouted: "Call for Ward!" At once the MO jumped into the ring to be told: "No, you fool, not you – the other Ward!" He was furious.'

Dr Stephen Ward survived the hoo-hah that followed. It also brought the debate round to osteopathy, of which he was an increasingly vocal champion. Somewhere in the Army bureaucracy it was decided that Lance Corporal Ward, following the support of his Colonel and other patients, should be awarded a commission in the Royal Army Medical Corps. He would be assigned to the new 'officer-stretcher-bearer' division to help out approved medics in battle areas.

But the RAMC men did not like this 'new-fangled medicine' and resented its practitioner. Osteopathy (which Ward believed he should be doing) was banned; he was to be more of an orderly than a medic. As he always believed you should, he went straight to the top. No matter Hitler was almost certainly still dominating their thoughts, he wrote to King George VI and Prime Minister Churchill advocating osteopathy. He petitioned his MP to ask questions in the House of Commons. Others simply questioned Ward's sanity – he knew they thought of him as 'a curious crank'. But officialdom's natural solution was at hand, the very faraway long grass. With some wonderment, he found himself on a ship to India. And he was not alone: 'It was the most amazing voyage of my life. There were 300 men on a ship carrying 3,000 women – nurses, Service girls, ENSA (Entertainments National Services Association) girls off to cheer up the troops. We were part of a slow convoy and the longer the convoy took, the happier we became. By the time we got to the Red Sea, some of the men began to feel the heat. This also affected the girls. There's something about shipboard life which completely changes a girl; she breaks down. All sorts of desires she would normally suppress come bubbling up. The most prim and prudish girls can be veritably insatiable. This was sheer bacchanalia. They actually fought for our attention, like cats on the prowl.'

Dr Ward arrived in India in 1944 reinvigorated and ready for more action. He was stationed at the huge British garrison in Poona (Pune), about 80 miles to the south and east of Bombay (Mumbai) and a vital rail junction. It was ideal Stephen Ward territory for it was also where Bombay society retreated to escape the big city. Affluent Indians and Anglo-Indians had created a cafe society to which British officers had automatic membership. Still championing osteopathy, the now Captain Ward continued to be tagged an oddball by the Army, but with his skill and social poise became a favourite with civic matrons and maharajahs. He was busy with patients and with dinner here or there and bridge evenings with the hedonistic and always girl-hungry Sir Pratap Singh Gaekwad, the Maharaja of Baroda, known to Ward as 'Boss' Baroda. In turn, he enchanted the jewel-acquisitive Maharani of Baroda (privately known to the English division as the 'Indian Wallis Simpson'). Captain Ward had the power to amuse the woman nicknamed after the divorcée for whom Edward VIII abdicated; he had the gift of being good company, never a nuisance, never an interference, quite ghostly. Guests who were always aware when he was there, to pass a cigarette or a remark, observed when he wasn't in the crowd at the bar no one wondered: 'Where's Stephen?'

Yet, he pushed himself forward when the timing was right. He greatly wanted to meet Mahatma Gandhi, the man whom Winston Churchill dismissed and disdained as a 'half-naked fakir'. Churchill was enraged by Gandhi's campaign for Britain to leave India in 1942 at the height of World War II. Gandhi, who had been jailed for his 'Quit India' movement, was free and attending the Mehta Clinic in Poona at the end of 1944 when Ward encountered him. He admired Gandhi's philosophy of non-violence and truth, of fasting and vegetarianism, a doctrine of self-sufficiency: they were both adherents of alternatives to the mainstream.

A crowd quickly gathered on nearby roofs and around the buildings when word spread that Gandhi was staying in a room at the clinic. Ward was walking with one of the Eton-educated 'Boss' Baroda's sons and his importance helped them make his way through the crowds. Word was given to Gandhi that a British Army captain wanted to see him. Ward was informed this was a day of silence for the Indian Congress Party leader. Nevertheless, they could acknowledge each other. When the introduction 'this is Captain Stephen Ward' was made, Gandhi approached, put his hands together over his heart in a *namaste* greeting ('the divinity within me bows to the divinity in you') and to everyone's great surprise broke his silence.

'Well, it is a change to have a visit from an English officer who has not come to arrest me.'

Ward was overwhelmed by the meeting. He was invited into Gandhi's room, frugality framed by three walls and an entranceway. In casual conversation, Ward enquired after Gandhi's health and the political leader complained of a stiff neck and frequent headaches – 'I offered to treat him on the spot. He accepted and I put my hands on his neck and started to manipulate. It worked and Gandhi seemed very grateful.' They met as patient and doctor three more times but then the Army's and Ward's attention was diverted to preparing for an onslaught on Malaya (Malaysia). The Allied invasion of Japan was never necessary and, as World War II ended, the dissident Ward went not to Kuala Lumpur but to Torquay.

Unsurprisingly, it wasn't quite so exciting. He had left the Services trailing a record that questioned his emotional stability but he laughingly dismissed this diagnosis as being made on 'stuffy attitudes'. He knew he had truly healed patients, 'but still everybody believed that osteopaths were curious cranks'. It was an incorrect statement for there were many devotees.

The American Ambassador to the United Kingdom, W. Averell Harriman, was one such devotee. The diplomat, who had been President Franklin D. Roosevelt's special wartime envoy to Europe and US Ambassador to the Soviet Union, believed his twice-weekly treatment was vital to maintaining activity. When General Walter Bedell Smith took over his post in Russia, Harriman had moved from Spaso House in Moscow to the American Embassy in Grosvenor Square.

With much less ceremony, Ward had removed from Torquay and, with the help of Jocelyn Proby, found a professional place in London. He set to work at the public service Osteopathic Association Clinic, which had rooms in Dorset Square, tucked between Sherlock Holmes' Baker Street and Marylebone. Professionally, it was fulfilling but it was a salaried post of less than £10 a week. The Ward parachute opened again. Well, *he* pulled it open. The US Embassy was anxious to find an American-trained osteopath for its new chief. Dr Ward had been at Dorset Square for about a year when the phone rang in the reception area. He just happened to be beside the jangling phone, as he later recounted to his friend Warwick Charlton:

'The American Embassy was on the line. Could we recommend the very best osteopath in town? I'm not the sort of man to lose a chance like that. I said at once: "Oh yes, Doctor Stephen Ward. I'll get him to phone back and fix an appointment." Then, I asked a friend if he would lend me his Park Lane consulting room for an hour or so. I rushed off to await my first private patient and in walked Averell Harriman, the United States Ambassador. I told him I hadn't been out of the Army for long and we began to talk.'

Harriman was more than pleased with his treatment and his recommendations brought Dr Ward an enviable number of private patients. Several more officials from the American Embassy, as well as other foreign diplomats who had heard of the talented Dr Ward and his 'healing hands' through the network of nightly consulate receptions, crowded his appointment book. Another well-connected sufferer was Bobbie Shaw, the son of Nancy Astor, Britain's first woman MP to sit in the Commons, from her first and tumultuous marriage as 18-year-old Nancy Langhorne to the rapacious Boston landowner and socialite Robert Shaw III.

These enthusiasts of osteopathic treatment were very much a friends-of-a-friend group, a cabal who would rave about good practitioners once relieved of their crippling pains. For Stephen Ward, now resplendent in monogrammed white shirts, it was better than a front-page advertisement in *The Times*. He had patients who invited him to some of the best receptions and dinner parties in London. This enabled him to open consulting rooms, within which he had a cavern of an apartment, which he rented in Cavendish Square in the West End. Harley Street was nearby and Cavendish Square became a magnet for Dr Ward's alternative and seemingly magical medicine. There were other alternative therapies around as well, but of a sexual nature: next door was the night-time action of post-war London, the territory of the Messina brothers and their rivals.

It was a tough game. London was scarred by many sights of deprivation, with cement blocks balancing bombed buildings, perseverance and a few pennies held families upright, and it was almost Government policy, albeit an emotional and cultural habit, that everyone would soldier on. It was just done differently by some. Stephen Ward was comfortable in all worlds, his own and those manufactured by others.

As with society, there was a hierarchy in the 1940s street-walker constituency. If you were a long way from Piccadilly Circus, your payment for providing 'a lumber' would be in shillings, and not many of them.

The going rate around the West End, Curzon Street, Maddox Street, Shepherd Market, and all the cutaways and corners between Bond Street and the extravagant sweeping curve of Regent Street and over to Oxford Street, with its back to Soho and front to Selfridges and all the glamorous stores, was 25 shillings. As it was, too, down Stafford Street to Piccadilly, around the Greek Cupid, Eros, and if one was to wander for some outdoor playtime (with tempting al fresco rates as there was no need to rent a room) in Hyde Park. Twenty-five shillings was five meals – rationing dictated you could not, by law, serve a meal costing more than five shillings a person. So, in many cases, the girls located throughout the two-mile rectangle of Soho were indeed singing, as it were, for their supper. At the brilliantly illuminated Piccadilly Circus parameter, Coventry Street opened out onto Leicester Square, which through the Empire, Odeon and Ritz cinemas marketed escapist dreams. At times, there seemed to be more buskers than starlings in the Square. Everything was on sale, from palm readings to a couple of ounces of black-market bacon to chats with the dead. Given that so many had lost loved ones during the war, mediums were popular.

No one traded in hearts of gold at this social crossroads. The prostitutes were asbestos-proofed. The men who ran or worked with them reflected in their look the sordid actuality of their game. Bobby McKew worked with Billy Hill, the clever and notorious gangland leader who controlled London during the 1940s and 50s, and said Hill would 'sort out' any of his people even seen walking on the same side of the street as a ponce or pimp; they were despised. In the remarkable shading of the criminal world, there was even a differential there: a pimp solicited for and shared the earnings of his girls; a ponce, or 'johnson', took money for 'protection', charged as much as £20 a week to allow a girl to work for him and pocketed half the cash she made. Even then, a prostitute still had to look after herself, protect her patch. A new 'innocent' walking into Shepherd Market had more chance of being clumped in the eye with a rival's shoe heel than doing business. If not that, the johnson warned her off, viciously.

The normal tactic was to butcher a girl's looks by slicing her with a shiv (knife), shredding her face unforgettably. Or a tiny container of acid would be dropped or slipped into her clothing. The ponce would punch the girl and, with his fist, shatter the acid phial, thereby burning and branding her. They operated like vampires; it was all done out of necessity, as 'part of the business' and without hesitation or fear of the consequences. It was truly the Wild West End.

About 25 per cent of the pimps and ponces were Maltese. It was not their fault – they'd been corrupted by the Royal Navy, they said. Prostitution flourished at the Valetta dockyard and someone had to control it. It's also where the nickname for the clients began: the 'mugs'. Those willing to pay for sex were known as 'steamers' and from there, in rhyming slang, came steam-tug and finally, 'mug'.

From Malta, they had the British passports and took their expertise, along with imported French and Belgian prostitutes, to the more profitable market of London. The masters of all this, and murder, were the Messina Brothers. Giuseppe Messina trafficked women in Sicily before moving to Malta in 1912 to establish a brothel. He married one of his girls, getting Maltese/British citizenship, and they had five sons. By the 1930s the family were in London with scores of European girls, who also held British passports through arranged marriages and were free from deportation. They had been lured by promises of a good life and forced to sell their bodies. The clock-watching Messinas imposed on them a ten-minute rule, the allocated time for wham-bam and on to the next customer. On a post-war victory day, one girl had 49 celebratory encounters.

Lavish police pay-offs during and after the war allowed the Messinas to run an open house. Named Debono, they took the surname Messina from the Sicilian province where their father was born. It was the only thing remotely sentimental about them. Towards the end of the 1940s, they had more than 40 brothels in and around Mayfair. Attilio Messina boasted: 'We Messinas are more powerful than the British Government. We do as we like in England.'

It did seem that way. Girls who upset the brothers were beaten and marked by electric cable; the more uncontrollable strangled with copper wire. Death, according to Robert Fabian, as 'Fabian of the Yard', a television hero of the 1950s, was an occupational hazard for the girls: 'When I was chief of London's Vice Squad, I had the names in my office ledger of every known prostitute in London, their phony names and genuine names, ages, photos, descriptions, habits, weaknesses, regular cronies and haunts, and even the names of their sorrowing, respectable relatives; this last for the purpose of identifying any of our Jezebels if, and when, she was fished up from the stinking mud of London River. Being murdered is one of the risks that a prostitute takes in her trade.'

Fabian, whom Bobby McKew said 'always looked a sartorial', delighted in cashmere overcoats and bespoke suits whenever he visited Billy Hill and was a showman of his time. He said in a 1954 interview: 'The police possess no authority and must proceed against this eyesore and this moral menace as foxily as an Oriental horse dealer.

'A police officer may know perfectly well that a girl who is parading shamelessly up and down Piccadilly is a prostitute, but he must wait until she "solicits to the annoyance of passers-by". She is never arrested for actual prostitution, nor for soliciting, but only for behaving in such a way that she has made a man step off the pavement to avoid her, or has grasped his arm, or has halted him in his free and lawful passage along the street.

'That is why the fine inflicted next day is always so ridiculously small. She is being fined for obstruction, just as a motorist, or a barrow-boy, or a pavement artist, might be fined, or a shopkeeper with his window-blind too low. So she pays her £2 and considers it merely a part of her normal business overhead, just as the rent of her "lumber" is, or the cost of her lipstick, or the heavy percentage she pays for her underworld "protection".

'The only real damage that a police officer can inflict upon her is to arrest her early in the evening, before she has had time to collect her quota of clients. And the punishment thus inflicted is not the trivial amount of the fine, but the loss of her fees.'

Which in Mayfair were considerable, possibly more than £100 a week – 20 times the national wage. A £2 fine was not a painful penalty The cashmere-clad Fabian bemoaned the other temptations of this world: 'I think it is one of the lesser recognised miracles of London that so few Metropolitan constables accept bribes, when by doing so they could easily double or treble their salaries.'

The punter was put at little risk – a kerb-crawler, having announced himself with a grind of low gears, could drive off, having said he was forced to slow from car trouble or to get a cigarette. A strolling 'mug' had only stopped to help the lady. Prostitution was not a criminal offence.

Where the law could work and declare two-year jail terms was against ponces and pimps, anyone convicted of living on a woman's immoral earnings. The harshness of English criminal law against the suppliers of the women, the slavers if you like, was that 'a man who was shown to live off or habitually be in a particular woman's company' had to prove his innocence of the charge of living on her immoral earnings, rather than the prosecution prove his guilt.

However, it was not something to which the Messinas or many others gave much thought. Nor did they take note of the 1885 Criminal Law Amendment Act, which ordered that to 'procure a girl under twenty-one to have sexual intercourse with a third party or to attempt or incite such procurement' could mean two years in jail. This, literally interpreted, dictated that, if a man asked another person to introduce him to a woman aged from 16 to 21 years old and he had sex with her, then the middleman, legally, was guilty of inciting procurement. 'Harry, meet my friend Sally' suddenly became a completely different conversation.

Yet that or many variations of it were part of Stephen Ward's London life. He was 'fitting in' to post-war conditions about which he and so many others had built up apprehension. For many, it was peace that had broken out, not war that ended. Daily life was a new battle complicated by fresh tensions and rules, such as strict licensing laws forcing pubs to close at 3pm. Excitement was missing after the war and there were long days for those who couldn't get jobs or were able to keep one. 'We'd get people from the Security Services, boys bored out of their minds, making us offers,' said Bobby McKew. 'They come along and say to Billy Hill, and not joking: "We'll drive the getaway car for you." It wasn't just for a laugh, they wanted paying, and paying well. But most of all they were desperate for excitement.'

Basements became drinking clubs with 'members' paying five shillings in a one-off fee to raise their voices to drown the silence; glasses to drown the loneliness. Anything was worth trying to vanquish the weariness of post-war London life. Distraction appeared the answer, though possibly the pleasure seekers needed purpose. There were a host of backstreet gambling dens (spielers) controlled by Billy Hill and his associates. Other doors gave access to illicit sex and drugs and opportunity for all manner of indulgence. Chinese restaurants began appearing, where after closing times there could be 'special tea' on offer, which was red wine mixed with port. It gave new meaning to 'fancy a cuppa?'

For some, it was a world of ration cards, broken dreams and brittle linoleum. For others, such as the property developer and millionaire Charles Clore who paid the then Duchess of Kent, the former Princess Marina and cousin of Prince Philip of Greece, to be his social adviser, it was an opportunity. In the late 1940s, he was known as 'Santa Clore' to struggling companies asking for investments. The young Maxwell Joseph was equally entrepreneurial. He started out in real estate but moments after the war ended moved his ambitions into hotels and catering. First, he had the Mandeville Hotel in Marylebone Village and then the Mayfair Hotel in Stratton Street, central to the action.

As was the first incarnation of Les Ambassadeurs and The Milroy club, which quickly became part of Stephen Ward's social geography. The Milroy ('Mil' from owner Jean-Jean Millstein, 'roy' from bandleader Harry Roy) soon established itself as the 'night-time headquarters of society'. These two establishments competed favourably with wartime favourites like the Embassy and 400 Club in Leicester Square. The towering, 6ft 4in tall Millstein became John Mills, but never lost his mangled diction. His early partner, also from Kraków, Poland, was Siegi Sessler. There was much talk about how they got their 'seed' money for both became serious players in London nightlife. Some said they had been Intelligence agents in the war and continued such connections as East–West relations chilled in a neatly carved post-war Europe. Others said they had aristocratic connections. Millstein/Mills most certainly romanced Rosemarie Kanzler, but that was when she was Swiss builder's daughter Leni Revelli and long before, after five husbands, she became one of the world's richest women.

'Any romantic notions about the money were just that – romantic,' revealed Kim Waterfield, a close friend of the equally sharp-dressing Siegi Sessler and a (paying) regular of Mills' hospitality: 'They were both in catering during the war, in charge of meat for troops. They made a fortune on the black market. They had the commodity that everyone wanted, everyone needed.

'Spying? Never – it all came from pounds of sausages.'

Which, like sex, always sells. Morris 'Morrie' Conley was a despicable piece of work. He made you want to have a shower within minutes after meeting him. It wasn't just distaste; like so many, he had an aversion to soap and laundry bills. Bobby McKew, who is not prone to over-estimation, said: 'He was a fucking monster!'

In the 1930s, Morrie ran the Mayfair furriers Caplan and Conley Furriers. He went bankrupt after pocketing an astonishing £10,000, but his talkative nature proved his downfall and he was finally jailed for two years. He got into gambling and back into jail when investigators discovered his fruit machines were rigged so the jackpot wouldn't pay out 'if you played them for 100 years'. Never give a sucker an even break, that was Morrie Conley – and what bigger 'mugs' than those seeking love?

Morrie's plan, like that of many others, was to 'help' the post-war male lonely hearts and the young women sweeping into London, looking for bright lights and a brighter than provincial life. He obliged them both – for profit.

'Those places where so many people went to lose themselves,' Stephen Ward's friend and patient Barry Stonehill told me in 2013. 'People believed they were missing out if they weren't out in the clubs. And there were so many to choose from. Les Ambassadeurs was our favourite. People went to the club where they got what they wanted.'

Young bucks around town would drink and gamble at Ruby Lloyd's Maisonette club or Frisco's, run by the West Indian Frisco ('I'm the biggest buck nigger in town') in Shepherd Market. For companionship and the sex that could easily follow for a small cost, the answer was one of Morrie's four Mayfair clubs. Sex was the money-maker. Morrie Conley would negotiate the fee between his girls and the clients but in time gave the job over to a string of club hostesses, 'madams'. Property investment paid well too; he bought up buildings and charged exploitative rents or pleasure in kind from his own girls. Morrie, they said, could get milk out of stone, and charge over the odds for it. He had superb black-market connections and everything was available at a price. The mantra was 'better drinks, better girls' but, in truth, it was only better bullshit.

His most popular enterprise was the Court Club at 58, Duke Street – a quick click of the heels from Grosvenor Square. Indeed, around Cavendish Square, Dr Ward's alternative 'Happy Hunting Ground', there was much to see, from the smart security at the American Embassy in Grosvenor Square to the Court Club, the monied ladies shopping and, in the early evenings, girls like the always accommodating, big-hearted (and chested) girl at Carlos Place, whom the doormen at the Connaught Hotel nicknamed 'Vera the Verandah'.

It was the street girls who provided companionship, not sex in a conventional sense, for Dr Ward. Before his encounter with the influential Ambassador Harriman when he left the Osteopathic Association Clinic, whenever he took off his professional white coat he would drink at the Coach Maker Arms on Marylebone Lane. He was always fumbling to find his ten-pack of cigarettes and taking time with his small glass of beer. Dr Ward's near neighbour, Lib Gosling's late husband Desmond, was a regular at the pub and she recalled in 2013: 'He would have a drink with

Stephen and they'd discuss the news of the day. Stephen was the same with the other regulars. He wanted to know what was happening, he liked to keep up with events. Desmond was there every night but Stephen Ward was not a boozer and he rarely stayed for more than two drinks. Desmond said he didn't relax – he seemed to be looking for friends more than a chat and he wasn't finding them in the pubs.'

But he found them on the streets. Ward went walking around Hyde Park Corner, along Park Lane and into Mayfair. He enjoyed being approached by the girls, no fear of Fabian there; he freely admitted he was turned on by nightlife, by prostitution. He would invite girls back to his flat and because of his manner and his look – a gent – they would go. He could manage heartaches as well as the other sort. Ward began sketching the girls and said he was fascinated by their world: 'I wanted to know what sort of things men demanded of them. I had listened to all sorts of gossip in the Army and I'd knocked around a bit but this was different. These girls were expert in all the kinks of sexuality. They knew more than any psychologist just what was needed by certain types of men. I was always amazed that they did it but then began to realise they were dispassionately interested in their job.

'A lot of them enjoyed it. People always moralise and say "pity the poor prostitutes – what awful conditions must have made them go on the streets?" Some were like that but most of these girls accepted sex as sex. To them it was a job. Whippings, beatings, the lot – what did it matter to them? I really believe they felt they were performing just as good and necessary a service as a doctor. Perhaps they were.'

When his practice prospered, only the timing of this routine would change. Ward would go out later in the evening, after dinner parties and other social events. By then, he truly was a man-about-town.

And it was an extraordinary town. At the high end of high society, it was eternally one of Jay Gatsby's endless parties, dawn populated by elegant couples in evening dress. By that time of day, of the girls selling themselves in Mayfair, with their shift over, there was only an echo of heels in the canyons created by the atmospheric architecture along Adams Row and Curzon Street and around Shepherd Market and Half Moon Street.

'Stephen could entertain anyone in society but he took a delight in encounters with the girls. The debutantes were on offer but Stephen liked his own girls,' recalled Kim Waterfield who raced around the same social circle. 'The point was he knew *exactly* what *he* wanted. There was always one special girl, one he was transforming into the woman of his desires.'

Certainly, Ward wanted to sketch out their futures as well as their faces, make them part of his all-encompassing, personalised society. It was all about Eve, but of course Eve can bite back.

Stephen Ward would arrive at a reception or party with at least two girls and, like a gangster carrying a double-barrelled shotgun indicating a refusal might offend, would present them first. So many were looking for a place in the post-war world. It was a time when the middle class seemed to vanish and the top and the bottom collided. Mark Sykes, a man of aristocratic antecedents and a leading charmer of the times, is certain the connection followed on from the war, where officers and other ranks relied so much on each other.

'It was a very positive thing at that time. It hadn't happened since Regency times – and it hasn't happened since. It was a time of toffs and spivs, the other lot didn't matter one bit. The upper classes and the lower classes always get on well because they hate the middle classes. They regarded them as terribly pretentious. Which they are, of course; they are.'

Opportunity, and the search for it, was the equaliser. It was a racy time. Bobby McKew received a pleasant shock on his arrival in London from Dublin in early 1950: 'Back home you'd be lucky after a couple of months to touch a girl's tit – in London, you only had to say hello.'

There were many other sporting opportunities for the young set who inhabited the incongruous world of Dr Stephen Ward. Of course, many others wanted to be seen as men of the world and dined out on Ward's risqué tales, as he himself did.

He took on the role in this society circle of something of the circus ringmaster. There became a set within a set and yet another set, and Dr Ward played with them like Russian dolls. The string that held the parcel together, giftwrapped it, were the girls. Mostly in their late teens, they were mature in their planning, which for the majority meant a good marriage: a 17-year-old girl was usually more intent on a wedding ring than on forging a career. Stephen Ward warmly adhered to that view.

The fashions, the precise make-up, the 'look' was aimed at sophistication, which meant older and more experience. Full-figured was the intention, and that was always emphasised, often with the help of Berlei corselettes and Twilfit bras and roll-ons, uncomfortable rubbery affairs with suspenders attached. Girdles and corsets were marketed, promising nipped waists (rationing also helped there) and breast uplift, which almost reached the neck, challenging the centre of gravity. Someone suggested that was where 'talking through your tits' began. Up close, with some, it was clear they were playing a part. Others had refined the role.

When quizzed about the age difference with the older men who courted them with cars, gifts and dinners, Stephen Ward invented a phrase for them: 'Say gentlemen are only as old as the girl they feel'.

Ward said that a lot, especially to his Thursday lunchtime chums. Some of them rather believed it.

CHAPTER THREE

DOCTOR IN THE HOUSE

'LIFE BEGINS AT OXFORD CIRCUS'

Jack Hylton & His Orchestra, 1934

When the future Queen gazed out at him, Stirling Henry Nahum's face was a picture of concentration, while she was radiant and relaxed as she is in the many images he captured of her on her wedding day. The photographer known only as 'Baron' was wonderful at coaxing the best reaction from *his* subjects, so good that he became a By Appointment accoutrement to the British Royal Family.

It helped that he was a close friend of Prince Philip and the Prince's pleasure-interested cousin David, Marquess of Milford Haven. It was Prince Philip's positive influence that secured his duties as the official Royal Wedding photographer on Thursday, 20 November 1947.

Any other Thursday, the Prince, his best man Milford Haven, Baron and his friend Stephen Ward and their cohorts would have been found in reprobate form, quaffing champagne, dining on lobster and oysters, and nominating their 'cunt of the month', an accolade awarded to the member of Baron's Thursday Club who had behaved the most foolishly in the preceding four weeks. It was always a close-run event. The membership of the gatherings, a weekly endeavour he created towards the end of 1946, was eclectic and liked to enjoy itself. The evening before the Royal Wedding at Westminster Abbey, Baron dined with Stephen Ward and three friends of the Marquess of Milford Haven. It was made clear then that the wedding would not stop Prince Philip being on parade on Thursdays – duties, of course, allowing. The Thursday Club met, up the post-lunch perilous and claustrophobic stairway, in Wheelers restaurant at 19–21, Old Compton Street, a favourite Soho dining spot of Lucian Freud, Francis Bacon and other tearaway talent. Nevertheless, Wheelers' owner Bernard Walsh kept the Thursday Club to strict invitation-only gatherings. Tables and chairs were squeezed together in the tiny second-floor dining room. As were the bunch of friends and their associates who were very much of their time. The Thursday rendezvous was their antidote to austerity, the champagne to brighten the grey days. Stephen Ward saw it as the ultimate acceptance. Baron had the endorsement of Prince Philip's uncle Lord Louis Mountbatten, great-grandson of Queen Victoria and the last Viceroy of India.

'Uncle Dickie' Mountbatten was precious about his image and, although he discarded more of Baron's photographs of him than he accepted, the final results were always celebrated. This patronage secured Baron in society. He had created attention working with the Sadler's Wells ballet company but after the war was drawn to social and celebrity photography. This helped with his other great interest: girls and their indulgences at sex parties. He led not so much a change in moral values but an acceptance of interests with greater parameters. Baron had photographic studios on Park Lane and an apartment on Brick Street, where he 'entertained'. He owned another, more private home behind Knightsbridge in Kinnerton Street, near the Nag's Head, where scallywags could get their legal misdemeanours, traffic tickets, the occasional fracas or a small burglary fixed by landlord Ned

Owen, who had the constabulary on his payroll. Baron had the conversational style of his Italian father, a wickedly entertaining shipping merchant, and the look of a faded silent-film matinee idol – all misgivings, velvet jackets and bow ties. He could have given tours of haunted houses.

Yet, he was the prime entertainment of the Thursday Club, his animation an amazement to lunch guests like filmstars Peter Ustinov, James Robertson Justice and David Niven, and the endearingly stuttering Lord Glenavy (Patrick Campbell). There were London newspaper editors (Arthur Christiansen of the *Daily Express* and the *Daily Mail*'s Frank Owen) and New York (Sam Boal of the *New York Post*), broadcasters like Gilbert Harding and men about town such as the lawyer Michael Eddowes. Larry 'Mr Harmonica' Adler, who was branded a Communist sympathiser in America, was a founding member: 'Around 1947 photographer Baron and others started the Thursday Club. It met once a week at Wheelers. Prince Philip joined. I, being blacklisted back home at the time, was dubbed the Subversive Country Member and, in my honour, whitebait on the menu was changed to *redbait*.'

The emphasis on lunches was humour, and very relaxed humour. Lewd talk, jokes on buggery a speciality, was most acceptable but serious chatter disdained. If the conversation veered towards politics or more conventional topics, the lunchers would burst into song, belting out 'Lloyd George Knew My Father' – which, in some cases, he probably did.

Stephen Ward would sit next to the Conservative politician Iain Macleod (who became MP for Enfield West in February 1950) and across from his and Baron's great friend, mentor and fellow female worshipper Vasco Lazzolo, a master of illustrations and paintings. Ward's other friend was the official war artist and expressionist painter Feliks Topolski. The Warsaw-born British citizen was a brilliant draughtsman and he and Ward were allowed to discuss their artistic skills, as well as women and buggery, at the lunches. He had a drawing of Ward having sex with a redheaded woman, his *'pinga grande'* in full flourish. Topolski painted many contemporary portraits, among them the authors Evelyn Waugh, Graham Greene and H.G. Wells. There was a suggestion he drew opera's turbulent Maria Callas, the only women ever invited to a Thursday lunch, but there is no confirmation portrait or sketch. Stephen Ward did sketch another of the guests, Harold Philby of the Foreign Office, but the work vanished with the subject. The Thursday lunch would go on until long into the evening and, with all such lubricated gatherings, the laughter would become louder, the jokes more outrageous and not so funny. It was in stark contrast to Prime Minister Clement Attlee's sober-minded, if not inclined Labour administration.

London had its own social marquee, which was divorced more by sensibility than geography from the rest of Britain. In turn, Mayfair ran its own kingdom. And made its own rules. Dining and wining, gambling and sex dominated life, it seemed. And so they did. Work was to finance such activities. Ward didn't worry too much about that. His charges ranged from five to ten guineas, a status-dictated sliding scale. The more patients, clearly the more he would earn; but he rarely saw his first patient until 10am and lunch was a pre-ordained 12.30pm. Often he would leave his afternoons clear of appointments.

He would take his sketchpad with him and drink coffee, smoke and draw at the Kenya Coffee House in Marylebone High Street, a stroll from Cavendish Square.

Dr Ward was always an amiable, looming figure. He had a smile that displayed remarkably good upper teeth and a manner as engaging as his bite. He was always closely shaven, groomed and clean. The only hint of the cavalier was his hair, which, when he needed a trim from the barbershop in George Street, flicked up above his ears in tiny tufts, devil's wings. He spoke like someone who had worked for a time with the BBC in Bristol, his tones not quite capital. He had an income of around £5,000 a year. He never appeared threatening; he was a doctor. To a Mrs Bennet with a sharp eye, he'd be a 'catch'. To the girls he met on the streets of London, professionals and the many others pursuing legitimate lives, he was a pleasant enough man, someone who made the day a little better. If they needed somewhere to stay, he had room at his flat, and his sitting room regularly doubled as a laundry room, with girls drying their underwear and their hair in front of the gas fire often in preparation for Dr Ward taking them to a society party.

'Everyone wanted to show off with their parties,' said Barry Stonehill, whose father founded the fabulously successful and rich J. Stonehill Wine Merchants in Moorgate, London, which fuelled high society. Ward, a buyer of plonk, would discuss the merits of fine wine with Stonehill at his Mayfair home. Barry Stonehill, the youngest son, was, he says, good at spending. An extravagant 6ft 4in and a little more tall, like an over-reaching quotation mark, with style to match his height, in a perfectly fitting white dinner jacket, he cavalry charged through social circles in California, the South of France and the Caribbean with roustabouts like the 'wicked, wicked' actor Errol Flynn.

In London, he had the sprawling penthouse apartment of Hereford House in North Row, Mayfair: 'Everything had to be amusing. I had a flowers and fauna party with an alligator and a monkey and birds in gold cages and all the guests. Someone was bitten by a monkey – that got the newspapers jumping about; all over Jimmy Pettigrew's "In London Last Night" in the *Evening Standard*. We had all the food catered, from Les Ambassadeurs, places like that. Where did the alligators come from? I hired them, same as anything else. The girls were guests. Stephen came to the parties and he always brought girls. Of course, he had the orgies with all the paraphernalia but we were more discreet on the sex front at our parties – more of that other sort of thing in Cannes and Havana or Nassau. *Abroad.*

'Stephen was a womaniser. I never saw him at a party without attractive girls around him – girls who were tall and slim, who were (or could be) models. "Gamine" is the word, lovely girls. They had fashionable figures, which would dress well. He was a clever and cultured man, interested in every topic imaginable, from spiritualism to black magic. We became good friends and had dinner together, talked about everything. He was interested, as I was, in Albert Schweitzer and his work in Lambaréné in central Africa, in the rainforest. We discussed all sorts of projects.

'Of course, he was one of the best osteopaths I've ever been treated by, and that has been a great many over the years. I consulted him all the time in London. With my height I've suffered slipped discs constantly and endured horrible pain. Some of the osteopaths have helped me immediately and Stephen was one of them. He had healing hands. He was gentle and with ease he returned my body to as it should be. I would leave his consulting rooms free of agony. He wanted to heal, not harm people. At the parties he wanted everyone to enjoy themselves, meet who they wanted to.'

Which is how Dr Ward met Eunice Bailey, whom many of her friends say was the only girl to truly break his heart. She was exceptional, with lush, long and dramatic red hair; a *natural*, and with the wit and manner to go with it. 'She was a stupendous beauty,' recalled Kim Waterfield. 'Eunice could go anywhere and enchant anyone. It was no wonder Stephen Ward was bowled over by her; everybody was. I got punched on the head when someone thought I'd slept with her – she made men mad with jealousy.'

When Ward glimpsed her at one of Baron's parties, he was predictably enchanted – and immediately told her so. It made no difference that he was out that evening with his latest interest, the American actress-singer-dancer Betta St John. She made her Hollywood debut (aged 11) in 1939, appearing opposite Marlene Dietrich in *Destry Rides Again* and almost a decade later created the role of the Tonkinese girl Liat in *South Pacific*, the stage bonanza of Broadway and, later, London, with which she would follow the production. She was dating Ward, whom she met through friends appearing on the West End stage. As Dr Ward, he was often called out to deal with the pains and strains encountered by actors and dancers. He enjoyed the entertainment community, for those involved liked, as he did, to put on a show. And it was a world of lithe and attractive girls. But, stunning as she was, Betta St John (originally Betty Jean Striegler from Hawthorne, California) could not compete with Alfred and Lily Bailey's daughter Eunice from Streatham, south London.

'She sparkled,' said Bobby McKew. 'They talk about all that "light up the room" thing – she had it, lots of it. And that gorgeous red hair.'

Of course, Stephen Ward knew exactly who should help him 'launch' Eunice into society and modelling: his friend Baron, whose subjects were as exclusive as Dr Ward's. First, he introduced 'my close friend Eunice Bailey' to society parties, where she mixed with film, theatre and radio names of the moment. These were parties where famous names would do readings and young actors or actresses might debut. This was a party crowd, where there was always someone who could help 'make you a star'. Influence was a strong currency.

Stephen Ward spent what he had lavishly on Eunice Bailey. It was a remarkable courtship. She met Prince Philip and other members of the Thursday Club at parties – there was one somewhere Monday to Saturday – and American theatre stars like Mary Martin, doing the London run of a Broadway success.

Always there were theatricals and artists in Ward's bohemian mix, which he would flavour with friends and patients like Ava Gardner, Peter Ustinov, Lauren Bacall and Mel Ferrer. Often around were the American comic couple Ben and Bebe Lyon, who made their home in London during the war and became a BBC radio fixture with *Hi, Gang!*, which broadcast throughout the

1940s. By then, Ward was renowned as an osteopath with a Who's Who patient list from European Royalty, the Hollywood variety, half a dozen of Winston Churchill's family, the House of Commons, the Lords, the Church and money men from the City of London.

'Sometimes going to his consulting rooms was like watching a Pathé newsreel,' noted Barry Stonehill, 'a famous face flickered past.'

Eunice Bailey did appear to be one of Dr Ward's 'special' girls. Many of those who knew him use the word 'besotted' to describe how he behaved with the women singled out from his crowds. He was indeed like one of the 1940s Hollywood moguls who believed they could bestow the miracle of stardom, huge public or social acceptance, on whom they personally chose. A tremendous conceit, it's been done many, many times and is operatic in its plot. Strange things happen when a star is born, not least the question of divided loyalties.

Dr Ward concentrated on coaching Eunice Bailey towards the modelling career she was clearly perfect to be fitted for. Baron photographed her, Dior anointed her their premier model and Salvador Dalí painted her. She and Ward dated in the more conventional sense. Dr Ward was not one for expensive dinners, if he was paying. They ate in cafes – he liked cracked pepper on scrambled eggs – and Eunice would be told to watch her figure: coffee was good for you. They'd sit around in his apartment and he'd read out items of interest, things 'good to know', from the newspapers. She was 18 when he met her as 1946 ended, and he helped her grow into a confident young woman. He was nearly twice her age but in 1949 such romances were not unusual. What *was* unusual was that Stephen Ward did not so much want to take a wife as make a success of the woman he said he loved.

It was clear to her friends that 'Eunice's doctor' was going to propose, and she told them she'd accept but he never did, never quite got round to doing so. His dithering cost him. He didn't lose touch but he lost Eunice to a younger set, to friends like Kim Waterfield and his brother Johnny and Johnny's 'great chum' Pitt Oakes, whose carpet-bagging gold-mine multi-millionaire father Sir Harry Oakes was murdered in the Bahamas in 1943. He was tarred and feathered and burned, killed by black magic or the Mafia, or a jealous husband. Whoever the culprit was, the result remained the same: his children got his money.

It was said that Ward was devastated to the extent that life was not worth living after Eunice Bailey moved on, but Bobby McKew recalls: 'The next thing he was with a new bird, a lovely girl called Patricia Baines. He trotted around with her, quite the thing' ... all the way to Marylebone Register Office, where they married on 27 July 1949. Twenty-one-year-old Pat Baines was a bright girl, who was already establishing her name as a model when she met Stephen Ward at one of Baron's bring-a-bottle impromptu parties. Ward's reaction was instant:

'I decided that I wanted her.

'I worked it out quite calmly.

'She would grace the practice.

'She would be useful.

'She was also desirable.

'I wanted her.'

He recounted it as if dictating a memo on his modus operandi.

Yet, not so secretly, Patricia Baines was that dreaded thing: somewhat middle class. Her father was a company director and she had been raised with conformity in London. They lived not far off Belgrave Square. Stephen Ward rented his Jaguar, rented girls, rented his consulting rooms and flat, earned well but spent what he got on appearances; he was canny with money but he wasn't careful with it in the sense of High Street bank savings. That was all too, well, middle class – just like Baines, who dreamed of being an ideal homemaker and had never heard that warning about covers and books. Her perception of the new man in her life was that he was a professional and social success, a talented doctor with well-to-do friends, a jolly *and* enjoyable companion: a perfect match.

His habit of chatting up prostitutes in the middle of the night was, understandably, inconducive to marital harmony. Yet, in their wedding-day photograph, they look as the happy couple should: he in his pressed suit, buttonhole and polished toecaps, she in a specially designed dress, with pearls and chiffon flowers.

From then on, marriage appeared to be a game of chance for Dr Ward. He missed out with Eunice Bailey, signed the register with Patricia Baines and, by the time they were honeymooning in Paris, he appeared to be fed up with every aspect of matrimony.

Whether deliberately or of necessity, he did not take enough cash for the trip. There was no honeymoon suite or champagne dinners – like the wine they drank, it could be called, at best, cheap and cheerful. Dr Ward's bride was distraught. Her husband was behaving like a monster, more suited to the bells of Notre Dame than even a low-rent Bastille pension.

Rather than forgotten, the honeymoon mishaps continued, aggravated on the return to London with the return of Dr Ward's evening sexual adventures. Fractured from the off, the marriage was unofficially over within a couple of months. Ward had liked the idea of Mrs Ward answering the telephone at his consulting rooms, of being on his arm at theatre and dinner receptions, of being part of his life. That was, of course, the snag: it was only *part* of his life. The other, vital, area was his social life and, some might argue, *anti*-social activities. He was addicted to sexual thrills and the company of young women; it mattered not if they were tarts or debs, or out-of-town goslings happily giggling their way into trouble. And some of his sketches, framed and on display in his apartment, far racier than flying ducks on the walls of suburbia; he didn't disguise his proclivities.

The problem wasn't that there were three people in Mrs Ward's marriage: there were three dozen – and counting. An open marriage is one thing, but Stephen Ward's idea was more 'Open,

Sesame'. He wanted it all, and he expected that he could have it.

His versions of this short, unhappy time depended on with whom he was talking. For some, he dealt with it invoking macho bravado. To others, it was love that just wasn't quite right. Years later from her home in Michigan, Pat Baines would say of that short and absurd time: 'He was virtually a stranger to me, even when we were married. I think he was in conflict with himself most of the time but he did have a lot of charm.'

When she moved into the George Street flat in Marylebone belonging to her friend, the actress Patricia Owens, in 1950, she told Owens and her boyfriend Bobby McKew: 'Stephen lives in a different country from the rest of us. He's a man who must live his own life. He has his own rules and can only live by them.'

Instead of saying he was charming, she went on: 'By the end of it, he frightened me.'

Dr Ward analysed himself somewhat differently when confronted with what he saw as a failure, snapping: 'I can't think why I proposed to her. I did so after only a few days. Now I like to forget it – it was quite disastrous.'

Which was something that distressed him. Romantic errors. Mistakes. It didn't lower his own self-esteem but he concerned himself as to how it would affect his value in the eyes of others, those he was anxious to enjoin and impress. Emotionally, he was sociopathic – his head did all the work, trying to escape the problem, his heartbeat stayed regular. There was no shame in being who you are: Stephen Ward's life came from his gut.

Still, anxious to salve the suspicion of others, he took the trouble to disguise this, proffering more conventional reasons for such a swift end to the marriage: 'She always wanted things – that was it, she wanted things. I simply couldn't stand it. I was glad to give her grounds for divorce, and, believe me, I provided lots of grounds. When the break came, Patricia told me: "You're not a man at all and I don't know why it took me so long to find out."

'What she meant was that I couldn't see why marriage should

mean things instead of feelings. She wanted clothes, she wanted a house; she wanted all the usual symbols. She wanted to buy furniture; she wanted to buy life insurance; she wanted to buy a car.

'That wasn't the way I saw marriage at all. Pat brought it home to me that marriage was things, things and more things.

'Once the recriminations began there was no end to them. She said things that were, to me, unforgivable. That I had given her a completely wrong impression of who I was and what I was. But that wasn't true. She imagined that because she met smart people with me and saw me at a smart party, because I lived at a smart address and some of the greatest names in the country were my patients, that I was rich.

'We kept on having rows. She said she thought I was so self-obsessed that I could never love or be loved. Now I sound like a woman's magazine.'

Which of course he did – to him, it seemed something of the right thing to say. And Stephen Ward's friends would realise it wasn't his fault. He told them he had been content to give his wife grounds for divorce, including adultery, but it was 20 months before their divorce was absolute, granted on the grounds of his mental cruelty. He was the one who delayed the divorce, who wouldn't let go, caught yet again between the vicarage and the brothel – or the dungeon.

Dr Ward and his friends Baron and Vasco Lazzolo had collections of pornography, as did another Thursday Club member, the big band leader Jack Hylton who always requested extra oysters for his libido. A popular club member, he often paid the bill and owned one of the largest classical pornography collections in Europe. Another enthusiast was boatmaker Beecher Moore, a pioneer of post-war racing dinghy sailing and sex lunches. He had priceless amounts of written and illustrated erotica. Moore and his wife Bobbie hosted some of London's most inventive

Sunday lunches in their private apartment in the Temple, with its stunning views.

Yet, Dr Ward was always looking for something different. He always had the girls, others had the locations and the equipment: whips, malacca canes, straps and assorted restraining and penetrative devices. Some enthusiasts enjoyed the wooden butter paddles employed in groceries – a speciality of 'Red Kate', who, at her mews establishment a couple of hundred yards off Piccadilly Circus, catered to the needs of those requiring humiliation and hurt in their ongoing quest for pleasure.

There was a good deal of money in pain. Police evidence of the day details that Katherine East was one of London's top ten richest women in her own right. She made far more than an MP or a Minister of the Crown, more than a Harley Street specialist or barrister – more, indeed, than most of her customers. Then again, she was providing a discreet service with its own particular ways and means of laying down the law.

Clients began to get their money's worth from the moment they reached her front door, cloaked in expensive crimson velvet. The curtain veiled the door's eccentric decorations of nails – dozens of them, with sharpened ends pounded out through it. An appointment, for a precise time, would have been arranged. Kate was waiting. And so too was the client – he would have to ring the front doorbell for several minutes before he got any attention. The humiliation had started. And the pain as the client knocked on the door and, in some cases, crashed his body against it. Kate knew just how long to wait before opening her porcupine door to greet her guests (many of whom decorated the pages of *Debrett's*) with the desired welcome: creative abuse. Weaklings of their own sordid desires, she despised them: 'You filthy, contemptible, ill-mannered pig! How *dare* you show impatience at my door!'

As this arousing tirade continued, the client had to walk stiffly through big-shouldered Kate's private bedroom into what she called her 'operations den'. Many times she was offered huge sums of money to allow a client to lie on her bed while she whipped them. Her refusal didn't offend: 'I would never be able to sleep in my room again, if I had let you so much as touch my bed!' Her services ranged between £50 and £100 – hugely expensive for a couple of hours' relaxation. To vary the form, girls (interns, as it were, many of them girls about town wanting some pin money and a giggle) would be brought in to whip the clients. Others were highly trained in the pertinent rigours. Rarely were there prosecutions. Red Kate was never charged with anything, but one 17-year-old girl supplied evidence of being taught how to deliver a whip with leather thongs and a two-foot malacca cane to eager clients, complemented by verbal lashings.

The Marquess of Milford Haven enjoyed a variance in lifestyle. At his parties, organised in Mayfair by Baron, there would be illegal gambling, chemin de fer and drinking, and then the cabaret of girls chasing around in little more than leather skirts, which would be flipped up in a 'when-the-music-stops'-type game. Men would be tied up in one room, girls in another; at some parties, they would produce giant plastic penises and make the girls bow down to them while guests playfully interfered with the exposed and spankingly pink backsides. Nothing was sacrosanct other than not paying your gambling losses, a gentleman's unpardonable sin.

'It wasn't romantic at those parties but it was always fascinating,' recalled Bobby McKew. 'I went along for the girls but others liked the other stuff. The younger crowd thought we were being very modern, very with it and unconventional. Some were there because they needed it.

'There was nothing evil or malicious about it – that's how they got their kicks. They didn't invent it any more than the Bloomsbury Set did. It was intriguing. Many of the men were older and they'd stand around naked. Some kept their black socks on, held up by suspenders. They'd lean on the mantelpiece and be talking about some debate in the House of Commons and someone would ask: "Do you mind if I suck your wife's pussy?" That would turn them on. There'd be a nod and they'd say: "She'd love it, dear boy, she'd love it." And off they'd go. And they did. Love it, that is.

'At one party I went off to find the lavatory and went into a bedroom by mistake. There was a man dressed head to toe in a rubber suit hanging from the back of the door. Hanging from it by his shoulders! On his face, over the rubber hood, he had a gas mask.

'I was wondering who it was and [film producer] turned to me and said: "Don't worry, he's relaxing."

'He saw the puzzle on my face and smiled: "We'll all have a drink later."'

Bobby McKew, Stephen Ward and the extraordinary cast of characters around them were heading into the 1950s, a period of devilment and danger, with nothing apparently to concern them but finding more fun. Still, there's no such thing as a free lunch, no matter what day of the week it is.

CHAPTER FOUR

DOCTOR IN HEAT

'BIG BREATHS!'
'YETH, AND I'M ONLY THIXTEEN.'

Doctor in the House, Richard Gordon, 1952

Fun and games were always on offer along Great Windmill Street, a couple of dozen yards up Shaftesbury Avenue from Piccadilly Circus. Each afternoon, a crowd waited heatedly for the 2.30pm opening of the Windmill Theatre and the delights of the Windmill Girls, nude ladies whose fullness had not been depleted by the rationing years. They were built for slow motion but even that was against the law.

The Lord Chamberlain, Lord Cromer, had acknowledged the argument that naked statues could not be called obscene and prosecuted. The Windmill could therefore present its ladies in motionless poses. The law: 'if something moves, it's rude'.

Audiences paid to view the glamorous girls arranged with care in exotic *tableaux vivants*; this was artistic material and the shows were themed. The mermaids were obvious, the Annie Oakley tableaux of the Wild West firecracker and friends inspirational. It was a harbinger of future delights like Soho clubland's 'Bonnie Bell the Ding Dong Girl', who performed decorated only in said bells, which customers could ring as she squealed: 'Dinner time, dinner time... all you can eat!' And snakes with naked ladies wriggling around and vice versa; there were whipping shows, all leather and body parts being lashed and entangled – all evidence there's no business like showbusiness. With such illegal antics elsewhere, the Windmill Theatre was mainstream; the police enjoyed free drinks and other hospitality after the shows, while Stephen Ward found new candidates for his specialised attention.

Also solidly established was nearby Murray's Cabaret Club in Beak Street, a basement establishment where more than 100 customers could crowd in to eat and drink, watch creatively costumed showgirls and buy them expensive drinks. Usually, there were at least 35 girls revolving through the small stage: make-up and costume changes were dealt with in premises across the street. It attracted a rich assortment of custom. At Murray's, there was always someone to have a drink with, an MP, a lawyer or a City gent, as well as the girls to look at. Or to engage with more actively.

As a wartime RAF officer, the television executive and film producer Harry Alan Towers became very fond of Murray's. All his life, he had a comfortable apartment in Weymouth House in Hallam Street, which he called a suite, a ten-minute walk towards Regent's Park from Oxford Circus. At one time, he would begin every evening at Murray's (ostensibly to work on film and television projects as his mother shared the apartment with him). He and his mother, Margaret Miller Towers, produced many of the successful radio programmes of the 1940s and early 50s. Shows included *The Lives of Harry Lime*, the eponymous *The Third Man* of Graham Greene's novella, which fed on the author's knowledge of one particular duplicitous character in British Intelligence. He also had a series created from Sherlock Holmes' adventures starring John Gielgud as Holmes.

Towers' love life was not even a one-pipe problem. He was always happy to relate his expertise with the world's brothels and his lifetime association with prostitutes. He knew what he liked and was willing to pay. He regarded the girls at Murray's and other London nightclubs (he knew the doorman or maître d' at every one) as something apart, available only if they wanted to 'extend their income'.

Percy 'Pops' Murray would recruit teenaged girls (looking always at least 18 years old) from around Britain and ensure expensive clothes and jewellery were made easily available for them… on hefty instalment charges. A hypocritical villain, Murray knew the girls would need extra money, although they were banned from leaving the club with a customer. Towers and others met their 'new friends' in the doorway of Lawley's, the Regent Street hardware store.

Towers, who would sip Bristol Cream sherry and hammer ideas out on a portable typewriter, was sharp. He told me how he had spotted on his second visit to Murray's that certain visitors to the club were taken to one of three booths tightly squeezed into corners. When he spotted the radio 'mikes', something he worked with every day, he realised the booths were all wired for sound. He believed there was a link to Scotland Yard but the arrangements made with 'Pops' Murray were organised by a different Government agency.

Scotland Yard's focus was on happenings next to the Windmill, for across the street were the West End offices of Jack Solomons, who controlled much of British boxing; his speciality was to import big-name American fighters, most of whom were managed by the American Mafia. Boxing meant money, both from the event and gambling on it. Of course, given the personnel involved, it could also mean trouble. It attracted all kinds of punters and often they made compatible connections. Which is why it was never easy to climb the stairs to the third floor at 41, Great Windmill Street, the offices of Solomons Promotions. The tea and billiards on the second floor were tempting, but it was the gossip there and the chance of a cash-making scheme that truly invited.

When he escaped the Siberian labour camps, after arriving in

London in 1949, Polish refugee Perec Rachman made some extra money stacking cues in the billiard hall, which he spent on prostitutes. A couple of years later, he was known as Peter and began taking an interest in the London property market. His associate Serge Paplinski enjoyed watching the boxers work out in Solomons' expansive gymnasium, as did his younger friend, the grinning Johnny Edgecombe from Antigua, who liked to be known as 'The Edge' and also did a little running around for the alarmingly charismatic, if roly-poly and balding Rachman.

Around Great Windmill Street, there were often opportunities for keen young men – a job, a mail van or some such 'nice little tickle'. Murder-for-hire was getting so expensive in London some said it was cheaper to do it yourself in this topsy-turvy environment where much influence was double-barrelled.

When the future first Earl of Snowdon, Antony Armstrong-Jones, offered advice on sketching to Stephen Ward, it didn't sit well with him and he dismissed Armstrong-Jones as 'one of Baron's trainees'. Which, indeed, the young photographer was, but, like Dr Ward himself, he was on a journey in society. Armstrong-Jones helped finance that by getting £10, win or lose, when enlisted to make bets on greyhounds at the racetracks around London. The enterprise was orchestrated by Billy Hill, and his lieutenant Bobby McKew explained: 'We used out-of-work actors at a tenner a time to provide different faces to make the bets on the dog races that were fixed. Eddie Chapman ran the ring and we doped certain dogs in every race. Dear Denis Shaw, the pockmarked actor who was always in the werewolf or vampire films frightening people, was an "innocent" regular for us. They always took *his* bets. He brought along Tony Armstrong-Jones as another "innocent" fresh face. Nobody knew who he was so he could do the job happily for us and get a few bob in return.'

Former Polish Army butcher John Mills had already made his fortune as a provider of high society fun and had broken off his partnership with fellow Army food tycoon Siegi Sessler. He had moved Les Ambassadeurs from its spot opposite Trinidadian bandleader Edmundo Ros' eponymous club in Stratton Street (the future Queen first danced in public to his music in 1946) to one of London's prime positions at the bottom of Park Lane, overlooking Hyde Park. He had background investors who were 'managed' by a lawyer with offices by the Connaught Hotel. On the top floor he placed The Milroy, with society favourite Paul Adam replacing Harry Roy as, in many ways, the leader of the band. For himself, Mills created a small apartment one more floor up, to which he added a movie room, where he could screen films for special guests.

Or further entertain them.

Number 5, Hamilton Place, built in 1810, stands on the site of one of King Henry VIII's hunting lodges and was purchased by Leopold de Rothschild in 1878. Rothschild waved money at the building and it is very much fin de siècle Louis XV. The Barbetti staircase remains a marvel of woodcarving and has led many guests to dizzy heights of enjoyment.

World War I veteran and accomplished scientist and inventor Captain Leonard Frank Plugge and his wife, Mrs Gertrude Ann Muckleston, took over 5, Hamilton Place when he sat as MP for Chatham until 1945. Plugge (pronounced 'Plooje') was a connoisseur of beautiful women and would engage an assortment of them to cater to his every need, his only prerequisite being that they were completely naked while doing so. 'Dirty Lenny' is how Kim Waterfield knew him: 'He kept a couple of mistresses in Dolphin Square and had what in the Deep South of America they call "weird ways".'

When 'Dirty Lenny' sold Hamilton Place with its magnificent garden to John Mills in 1950, he was a central member of the rich, titled and aspiring in the 'Princess Margaret Set' and a good friend of Stephen Ward's. And it was Les Ambassadeurs to which that fast-living crowd went, almost every evening, in almost every circumstance. The American-Polish film producer Gene Gutowski was a habitué, who recalled in 2012: 'There was dancing to the orchestra of Paul Adam. Dark suits were obligatory, as were black shoes. I was once turned away at the door for wearing a dark-blue blazer: "This is not Miami, Mr Gutowski," the man at the front door admonished me.'

Kim Waterfield recalled one evening with Stephen Ward in 1952: 'I'd just flown in from New York and got a hire car at the airport, a self-drive Humber Hawk. And where did I go? Les Ambassadeurs! Where else? I couldn't pass it – that sweeping staircase and all the beautiful girls.

'People talked about Hollywood, they talked about Rome, but London had the most beautiful and wildest girls in the world.

'It was a long flight, but it never occurred to me not to go to Les Ambassadeurs. I went to freshen up and the attendant there could see the travel weariness in me. "Would you like something to help?" he asked and produced a couple of Benzedrine – it's what kept so many of the crowd going until dawn.

'The Milroy club was *the* nightclub, principally because that was Princess Margaret's haunt. Les Ambassadeurs and The Milroy club were the smartest places in town. We were young and arrogant and thought that people who went places like the Stork Room were the riff-raff – Les A was where you dined. I got there and was talking to John Mills, and Paul [Adam] came over and we ended up with Stephen at the bar. Sunny Blandford [heir to the 10th Duke of Marlborough] and people like that were about – it was the time they were gossiping that Sunny was going to marry Margaret. I should have asked her, for later in the evening, with the drinks and the travel and the chemical help, I was a little disoriented and walked into the wrong toilet and almost into Margaret's stall! Happily, all was well.

'Paul Adam was her favourite bandleader. He'd set up a song for her as soon as she and her entourage arrived. Princess Margaret always loved it when he'd sing "Chicago, Chicago, That

Wonderful Town". He'd always sing, "You gotta go *down*, you gotta go *downnn...*" with all the innuendo absolutely intended.

'The Milroy wasn't theatreland, it was very much films – American film producers, very heavily Americanised. These Americans were of a certain age and they had beautiful starlets with them and at a certain time the girls would make their excuses and say, "I've got to be home with Mummy" or "It's the night I wash my hair", and they'd sneak straight up to The Milroy. It was still the time of rationing and it was part of the culture that you brought a bottle.

'Paul was a master at the music but he was louche, swinging his cock more than his baton. Paul was Stephen Ward's great chum. Paul was married to the very beautiful actress Zena Marshall, but they divorced and Paul married Jane Hart from Hampshire. In turn, Stephen was besotted by Jane, adored her.'

'Stephen was a good friend,' the onetime Jane Adam told me in 2013 at her coastal home in the west of England. 'My husband went to him as an osteopath and that's how I first got to know him. We'd go off and have a coffee with him afterwards. I found him quite shy but he was difficult to describe. He was easy-going and easy to be with, there was no dark side. He always said he was looking for beauty in his life.

'He didn't stand out; he didn't push himself with me. I wasn't romantically involved with him but we'd go to Richmond Park, where he liked to take photographs of the deer. He enjoyed it there, feeding the deer, taking his photographs. He was a very good photographer. And an artist, he did a very nice drawing of me. He was a talented osteopath but he never had any money. He was always scrounging cigarettes, preferably Senior Service. I went with him to Milroy, where Paul had his band and he always got a warm welcome – people really liked him.'

Kim Waterfield endorses this impression: 'One was always pleased to see Stephen – he was always a delight. He was meant to be a bit tight but I don't recall him paying the bill or not paying the bill and, whichever way it went, it being a problem. It was certainly considered a great discourtesy to allow a girl to pay a bill and someone who didn't stand their round stood out. Stephen liked girls and that was that. I enjoyed him, easy-going person.

'He was something of a snob, but who wasn't? He was not a name-dropper and he spent a lot of time with the Queen Mother, who was such a popular figure but he never said anything about it. He had a good way about him. There was no question he was a nice, clean-looking man. He had a strange presence. He might have been there and he might not have been, and no one said: "Where's Stephen?"

'What you see isn't always what you get. Stephen deployed a cigarette holder in the evenings and he held it in an arch way and the first time I met him, I thought he was an old queen. He was older than us but I soon discovered he wasn't an old queen.'

Bobby McKew saw much evidence of this: 'Stephen would be in the coffee shops down Park Lane and he'd have his sketchpad and he'd look at a lot of girls and he'd draw them, and eventually the girl would come over and sit with him. He was a good-looking man and women found him attractive, there was no argument about it. Every time I saw him, he was with a different beautiful girl and I hated him. Then I got to know him. Paul Adam used to go round to Stephen's and get him to massage him. I went round there, but not for a massage. With Stephen, I always felt that he was offering you his girls, but in turn he wanted to fuck one of yours – free love.

'He was one of the crowd; he drifted about – he wasn't a great friend in that sense. He wasn't the type you'd instantly think of to invite out for the evening but, when he was out and about, he was good company. He knew everyone.

'I went to The Milroy and Ava Gardner was having a party. Paul Adam was there and lots of others, and Ava's sister, who wasn't all that, even after a few drinks, was sitting next to me and I was talking to her for ages. She said she didn't drink – she had her own jug of water. When she went over to help Ava with something I poured a glass of water and it was straight vodka – that's how she survived life with her sister. They were on the town every evening. We all went out every night. If we weren't at Les A or The Milroy, or The Star, we thought we were missing out.'

For many of Stephen Ward's crowd, The Star of Belgravia was the centre of the universe – no one who wasn't interesting seemed to go there. The painter Lucian Freud would spoof for drinks with underworld players like Bruce Reynolds; Billy Hill, the laconic leader of the London underworld, could be at one end of the bar and Scotland Yard Commander Wally Virgo at the other. Or next to Stephen Ward's patients: the Maharaja of Cooch-Behar, wartime veteran Jagaddipendra Narayan Bhup Bahadur and the Maharaja of Baroda, Sir Pratap Singh Gaekwad. 'Boss' Baroda kept in touch with his friend Stephen Ward, meeting for drinks at The Milroy and The Star.

'When I went out with Boss,' explained Bobby McKew, 'we were always with two or three or more gorgeous girls. I'm not sure Boss was ever that interested in sex with the girls, but he always wanted them around.

'One flash character who ran an Aston Martin dealership reckoned I was pimping for Boss. He approached me and asked, "Bobby, where do you get the girls for the Maharaja? I'd like to meet them very much." He thought I was a ponce! I was furious, but I didn't show it. I said the girls all came from a good contact, a Wilhelmina Hill. I gave him the phone number, Bayswater 7338, and told him to call. I said, "If a man answers, don't worry about it – he's the caretaker." So this guy starts ringing Billy Hill and asking about the girls. About a week later, he came up to me and apologised. He said he knew who he had been telephoning – he never asked about girls again.

'Bill's terrifying reputation went around the corner before him: the perception of what Bill might or could do scared the wits out of people. Paul Adam had an interest in a club in Stratton Street run by a devilish woman. Paul was complaining about getting money owed to him from her. I was putting myself about and I said I'd go around there with him. I was leaving Bill's place in Moscow Road and he asked where I was off to; I told him. He was bored and said he'd come with me.

'When Bill walked into the club the old bird clocked him immediately. A white poodle came running over to Bill and he feinted a kick at it and it ran off, scared but not hurt. The club woman went white. She thought he'd kicked her dog – and she was next. Bill just stared at her and said: "Pay the money or you go down a hole. *And* the dog goes too."

'That was that. At the stairs the poodle appeared and Bill leaned down and picked it up in his arms. He looked it in the eye and said: "I didn't mean it, I didn't mean it." He tickled the poodle's ears and we left.

'When I went to The Milroy with Boss that evening Paul had got his money. He was in a great mood. When he saw Boss and I, he turned to the orchestra and off they belted out the "The Rich Maharaja of Magador". From then on when Boss arrived, Paul would play that song.'

When in London, Boss Baroda would visit Dr Ward two or three times a week for treatment. He was then one of many illustrious patients in the inscribed, blue-jacketed appointment book: half a dozen Churchills including Winston and his son Randolph, politicians Sir Anthony Eden and Hugh Gaitskell, oilman Paul Getty and his always amusing business tycoon friend Nubar Gulbenkian, a range of musical maestros from Paul Adam to Sir Malcolm Sargent to Sir Thomas Beecham, and the famous from stage and screen such as Frank Sinatra, Mary Martin, Elizabeth Taylor and her then husband Mike Todd, Danny Kaye, Robert Taylor and Douglas Fairbanks Junior.

Socially, his circle had a similar range. And there were always new girls on the scene. As well as familiar faces like Eunice Bailey, who, on 5 July 1952, had married Pitt Oakes who was indulging most of his inheritance in strong drink.

'Stephen would be at parties or gatherings when Eunice was there and they'd be polite and kind to each other,' recalled Kim Waterfield.

Ward, as others tell it, looked at Eunice Bailey with unsoothable longing in his eyes. He must have wondered what might have been. Pitt Oakes was fun for a time but, when the drink took proper hold, it burned out any personality from him. The friends were at a party in the South of France, at the Cannes Martinez Hotel. The fun had become boisterous and the newly wed and drunken Pitt Oakes was walking a 'tightrope' along the balcony overlooking the glittering La Croisette Boulevard. 'Eunice came up behind me,' said Bobby McKew, 'and whispered in my ear, "How much to push him off?" And she meant it.'

Bobby McKew was by then living with Pat Owens, flatmate of Pat Baines, the former Mrs Patricia Ward. Pat Baines had gone to America and Pat Owens talked of following her, but to Hollywood. Ward would meet them for coffee at the George Street flat or, more likely, bump into one or other of them around the neighbourhood. Pat Owens was a lively and talented girl. She had appeared in *The Happiest Days of Your Life* (1950) with Alastair Sim and Margaret Rutherford. McKew thought she was terrific. He knew many of the aspiring thespians around London (his father was in the movies). Robert McKew Senior worked for Rank and was in charge of distribution to Irish cinemas.

Some of the Rank film crowd naturally gravitated to within the Milroy circle, including Kay Kendall, who Stephen Ward first met when she worked at Murray's, where the girls appeared in two shows a night and earned around £8–£10 a week minus 10 shillings for hair and make-up. The floorshows and costumes were elaborate, the nakedness most daring. Comfortable with the spotlight, Dr Ward escorted Kendall to dinner and showbusiness functions. With Pat Owens on his arm, so too was Bobby McKew. He took her to Dublin to meet his family and suggested they also visit her father, who she had said was living in Ireland.

'Pat didn't think that was going to happen – she only had a Post Office address for him. I thought it was strange and I suppose I went on about it a little. I didn't like things not making sense but then she told me the truth.'

Welsh-born Arthur Owens (also known as Arthur Graham White, codename 'SNOW') was Hitler's main spy in the UK during the early years of World War II. A civilian Royal Navy contractor, he had been recruited in 1936 before being 'turned' into a double agent by MI5 in 1941. Despite this, his loyalty was always questioned and finally he was interred at Dartmoor Prison until the end of the war. He travelled to Canada as 'Mr Brown' but spent his last years in Ireland.

'I think Pat just closed her mind to what had happened with her father; she concentrated on her career. Lots of girls wanted to escape their pasts,' says McKew.

In such circumstances, Dr Stephen Ward was always happy to help – 'Beauty is an odd thing. I would say I was one of the most successful men in town with girls. I'm not handsome, and I've no money. What is it then? I believe it is my basic interest in women as people. I know I understand a woman's mind.

'Sex isn't everything. I've had relationships with beautiful women and never had sex at all. I used to encourage all the girls I knew to talk to me, and to discuss their problems with me. I was really interested and in any case I liked to feel involved with them all.

'One man's passion is another man's poison.'

Passion was Ward's manifesto. He was also a diligent friend and stayed in touch with those who intrigued him. While he didn't push himself, he was persistent in his friendships.

Paul Adam's wife Jane, a showgirl and actress under her professional name of Jane Hart (shortened from 'Hartcut'), worked on *Lady Godiva Rides Again* (1951) with a string of British luminaries. Stephen Ward visited her at the set in Folkestone several times.

Among the cast were Diana Dors, Kay Kendall, Joan Collins (her film debut) and the usual comic suspects: Alastair Sim, George Cole, Stanley Holloway, Sid James and Dennis Price. Dors (who had for some years been involved with Kim Waterfield) met a confident and scheming rogue called Dennis Hamilton during filming and after five weeks married him at Westminster's Caxton Hall on 3 July 1951. Despite the security of marriage, or maybe because of the insecurity of it, she was a little wary of making new friends but she became very fond of Jane Hart, correctly rating her as one of the great beauties on the scene. The bountiful Dors, emerging filmstar and Britain's 'blonde bombshell' antidote to Hollywood platinum, was returning to London with other cast members. Hart said her friend was driving down and they would give her a lift back to town. Sixty-two years later, Jane Hart told me: 'I didn't expect what happened – but it did. Absolutely. Stephen had arranged to pick me up.'

Stephen Ward roared up to the cast hotel in Folkestone. But Diana Dors didn't like the look of him. She thought he was 'something of a show-off' and explained: 'Before lunch he insisted that I go for a quick ride in his new sports car, and he drove around the country lanes at such speeds that I was terrified.

'Just as we prepared to leave for London, he turned to Jane and announced he couldn't possibly give me a lift back. There just wasn't enough room for three of us. So off they went.'

Dors was a big star. Of course, Stephen Ward was not starstruck – and he most certainly wasn't interested in film titles.

Lady Godiva Rides Again was a beauty contest comedy but Ward took a serious interest in the girls parading in their bathing suits. One such girl was someone he knew by sight: Ruth Ellis, who regularly worked as a hostess for Morrie Conley. Ellis's great friend Vicki Martin had always wanted to be a movie star, a celebrity, to be *somebody*.

Stephen Ward helped her achieve that dream, the one she had brought a couple of years earlier, as Valerie Mews, on the No. 701 green bus from a suburban Staines, Middlesex to Park Lane, Mayfair. A one shilling and seven pence bus ride of 18 miles resulted in a remarkable metamorphosis.

With no plans, no future, no friends and nowhere to stay, Mayfair at 9pm – all bright lights and rushing around and noise and the heavy smell of soot in the air – was alien country. It all loomed, but Valerie Mews refused to be intimidated – she had left her grandmother's bungalow at 4, Chandos Road, Egham, for opportunity.

She got, if we can call it such, a lucky start.

CHAPTER FIVE

DOCTOR ON THE MOVE

'ARE YOU HAVING FUN?'

Flanagan & Allen, 1949

The coal fires of London gently puffing out putrid fumes and lung disease would slowly dim the light over the city until the sun flicked off the switch proper, but from her seat on the 701 bus Valerie Mews had a clear view of her future. It was as bright and unthreatening as she was.

She was, like many of the girls arriving in the capital, so very young: just 17 years old when she took her first step into Mayfair and turned towards Hyde Park Corner. Turning back on herself, she knocked on the doors of the clubs and restaurants around and off Piccadilly Circus and was greeted cheerfully, if not helpfully. Still, through the shadow and fog and the biting smell of sulphur, Valerie found herself in Duke Street, off Grosvenor Square, and being invited into Morrie Conley's Court Club. She could have a job and a bed and the club manager Ruth Ellis would help her settle in. Together, the two girls roomed in Tooting Bec. The double act extended to weekends when they would attend country parties and, off-duty, profitably see some of the Court Club regulars. Time sped feverishly forward in their young lives.

Next, Ruth won a promotion and was to manage the Little Club at 37, Brompton Road, just along from Harrods in Knightsbridge. Valerie needed to find a new flat and roommate; she needed a little more luck.

Call it happenstance.

A driving April shower rushed Valerie Mews into an Oxford Street doorway to seek shelter. She left just a few minutes later and was on her way to becoming Vicki Martin. Stephen Ward had chosen the same doorway to duck into, they'd smiled at each other, connected and soon they were off in a taxi to Cavendish Square, with promises of cups of very hot coffee. Valerie/Vicki was soaked, but she smiled and it captured anyone who saw it. 'I don't know if she had a slight astigmatism, but it felt like she was always sharing a joke with you,' Kim Waterfield recalled. 'She could be talking to someone else but Vicki always seemed to have her eyes and her smile on you. She was captivating and exciting; she was highly lovable – there was something terribly inviting about that look.'

Ward didn't miss that potential, even in the storming rain. This girl had promise, the cheekbones, legs and body of a great beauty, yet her voice was high-pitched, sharp enough to cut diamonds, and she chattered and chattered. Valerie Mews thought she knew the world; Dr Ward knew she didn't but he would make sure *Vicki Martin* did. They chose the name from *The Listener* magazine while turning the pages of the BBC publication and reading aloud to teach the teenager a more upmarket sound. She sat, warming herself and curled up like a cat, with one of his frayed white towels wrapped round her hair. As it dried and they talked, Ward produced his sketchpad and drew Valerie, whom he informed would be a model, be a star. Dr Ward maintained: 'I used to try to keep her laughing, just for the joy of seeing her face light up.' He packaged that joy into a more society-friendly bundle.

His vainly denied conceit was that he was intoxicated with the belief he could do it. He was helped, of course, by the fact that

Vicki Martin's athletic look and easy-to-know personality were absolute deterrents to any too inquisitive enquiries about her antecedents. The circle of men she was launched into wanted to touch her, not interrogate her. 'She was never unwilling to have fun,' said Bobby McKew. 'She had the look that launched a thousand lusts.'

And took care of many of them.

Like the debutantes he danced with and treated, Stephen Ward's protégé 'came out'. It was orchestrated at Siegi Sessler's club at 46, Charles Street – a quickstep from Berkeley Square. That evening, Sessler arranged extra cognac in the peppercorn sauce for the finest cuts of prime beef as 'a present for Stephen'.

The always immaculate restaurateur was as renowned for taking illegal bets and laying them off, and on Monday nights provided the location for high stakes chemin de fer evenings and his *Zrazy Zawijane*, beef roulade. Sessler, having gone his own way and being on bad terms with Les Ambassadeurs' John Mills – 'We are Poles apart' – had found his niche. His restaurant-bar was famous for being famous (one wag dubbed it 'Madame Tussauds for live people'). The faces were familiar, a Hollywood casting director's wish list: Humphrey Bogart, Bob Hope, Bing Crosby, Marlon Brando, Marilyn Monroe, John Wayne, Cary Grant, Bette Davis, Clark Gable, Doris Day, Joan Crawford, Ingrid Bergman and Elizabeth Taylor with Mike Todd.

It was also where money, old and new, went. Film producers sat at the next table to European royalty and English landed gentry. Siegi was personal friends with many of the Princess Margaret crowd, as well as the Aga Khan, who kept an elegant Mayfair townhouse – 4, Aldford Street – as a pied-à-terre. There, his son Prince Aly Khan entertained conquests, giving them drinks from a walnut cabinet hidden behind a wall panel to avoid his parents' disapproval. He was less concerned about the opinion of others, saying of society Englishmen: 'They call me a nigger and I sleep with their wives.'

Vicki Martin slept with many of the wives' husbands. Stephen Ward's good friend Fred Mullally (a jack-of-all-trades journalist) was running the public relations outfit, Mullally & Warner, with high-end clients like Vera Lynn, Audrey Hepburn, Paul Getty, Douglas Fairbanks Junior, Johnnie Ray and other visiting American entertainers such as Frank Sinatra and Frankie Laine. He helped Siegi's become the place to eat (the food was excellent) and, more importantly, to be seen. Mullally helped Stephen Ward arrange Vicki Martin's first sashay along the society catwalk of Siegi's and recalls: 'The euphoria hadn't quite mounted to its heady pre-dinner peak when Stephen and Vicki made their entrance. There were girls in the room far lovelier than Vicki, and all of them were more expensively and elaborately dressed.

'It just didn't matter. They all lost their escorts to a girl of the people, with short, cropped hair the texture of hemp, a laughing, unguardedly avid face and a body you'd commit crimes for.'

Ward regarded the men swarming around Vicki as a triumph, *his* triumph. That first night in the flat she'd slept on his divan and crept into bed with him, not long after the sun began showing. There was the intimacy of a 'cuddle' but not what Dr Ward called an 'erotic cuddle' – he had remarkable control and several of his girlfriends told me that one type of 'cuddle' did not automatically lead to the other. This, above anything, singled him out as someone they could trust and confide in, without him exploiting their differing emotional upheavals; he was a shoulder to confess on. He himself recalled: 'Vicki was grateful I did not force myself on her, although she made it quite obvious that, if I wanted her, I could have had her. I didn't want her like that – I was entranced by her.'

For more than a year, Vicki Martin lived with him and became a society favourite – a dashing young man in a red sports car here, an older chap with a Rolls-Royce and a big-shouldered chauffeur (and an even bigger international bank balance) there. In the autumn of 1954, she was photographed by Baron, whose photographic talents were never in question. He had spent that summer on location with Marilyn Monroe. He had captured the christenings of Prince Charles and Princess Anne and narrowly missed out on being the official photographer at the Queen's Coronation on 2 June 1953. Prince Philip had recommended his Thursday Club friend but his mother-in-law wasn't having that naughty Baron at her daughter's big day. Elizabeth, the new Queen Elizabeth II, would be photographed by her mother's conventional, if chocolate-box favourite, Cecil Beaton. As, of course, would HM the Queen Mother.

Yet, Baron's regal elevation was such that his pictures of Vicki Martin stamped her passport for other modelling assignments. She was photographed by Ward's friend, the louche Anthony Beauchamp, who in 1949 married Winston Churchill's daughter Sarah in America. Beauchamp (originally Entwistle) was a libertine and his musketeer philosophy, all-for-one-and-one-for-all, made him a sought-after fellow traveller for Dr Ward, who was a guest at his wedding. Vasco Lazzolo, fresh from sculpting and painting Prince Philip, had Martin sit for an oil painting. She briefly appeared in a film, a melodramatic nonsense about the fashion industry, *It Started in Paradise* (1952), starring Jane Hylton.

Vicki attended the races, she went to the society places; she went to town. Dr Ward had lighted the blue touchpaper and Vicki Martin took off like a rocket. She became a regular everywhere, including at The Star in Belgravia, where she would insist on being served pints of beer. Often there with them were Bobby McKew and Georgina Egan, an elegant and successful fashion model whom McKew had introduced to the Maharajah of Cooch-Behar at a Belgravia dinner party. They all knew Barry Stonehill and Errol Flynn – all 'the boys'.

Vicki had first met the Maharajah of Cooch-Behar at her launch party at Siegi Sessler's club and they talked together at the bar of The Star. Unmarried, he was also a friend of the Aly Khan, Barry

Stonehill and Errol Flynn. He had his own racehorses, apartments in London, homes in India, a tax-free income, a multimillion-pound trust fund, a palatial future assured and a terrible fancy for Vicki.

She earned good money as a model and men would give her cash for taxis or a new dress, or maybe that little something in the jeweller's window. Mostly, they expected something in return. In the 12 months she lived with Ward, she gave him money if he was short and he returned the financial favour. She had mentors. 'There were meant to be some powerful people in Vicki's life,' said Bobby McKew, before qualifying: 'But the whole crowd she mixed with were important people.'

Cooch-Behar set about courting Vicki and started by asking his friend Stephen Ward to bring her to dinner at Les Ambassadeurs. Earlier that day, he had a couple of rose gardens sent around to her from the flower shop at The Dorchester. Soon, Vicki had moved from her launch pad at Dr Ward's to her own apartment in Upper Berkeley Street, where she was visited several times by Ruth Ellis. With all that had gone before, Vicki appeared to have found a soulmate. Cooch-Behar wanted to marry her but there was one snag: in doing so, he would go against his family and forfeit a huge amount of the income that paid for his lifestyle. Still, he was up for it, telling Vicki they would have to live in India. She agreed, but, when Cooch-Behar went off to India, she confided in Ward. He counselled that they might both regret such a decision – was it not better to go on as they were, carefree and in love? Which is what they did, living and driving fast.

Vicki liked speed and fast drivers, such as 6ft 2in blond Mike Hawthorn, the Yorkshire Formula One racer who won his first Grand Prix at Reims in 1953. Hawthorn had much style – he raced for Ferrari wearing a bow tie, on and off the track. He held court at the Steering Wheel Club, near Shepherd Market at 2a Brick Street. There, he would drink and talk with Stephen Ward and Vicki, and other drivers: Innes Ireland, Graham Hill, Peter

Collins, Roy Salvadori, Alberto Ascari and Stirling Moss. This lively and high-spirited crowd attracted racing fans and keen drivers like David Blakely, who had an apartment at 28, Culross Street (behind the US Embassy in Grosvenor Square). They would laugh about Vicki's driving record. She'd been involved in a dozen crashes, one very serious that put her and Cooch-Behar in hospital.

On the way back to London from the Newmarket races, they'd been spinning along the country roads near Baldock, Hertfordshire in the Maharajah's blue Bentley when a white van sped around the corner and in the bang turned the Bentley turtle. Cooch-Behar was badly hit around the head and unconscious for some hours. Vicki suffered cuts and bruises all over her legs and a twisted right ankle. While her boyfriend came off the seriously ill list, she dealt with Fleet Street, 'The Model and the Maharajah'.

The shock of the crash and the ensuing injuries all but forgotten, Vicki's passion went into the telling of the story from her bed at the Lister Hospital in Hitchin: 'I am so very fond of him as I feel he is of me but there is little hope of our romance coming to anything. You see, it is the Tiger's mother – I call the Maharajah "Tigre" and he calls me "méchante", French for naughty girl – who is putting her foot down.'

Vicki instinctively invited kindly treatment.

Kismet wasn't having it. Tragically, nine lives gone, on 9 January 1955, Vicki was involved in her 13th car smash. Three nights earlier, Stephen Ward had taken her to Les Ambassadeurs for dinner. John Mills had been there and Paul Adam had played a couple of numbers dedicated to her. It had been an evening without moderation, which was her style.

She was in the front of the car with the Canadian journalist Terry Robertson. At around 4am on that Sunday morning and a little on the outskirts of Maidenhead, Berkshire, their car hit another head-on. In that car were the 'honeymoon' couple David Salisbury Haig, a scientific officer of the National Coal Board, and his wife Helen. They were returning from a dance in London. Haig, 41, was killed outright and his wife injured; they had been married for six weeks. Robertson's legs were badly damaged and head injuries blanked his memory, but Vicki took the brunt of it and her heart gave out while she was being treated in hospital.

First at the scene was Sir David Salt, of Cookham, Berkshire, and he introduced the first question mark: 'The girl was dying on the road and I have since wondered how she came to be on the road, because the door of the car was shut.' Early news reports said Vicki Martin was the driver but the police later issued a contradictory statement.

When he heard the news of Vicki's death, aged 23, Stephen Ward's first thoughts were of Valerie Mews and he drove over to Chandos Road, Egham, to inform and comfort *her* grandmother.

A funeral service was held for Vicki Martin at the West Chapel of Golders Green Crematorium on 18 January. It was a tearful affair and Stephen Ward stood as some of the richest and most powerful people in the land wept. From India, Cooch-Behar sent her favourite red roses, a giant wreath of them, with a card: 'Goodbye to méchante. My love always, Tigre'.

This ceremony was followed by Valerie Mews' burial at Englefield Green, the closest village to Egham with an available cemetery. The alchemist Stephen Ward was there and Paul Adam held his arm amid the smaller crowd of mourners for the golden girl he'd created, given the confidence to take off and live just a little too fast.

Adam later told his friends that he was certain that the strength and dignity Ward had shown had helped others. Ward's grief, he said, was more internal. Certainly, Stephen Ward was a reflective man. He would voice strong views but then be silent. Some of those with whom he debated about morals and politics thought his silence was him mellowing; usually, he was ruminating, preparing for another attack. It was a difficult world to be in, this one of global chilling and personal grief. The news each day brought nothing but more concerns on domestic and world affairs.

An inquest into Vicki Martin's demise was opened two days after her death and then moved to 2 March 1955 for a full hearing. The results were kept private, the files closed. Stephen Ward did not know what to think – there were some things he could not control.

Also, Martin's first friend in London, Ruth Ellis, was in serious trouble. 'We all met Ruth at Carroll's (or then the Little Club), where she worked for Morrie Conley,' recalled Bobby McKew. 'She was someone you nodded to, might buy a drink if there was a crowd of you. She was older than us, so not part of the crowd. Nobody saw it coming.'

Ellis had become heavily involved with David Blakely, the racing car enthusiast to whom she'd been introduced by Mike Hawthorn. They had tried to live an 'open' life, both sleeping with other partners. After one violent argument on 8 January 1955, the evening before Vicki Martin died, Blakely had punched Ellis in the stomach and she'd miscarried. The tumult continued day-to-day until Easter Sunday, 10 April 1955, when Ellis confronted her lover outside the Magdala pub in Hampstead. She saw Blakely's car and waited. He was inside, drinking with his friend Clive Gunnell.

When they appeared in the street, she shouted: 'Hello, David.'

He ignored her.

'David!' she shouted.

He fumbled for his car keys.

Ellis aimed a .38 Smith & Wesson Victory revolver at him. She got off one shot.

It missed.

He ran. She chased… and shot again.

The second shot grounded Blakely, who was screaming in anger, shock – and fear. His lover approached. She stood over him, a point-blank executioner. She fired three more times: one shot in Blakely's back, the next one a quarter of an inch away from the target.

She tried to get off the final bullet – click, click, click. The pin of the revolver kept meeting an empty chamber until the last bullet pumped out into the stone pavement and ricocheted across the street, hitting a bank manager's wife in the hand. Amid the screams, Ellis turned to Blakely's drinking companion and said: 'Will you call the police, Clive?'

Stephen Ward, even more than most of the country, followed the aftermath closely. He could understand this crime of passion, the catalyst for it, if not the true madness of the despair of love for he did not have that depth of emotion.

Ellis appeared on 20 June 1955 at the Old Bailey in her everlasting image: bright dyed-blonde hair, white silk blouse and neatly cut black suit. From the dock she wrapped up the evidence for the prosecution: 'It's obvious when I shot him I intended to kill him.'

That statement secured a guilty verdict; the death penalty was mandatory. Ellis was taken to the condemned cell at Holloway Prison. Appeals for a reprieve failed and, on 14 July 1955, hangman Albert Pierrepoint dropped her body down 8ft 4in from one cell to another; the execution took 12 seconds. Her body was left hanging for an hour. By late morning, the London evening papers were supplying details.

Stephen Ward regarded it as more evidence of the decline of Western civilisation. And he said so, as did Ward's great friend and patient William Waldorf Astor III. A former MP, 'Bill' Astor had gone to the House of Lords on his father's death in 1952. With another young, aspiring politician John Profumo – at 21 in 1936, he was chairman of the East Fulham Conservative Association – Bill Astor supported the Conservative cause in west London, shortly before the war.

By 1938, Jack Profumo was involved with a woman called

Gisela Klein, a name strangely absent from UK official files for she was under surveillance by MI5. She vanished from Britain a few months before the start of World War II (CIA documents show a similar woman, using a string of aliases, working in Intelligence in post-war Germany). As an MP and Conservative candidate, Profumo had campaigned for an end to corporal punishment (he'd been birched at Eton) and capital punishment. Not many months after Ellis's execution, Bill Astor had spoken emotionally and pertinently in the House of Lords against the death penalty. He and his brother, David Astor, who ran the *Observer* newspaper, were strident in their viewpoint.

News to stimulate political debate was on the radio and front pages every day. The Hungarian Revolution against Communist repression was squashed by tanks in the streets. The crisis when President Nasser of Egypt nationalised the Suez Canal Company on 28 July 1956, and British Prime Minister Anthony Eden dithered, before finally sanctioning an abortive invasion.

Bill Astor listened to Dr Ward on high-handed American foreign policy. Ward had constantly picked out the power of US commanders like General Douglas MacArthur, who had to be reined in by President Harry Truman after he bragged during the Korean War about unleashing a nuclear hell against China. The H-bomb was a horrifying thing. It was not, believed Ward, the way to achieve peace and freedom in the world, 'this bomb waving'. In political discourse, Astor, an Intelligence officer with the Royal Navy during the war, was comfortable. On social matters, he appeared, at best, confused. Despite his strong beliefs, he could behave like a befuddled gnome, all big ears and a silly smile.

The eldest son of Nancy Astor, for ever famous as Britain's first female sitting MP (elected 28 November 1919), missed out on much of what should have been his legacy but he had still inherited the family name, family jewels and family foibles. His passion was horses and he had his stud farm at Taplow, near Maidenhead, where Vicki Martin had died. When he hurt his back after a nasty fall hunting, it was his half-brother, Stephen Ward's early London patient Bobbie Shaw, who sent him his 'Dr Magic'. By the early 1950s, they were great friends, Dr Ward easing Astor's physical and emotional woes, and Astor in turn bestowing his social blessing and helping his physician's cash flow problems. In time, Lord Astor bought the building at 38, Devonshire Street, where Dr Ward, who had financial difficulties with the taxman, had moved his consulting rooms and taken the apartment above.

The two men enjoyed similar pursuits and lively conversation about world politics, especially Anglo-American relations. It was, it seemed, a beautiful relationship. Lord Astor hunted every weekend and, to alleviate the aches from hours on horseback, he would dispatch his chauffeur to London to collect 'my doctor'. It became a habit: Bill Astor would enjoy his sport; Dr Ward would massage his body into feeling better – and introduce him to girls who helped out in that area too. In turn, Lord Astor introduced Ward to his friends, including John Profumo, who in 1950 had been elected MP for the second time, representing Stratford-on-Avon, Warwickshire. Profumo attended one of Dr Ward's cocktail parties, where he said he 'always had a lot of pretty girls about the place'. The Conservative Party favourite found Dr Ward 'hugely charismatic' and regarded him as 'a go-getter of girls'.

John Profumo liked girls. He had what the gamblers called a 'big edge': a gentrified pedigree and the comfortable style to use it. He was, in the patois, a right smoothie. He and his friends led an after-dark life around London, casting around in the twilight zone. They were not shy about approaching and talking to the club hostesses and having 'nightcaps' with them. They visited clubs like Murray's and the Stork Room; they were not alone there, despite Kim Waterfield's somewhat disdainful view of Al Burnett's club. He revealed: 'Stephen liked the Stork and was there a great deal. Many famous faces were.'

The Stork Room did not have the formal dress code nor the pretension of Les A and The Milroy but it was where Princess Margaret went 'slumming' with the usual A to Z of movie stars, from Ava Gardner to John Wayne. John Profumo met Elizabeth Taylor and Marlene Dietrich there; also Vicki Martin and Cooch-Behar. Stephen Ward had visited the club with Vicki and was seen there talking to Michael Bentine, a patient and star of *The Goons*, with another 'Goon' and club regular, Peter Sellers – or, being 'snapped' by the camera girl in a tight, gold lamé suit, Kim Proctor.

The Stork Room could legally accommodate 200 guests and just about the personality and libido of Al Burnett's friend Jack Hylton. The grand impresario – 'think champagne and you'll be champagne' – dominated London's theatreland and much of British light entertainment. Mr Showbusiness owned the Palace Theatre in The Strand and the Victoria Palace. He had a string of acts, including the hugely popular Crazy Gang, under contract. Stephen Ward treated his bad back several times a week.

Jack Hylton of Jack Hylton and his Orchestra (the first British band to broadcast to America in 1931) was friendly with Benny Huntman, a boxing manager who worked closely with Jack Solomons at Great Windmill Street before he moved his operations to Joe Bloom's Gym on Earlham Street, Covent Garden. In turn, the bandleader was *very* friendly with Huntman's sister-in-law, Pat Pope: he was obsessively in love with her. He would turn up at her flat at midnight and beat on the door, insisting he would die if he did not have her. She was in the chorus line dancing as 'Pat Taylor' when the man Benny Huntman's son Roger knew as 'Uncle Jack' began his long romance and he told me in 2013: 'I was just a kid, but in 1951 I was at Uncle Jack's place at Albany House in Mayfair and we were allowed into his meeting room. He was saying goodbye to Stephen Ward and Lord Mountbatten. I was told to shake hands and say hello. Ward was Uncle Jack's personal physician – not his doctor, but the one who kept him running around. How many times a week he treated him depended on what Uncle Jack had been up to.'

And he was a busy man. As were John Profumo, a politician being touted as a future Foreign Secretary and, possibly, British Prime Minister, and the ever more popular Stephen Ward. They, like many other habitués of London's nightlife, found a new venue for their general interests and pursuits. It was called the Eve Club and took its enviable place at 3, Burlington Gardens in basement premises off Regent Street. Almost everybody there was working at least two jobs and an amateur at one of them, especially the spies; it was a new and expensive hunting ground for Intelligence and sexual predators. Like *Casablanca*, they could have created it on the back lot at Warner Brothers. It was just the dialogue that wasn't so well rehearsed.

Jimmy O'Brien had worked his way up to general manager at Murray's when a Romanian refugee called Elena Constantinescu suddenly appeared in London in 1947, announcing she had fled the evil of Communism. That won the tiny 20-year-old a job as a cigarette girl at Murray's. Her look and attitude got her work as a dancer, a Murray's girl, and a new name: Helen O'Brien. The 'O'Brien' didn't dispel her heritage and she smoked gold-tipped black Balkan Sobranie cigarettes. With her sharp eyes and neatly bobbed blonde hair, she appeared through the drifting clouds of smoke in the role of the mysterious émigré. It had been enough to entice Jimmy O'Brien and, as a couple, they deserted Murray's and opened the Eve Club on Valentine's Day, 1953. The floor was lighted, a London innovation to enable guests to admire a dancer's ultimate assets; on it they presented Folies Bergère-style shows – if a girl wasn't from Paris, she was supposed at least to sound as though she might have visited. The girls couldn't be totally naked or swing their hips, or anything else... on stage.

The 'hostesses' were encouraged to keep the lonely from overseas, the Albert Embankment, King Charles Street and others from around the corner in Westminster and Scotland Yard, happy boys. A High Court judge called the Eve 'a sub-division of the Foreign Office'. Helen O'Brien was discreet without taking anyone for a fool. The police got paid; problems weren't admitted. The girls appeared in brochures: 'Her attractions are stunning, her talent is extraordinary and her telephone number, sir, is none of your business'. As a club, with membership of one guinea a year, the drinks kept being legally poured until 3am. The only prohibition was on flashbulbs to protect the blue eyes of Sinatra and the dignity of others.

There were no hypocritical rules for members (the club's book listed European royalty, a sultan and an Ecclesiastical bishop, who married a hostess) about canoodling with the girls. Men would buy drinks for the girls and perhaps offer a £5 or £10 note by slipping it into a handbag or cigarette pack when they left the table. Helen O'Brien would sip champagne in the velvet booth known as 'Table One' and cast her eyes over the usual suspects. O'Brien witnessed secrets being exchanged; as well as telephone numbers and other information. She was quite clear: 'Of course there was sex, but not on the premises. We were not a whorehouse. If a girl and a client wanted to begin a relationship beyond the club, we knew nothing about it.'

Acutely aware of the Cold War and what was happening in Romania, O'Brien was fervently anti-Red. Nevertheless, she let them, as it were, under her bed. She put patriotism first and welcomed Eastern bloc 'diplomats' as generously as she did Intelligencer Officer Horace Marsden and the other 'funny people'. MI5 agents tried to recruit her but she never said (nor did they) if they were successful. The KGB boss in London did have personnel in most of the London clubs every night. His Embassy at Kensington Palace Gardens had a secure 'entertainment' room; a combination safe held several thousand pounds in cash for expenses; a fridge-freezer bottles of vodka and schnapps for diplomatic refreshments.

At the Eve, the spooks regularly bought drinks for each other. It was a bewildering atmosphere; you might be drinking with Boris from the KGB and Judy Garland, or Shirley Bassey and Carrington from the Foreign Office – potentially a remarkable chorus line in the risqué twilight. Yet, possibly not so much fun as doing the conga at John 'Jack' Profumo's stag night at the Eve Club on 29 December 1954.

CHAPTER SIX

DOCTOR IN CLOVER

FIDARSI È BENE, NON FIDARSI È MEGLIO.
(To trust is good, not to trust is better.)
Italian saying

She was shouting, wailing, and the pitch of her east Glasgow accent was as piercing as that wrong guitar note.

'I'm taking them with me. They belong to me! I'm going and they're going too!'

How so much noise and outrage escaped from the neat and well-formed figure of so small a person astonished Stephen Ward, who stood in his apartment bombarded by this tantrum. Crash, bang! Crash, bang! Bobby McKew and his girlfriend Patricia Owens stood there with him, both trying to look the other way.

Maureen Swanson was moving out. And her pots and pans were going with her. They had been dating for a year. 'She was a feisty one,' said Barry Stonehill, 'but a girl who knew what she wanted. She was devoted to Stephen Ward – I suppose needs must.'

'Pat Owens saw a lot of Stephen Ward and Maureen. She was a right little Scots girl,' said Bobby McKew. 'They were very social and invited people round for drinks. Well, you took the gin – Stephen had the tonic, maybe some vermouth. He had drinks, but kept them locked up for special occasions. I wasn't special enough. Stephen didn't really drink. He'd have the same glass in his hand all evening. He was always sharp, heard everything said around him.'

With Maureen Swanson, he inhabited the film as well as the social world. In 1951, he was commissioned to draw the 19-year-old actress, who had won the juvenile lead in the musical *Carousel* at the Theatre Royal, Drury Lane. She was smitten: 'He was a very attractive, very dashing man about town.' The relationship took off.

Ward told friends he was in love with Swanson: 'For a time we both thought quite seriously of getting married, but Maureen was not easily swept off her feet. I used to try to advise her about her career, particularly when she went into films but she had her own ideas about what she wanted from her career and from life. We quarrelled frequently.'

'They could bring the roof down on that flat,' said Bobby McKew, but it was always 'quick and noisy and over'. The young actress – who the fanzines described as a 'physically alluring amalgam of Rita Hayworth, Jane Russell and Susan Hayward' and 'the next Vivien Leigh' – was nevertheless groomed by Dr Ward for other things.

Yes, she made films – *Moulin Rouge* (1952), *Knights of the Round Table* (1953), *A Town Like Alice* (1956) – but Ward pointed her towards other titles. Her stunning looks attracted the Marquess of Milford Haven, the Earl of Suffolk, Lord Hanson and the King of Jordan. Fleet Street took note: 'Miss Maureen Swanson is now on speaking terms with a fair cross-section of the aristocracy, including a viscount, a marquess and half a dozen dukes, and thanks are due to Viscount Ednam, Mr Billy Wallace and the Marquess of Milford Haven. All three are good friends of hers and over the past few weeks some of the most exclusive drawing rooms have been improved by her decorative presence. Viscount Ednam is the one peer that the lady will not talk about.'

Ednam, heir to the Earl of Dudley, head of one of Britain's wealthiest families, was married though separated from Stella Carcano, daughter of a former Argentine Ambassador to the UK. That he was heavily involved with the 'pocket-sized Venus from Glasgow' was not something any of those involved wished to flaunt.

Yet, Stephen Ward, though himself devoted and 'in love' with Maureen Swanson, did everything to encourage and promote her romance with Billy Ednam. Before Swanson (and her three pots and two frying pans) left him, another young actress witnessed the closing weeks of the year-long affair. Award-winning British actress Shirley Anne Field was the recipient of a Ward offer of an 'erotic cuddle'. She said he was 'handsome in an English way' – good hair, fine features. In the late summer of 2013, she smiled at the memory of it: 'I met Stephen when I was a young student going to an acting school. I stopped off with my friend Sylvia at this coffee shop on Park Lane and this rather nice man, who we thought was middle-aged, said hello and started talking to us. I was utterly charmed by him.

'I drank Coca-Cola and thought it was rather racy. He asked us if we knew Maureen Swanson and of course we did – she was working and we weren't! And he didn't just know her; she was staying at his flat. He talked to us about Maureen, who he'd got involved with this guy, who was going to inherit a lot of money. He said she'd met Billy Ednam and it would be wonderful if Maureen could "capture" him. She was good on the camera but tiny, but naturally we were curious. He told us he could help us meet the right kind of people. I said I couldn't see how meeting some rich bloke would help my acting career. He laughed: "Sweet, little thing, influential friends can always help."

'He said he'd meet us again the next evening and he took me for a sitting to be painted. He was very professional. He lived near Harley Street and the apartment was big and comfy, but not polished or smart. It was very much lived-in. He put me in the bay window with the light behind and he began the painting. The phone rattled on and sometimes he answered and made appointments with his patients or he ignored it. I had to sit still.

'A girl came in, dressed to kill in an evening gown. She was off to dinner at Les A with Billy Ednam. Stephen said: "This is my lovely Maureen." He gave her a really mouthy kiss and a car horn sounded and she was off to the other man. Stephen said he loved her very much and it made me sad for I didn't really understand.

'The painting went on for a time and I posed two or three times a week. Sex was always on offer with Stephen: "Now then, darling, how would you like a nice erotic cuddle?" And I'd say: "Not tonight, Stephen," and that would be it. He'd give me the taxi or the bus fare home, probably the bus fare being Stephen. He was always short of money. He would have liked more. I asked him what Maureen would think if I'd stayed and he told me: "She won't mind, my love. The more the merrier."

'Stephen would invite me for dinner. I'd walk up the stairs to get to his apartment and he'd say: "Now, darling, you can either have a pair of shoes and some nylons or go out for dinner. Or you can have a poached egg on toast." I had egg on toast – the shoes and nylons were so important to us.

'He never pushed himself in any way. I only knew Stephen in a kind way – I don't mean that he wasn't a ladies' man, for he was, and I don't mean I didn't succumb to that, for I did, but he had a sort of ethics that I admired. I never, ever thought he was a wicked man. Never.

'He was very sad about this love of his life he'd lost, this little Maureen from Glasgow. He was so old-fashioned, we all were. He always said: "Now, dear, you could marry a Lord".'

It was a Lord, Bill Astor, who ruled the almost 400 acres of rolling Berkshire estate of Cliveden, sloping down to the River Thames, where Stephen Ward was becoming a regular visitor, one of the many for whom the sight of the formal parterre to the south of the house always took the breath away. It made his heart sing to be there: he was on stage; he loved it, every part of it.

'He was mad about the aristocracy,' said Field. 'He couldn't believe it when I said I wanted to be an actress and not Lady Somebody – he just could not understand it.'

Dr Ward didn't want to understand too much of the past of Cliveden, so he refused to dwell on Nancy Astor's 'Cliveden set' comprising a politically active social circle soft on Hitler, a group of high-minded aristocrats and politicians, the hollow men who were seen as keen to appease the German leader and to promote Nazism. Nancy Astor said Hitler himself looked too much like Charlie Chaplin to be taken seriously; she would know. Between the wars, Chaplin and an astonishing list of names including T.E. Lawrence, late of Arabia, Gandhi, Winston Churchill, President Roosevelt and writers like Henry James and George Bernard Shaw were entertained by her on Cliveden weekends. After a 1936 visit, the diplomat and writer Harold Nicolson thought: 'There is a ghastly unreality about it all... I enjoy seeing it. But to own it, to live here, would be like living on the stage of the Scala theatre in Milan.'

For Stephen Ward, it was like coming home. To assuage death duties, if not his eldest son and heir, Bill Astor's father gave Cliveden to the National Trust in 1942, and that included several riverside cottages of which Spring Cottage was the largest. Pamela Cooper, the former Viscountess Ruthven, and her second husband, Derek Cooper, were close to Astor (he had offered them Spring Cottage). She recalled: 'I couldn't take on his cottage so instead Bill offered it to his osteopath, Stephen Ward. He was amusing to talk to and always appeared anxious to please.'

The offer, in fact, came more directly from Philippa, the second Lady Astor. Bill Astor married Sarah Norton in June 1945, but, after having three miscarriages, giving birth to healthy son William and suffering post-natal depression, his bride left him for a younger (by seven years) man, Lt-Col Thomas Michael Baring, an officer with the 10th Royal Hussars. All attempts at reconciliation failed and the pair officially divorced in 1953. Before her death, aged 93, in February 2013, Sarah Norton recalled: 'I adored Nancy, his mother, who treated me like a daughter. When we got married, I hardly knew Bill. He was very generous, but the age difference between us was too great [he was 37, she 25] and, after the restrictions of the war, I needed to break loose. We were amicably divorced. Nancy said to me: "I think you're a goose to leave a millionaire!" She was never unkind to me, though she did want the family jewels back, which I gave her, of course.'

In 1955, Bill Astor married Philippa Hunloke, daughter of Dorothy Macmillan's sister Lady Anne Holland-Martin. She was the goddaughter of Churchill protégé Harold Macmillan, the British Foreign Secretary.

Macmillan, who saw his then Government role as 'forever poised between the cliché and the indiscretion', maintained weekends at Cliveden were like staying at a grand hotel. On arrival, friends were received by at least four staff and their cars driven off to be washed, wax polished, refuelled and garaged until departure, much like the guests. Visitors had one of Astor's Bentleys and a chauffeur for any weekend outings.

The new Lord and Lady Astor had honeymooned in Ireland and the South of France – which is where the acrimony and their daughter, Emily Mary Astor, began. They had met and married within a few weeks and in much the same time separated emotionally.

Stephen Ward on his visits to Cliveden became a contact for the couple, a carrier of their half-hearted thinking that the marriage could be made to work. It was all about being seen to make an effort and Dr Ward obliged as a go-between. In July 1956, with the Suez crisis peaking and her marriage almost at an official end, Philippa Astor took Dr Ward and a couple of other guests for a boat trip on the Thames. From the water she pointed out the partly timbered faux Alpine jumble of Spring Cottage, with its leaded windows and first-floor gabled balcony, which looked as though it had survived many student ski seasons.

Lady Astor had considered the double-fronted property as a marital bolt-hole, but on a visit declared it was 'so sodden you felt like living death after being in it for more than ten minutes'. Dr Ward instinctively grasped the potential of this riverside escape: it was only a mile-long walk through beech woods from the main house. As a bonus, it was surrounded by an unkempt garden fed by a little stream, a burn of rocks.

The next day, he took a walk to Spring Cottage. There are numerous versions of how Stephen Ward took over the cottage – never mind what happened there – but his own version is highly acceptable: 'I walked through the wilderness of the grounds on my own before breakfast. I tramped through the weeds and the undergrowth and pushed the door open. It was easy enough. When I got back to the big house I at once told Philippa. I think she was amused by my enthusiasm. "Oh," she said casually, "if you think you can take that garden on and lick the place into shape, I don't see why you shouldn't have it. I'm sure Bill could get the National Trust people to agree."

'Bill got the Trust people to put things ship-shape – only the main structure, because I wanted to do the rest and the garden myself; I had ideas about a rockery. Well, that was the beginning of it all.'

It wasn't going to be *Wind in the Willows*. However, there were children's games like hide-and-seek – in the nude and around the rockery and in the woods. Blindman's Bluff in the buff was another favourite. The volves didn't knowingly get involved.

'The thing about going down to Cliveden was that you did what you wanted,' recalled Bobby McKew. 'You could run around naked, asking Lady this or that for a fuck, or you could sit on the riverbank and relax with a drink. People would walk around naked and nobody thought anything about it. It made hide and seek a lot more fun to play. When I went there, I joined in.

'Nobody ever cried rape or anything – it was all very polite. If you suggested a fuck and they didn't want to, then you didn't bother. There wasn't any pressure on anyone. You could keep your clothes on! And someone would appear. Girls would emerge naked in the water and you'd have to "hook" them with a rod and line. You didn't go for the food (which wasn't up to much) and you took your own drink, but that was fine. Whether it was a good or not-so-fun weekend at Cliveden depended on who was there, like anywhere else. If anything, the girls were wilder than the men.'

The London gentlemen tended to be older. On dull days, they said that you couldn't always tell if some of the guests had clothes on or were naked; either way, they needed ironing. Shirley Anne Field said: 'I was often invited to Cliveden but I wasn't keen to stay in a cottage on an estate and meet all these elderly people, a little crinkly for me.

'I was the only one focused on a career, everyone else wanted to marry lords or dukes or get involved with them. But Stephen kept asking and I went. One weekend I met up with Jeanne Baldwin, who worked for Rank and I knew. She was Maureen Swanson's best friend *before* her marriage. At the cottage, one bedroom was for the girls but some mornings Stephen would get all the girls into his big bed and bring us breakfast. He was proud of the cottage but it was quite shabby, nothing remotely grand. Grand was the big house – Buckingham Palace material.

'I went over there with Stephen and Jeanne Baldwin, and Bill Astor was all over me: "Why don't you come and stay, we have this room and that room? It would be lovely to have you stay – you can have any room you want." I'd arrived with Stephen and Jeanne Baldwin and thought it a bit rude of me to be invited and not them. It's a big house. I looked at all these elderly politician people sitting around. They all looked boring to death to me, even if they were running the country. I decided I'd be happier in the cottage with Stephen and Jeanne, even if all they talked about was cars; they were both mad about cars, spent their money on them.'

On other visits to Cliveden, Field met Margaret Ann Bissett

Brown, who as Maggie Brown was a wonderfully successful international model, another of Ward's redheads on stilts. Behind his back, people described him as some sort of magician and you can see how it began: there was no why or how but he had hypnotic power over women. Maggie Brown was an Everest of dreams and in every argument about the most beautiful woman in London. Ward encouraged beauty, which was often all long legs, long waists and long necks – a bevy of swans from provincial ducklings. In an interview, he put on record their first meeting: 'I met her at a cocktail party, she bowled me over but she had a boyfriend at the time and told me so. A year later we met again, quite by chance, and she said she was unattached. She worked terribly hard and took her job seriously.'

Brown moved in with Dr Ward in London and paid towards their living expenses. If possible, they would go to Cliveden as early as possible on a Friday afternoon and spend Saturday working on the cottage and garden. She painted the interiors; he brightened up the riverbank, planting irises, marigolds, primulas and had campanulas drifting in the summer day's water. Friends had an open invitation to visit but it *was* potluck – *whatever* was on the stove was on offer. The ones they wanted to see brought picnics and drink and cigarettes, others only their problems.

It was bliss for Dr Ward: at Spring Cottage, he had one of the smartest girls in town with him as a girlfriend and hostess. He kept a photograph of them both sitting on a settee there in his wallet and would show it to strangers. Behind the sofa, he had painted a mural of the cottage in its chocolate-box setting. To some visitors, Spring Cottage was all about English afternoon tea. The running around the log fire naked after tea was less conventional. And it wasn't a luxury spot.

'It was always an open house at the cottage but it was like camping,' recalled Shirley Anne Field. 'You slept quite rough. There was no telephone; there was power for the lights but the cooking was done by gas and sometimes the bottles of gas would run out mid-fried eggs. Stephen had back-up gas bottles but the eggs didn't stand a chance. It was camping and that was the fun of it – getting on with it together.'

There was a lot of laughter and fun at the cottage. Up at the main house, Bill Astor was often lonely. He'd trek over to Spring Cottage, looking for some amusement. Stephen Ward could certainly do that. He'd arrange a game of Blindman's Bluff in the woods with the girls and after a time Astor wouldn't be lonely any more. Ward could also do intellectual entertaining – almost everyone praised his conversation and wit. He did think before he spoke for he learned early on that you cannot retrieve what is said. His charm had no parameters; he could deploy it anywhere. At Cliveden, he tried it on Philip de Zulueta, private secretary and confidential adviser on foreign affairs to Harold Macmillan, who rented one of the two other cottages made available at Cliveden; the other was taken by the bouncy and likeable Fleet Street writer Alan Brien. When Macmillan visited his private secretary, Ward and Brien were sometimes invited over.

Ward's financial arrangement with Bill Astor in regards to Spring Cottage was simple: he paid £1 a year peppercorn rent, looked after the upkeep of the cottage and provided free osteopathic services for Lord Astor and any of his Cliveden guests who might require or wish to sample the skills of Dr Ward's healing hands. In turn, Astor allowed the Spring Cottage crowd to use the impressive Cliveden swimming pool.

It appeared Stephen Ward could feast on two rich cakes: the Bohemian style of Spring Cottage and the grander version at Cliveden, where he would attend dinners with the aging Nancy Astor and a social galère of names, including the man he now knew as 'Jack' Profumo. The MP was accompanied by his wife, the actress Valerie Hobson. A sought-after beauty, she was often flirted with. It had been that way all her life; she liked and enjoyed the attention of men. It was a rebellion against her strict

Protestant upbringing. The daughter of a Navy officer who liked to be called Commander Hobson, she was born on 14 April 1917, at Larne, Northern Ireland, but went to school in London. Mesmerised by the theatre, she attended the Royal Academy of Dramatic Art (RADA). At 18, she secured a contract with Hollywood's Universal Studios but it was a mess, just saved in 1935 by her title role as *The Bride of Frankenstein*, with Boris Karloff as the monster. Valerie worked with stars like Claude Rains, Douglas Fairbanks Junior, Ralph Richardson and Laurence Olivier. More in character, she was cast as a sultry femme fatale in Michael Powell's *The Spy in Black* (1939). She met Anthony Havelock-Allan, a new power within the British film industry. Havelock-Allan was an enthusiastic ladies' man, having left conquests across Europe and throughout London. When he met Valerie Hobson, he had three affairs on the go and happily made it four, but she was the one he married in 1939.

Havelock-Allan was equally prolific as a film producer and a philanderer. Valerie Hobson responded in kind and actors of the time say she was 'playful'. After her marriage, she soon became pregnant, but didn't want to have the child. She took the back-street option in her own home, a steaming hot bath and a bottle of gin. Five years later, she gave birth to Simon, a Down's syndrome child. She appeared in landmark films: David Lean's *Great Expectations* (1946) as the adult Estella, and as prude Edith D'Ascoyne with Alec Guinness in *Kind Hearts and Coronets* (1949), also starring Thursday Club veteran Dennis Price. Stewart Granger, who liked to play his swordsman *Scaramouche* role with the ladies, in 1988 told me she wasn't so prudish when he had an affair with her during the filming of the 1947 melodrama *Blanche Fury*, in which she had the title role. 'Hot as a scalded cat,' he called her.

John Profumo first warmed to Valerie Hobson at a fancy dress Hogmanay evening at London's Royal Albert Hall in 1947. She was a 29-year-old movie star, he a former Tory MP waiting for another seat; that New Year's Eve he was dressed as a London bobby and she as Madame Recamier, the famed eighteenth-century Paris hostess. He became an ardent admirer of the married Ms Hobson, as was the racing driver Whitney Straight, whom she considered a safer prospect for an illicit affair: like her, he was married. Jack Profumo became the man in the middle, the other man in her adulterous affairs. At the same time, her husband was involved in a serious affair with another, younger actress: Stephen Ward's close friend Kay Kendall.

Profumo and Valerie Hobson began a secret affair; the naughtiness of it intensified his passion. There were private notes, suggestive letters disguised as film offers. It was in July 1949 that Hobson discovered she was pregnant again: the father was Profumo.

There was no question of a bottle of gin this time: she went into a nursing home in Hendon, north London for a medical abortion, suction dilation and curettage, spending three days there looking out over the River Brent before deciding to end her affair. Her lover was up for election in the new seat of Stratford-upon-Avon and, with no scandal about love affairs or a divorce action, he was safely elected in February 1950.

In her life as Mrs Havelock-Allan, relations with her husband were not always warm, but one night, after attending the opera, they became close again and she became pregnant. Soon after the birth of their son Mark on 4 April 1951, they divorced, with Havelock-Allan, the great seducer, playing the guilty party under the law and getting himself caught in a contrived act of adultery.

Not long after the ink had signed off the 1952 decree nisi, the newly single actress was considering a proposal from the Marquess of Londonderry and the attention of others. They were over-taken by Jack Profumo who, although she admonished him for treating all pretty girls as 'fair game', had reawakened her interest in marriage. Their wedding, seven years to the day after they first met, was at St Columba's in Pont Street, Knightsbridge, on 31 December 1954. It got some attention, for Valerie Hobson had revived herself as a celebrity attraction as Anna opposite Herbert Lom in *The King and I* at the Drury Lane Theatre, where her fame had begun working for Oscar Hammerstein. It must have made her think before she announced she was abandoning her career for marriage, being a good Tory wife. It was a sacrifice.

But sacrifices had to be made in political marriages. Jack Profumo knew the advantage of his wife's abdication from stage and screen. At Conservative gatherings, he pointed out in his speeches: 'When I married my beautiful and talented wife, I quickly found that I had become a most popular speaker. People used to invite me to open their bazaars, adding, "You'll of course bring along your charming wife." I tumbled to it all when a socialist asked me to open his bazaar –"You'll of course bring along your charming wife". When I told him that that would be impossible, he replied: "Don't bother then. Come along yourself – next year!"'

Profumo was a highly suitable leading man. He was a dashing second lieutenant in the 1st Northamptonshire Yeomanry in 1940 when he became, at 25, Britain's youngest MP, winning Kettering. His first vote was a courageous one. That May he joined 33 other Tory MPs, including Harold Macmillan, in going along with Labour in censuring the Neville Chamberlain Government for its failure to supply British troops in Norway. One minister spat on Profumo's shoe after he passed through the lobbies; the Tory Chief Whip told him that he was 'an utterly contemptible little shit' – Harold Macmillan always remembered that Profumo moment. In wartime, he was mentioned in dispatches, created an OBE and rose to the rank of Lieutenant-Colonel. His background helped: his father was a baron of the former United Kingdom of Italy but he had spent most of his life in England, and all of it privileged. He had money. A major shareholder in the Provident Life Association company, like

Churchill he had been to Harrow and gone on to Brasenose College, Oxford, where he studied political economics and agriculture. When the Tories took a severe political kicking from the Labour Party in 1945, he lost his Kettering seat but was compensated by being promoted to Brigadier and went as chief of staff of the UK mission to Japan.

He then worked for Conservative Central Office advising on broadcasting methods, how to avoid making the wrong impression, saying or doing something silly – blunders that might embarrass the Party. John Dennis Profumo, although a man who could be intellectually laundered, was an enthusiast and continued to be so when his bachelor life ended, aged 38. Never fearful of the rustling of lace curtains, he went about his business unafraid of censure.

Stephen Ward sensed equality at Cliveden and it was hard to blame him for being a little smug. He was on intimate and first-name terms with the major players in the land; then there were all the lovely girls in swimsuits and tight sweaters and slacks who joined him at the Cliveden swimming pool. It invited a crowd and fun and games. His carousel of cachet spun every which way.

When the call came from the Astors, he jumped. But for him this was an essential part of this paradise: he rubbed its back. He was always especially impressed to see Ministers of the Crown. He and Maggie Brown would be invited to events at Cliveden and both dressed formally and immaculately. Dr Ward knew when to hold back his effervescent personality. He let the show do all its own work on 18 June 1957, when Bill Astor's friend Douglas Fairbanks Junior was given the estate for the coming out of his daughter Daphne.

It was a remarkable event with nearly 500 guests from around the world, including the top team: HM the Queen and Prince Philip, Princess Margaret, Princess Alexandra and the Duchess of Kent. Baron, photographer to the Royal Family, had died of heart failure, aged 50, in September 1956. That evening, the man Stephen Ward knew as 'Baron's assistant', Antony Armstrong-Jones, took the official photographs. Uniformed police, two private security guards and Fairbanks' private secretary kept out the uninvited, including Fleet Street. Guests had privacy to drink champagne at the four bars and enjoy a fanfare of a buffet co-ordinated by John Mills from Les Ambassadeurs. When dancing began at 10.30pm, the live music was provided by Paul Adam. Many of the guests said hello to him; many women smiled knowingly.

Prominent among the Americans was John 'Jock' Whitney, the newly appointed US Ambassador to Britain. His post meant close contact with the man whom the Americans were delighted had replaced Anthony Eden, purged by Suez as Conservative leader and Prime Minister, the Tory grandee Harold Macmillan.

That evening, every window at Cliveden had a bright light shining in it. High, flaming torches every couple of feet marked the driveway. There was a reverse Cinderella at midnight. All the lights were extinguished for the fireworks display, to which Bill Astor had invited patients and nurses from local hospitals, all the staff at Cliveden estate and the drivers and security people. Downstairs were brought in through a side gate and given beer and sandwiches. It was all so very conventional. Maggie Brown sought convention too – she tolerated the playful games at Spring Cottage.

Shirley Anne Field was there one weekend when the cottage crowd were invited over to the big house for a formal dinner. 'There were a group of Bill Astor's pals and not one was anywhere near my age. Stephen looked at me; he knew I was fed up and he told me to make an effort. "If you're to be a success, it's no use showing you are bored!" I told him I couldn't care less if I was a success at Cliveden or not. After dinner we swam in the pool. We younger girls were in bikinis while the women guests from the main house had on what I'd call school swimsuits.

'When we trooped off back to the cottage we were more of a

crowd. One newcomer, Billy, was a man in shipping, who wanted to play nursery games. His favourite, he said, was his own version of "Blindman's Bluff". We had to tie him to a chair and shout and scream at him for being a naughty boy. I thought it was silly, but Billy loved it and found it very exciting. Stephen said Billy's trouble was he'd had too many nannies.'

Ward's problem was he had too many options. Evening excursions on the streets in London were increasingly routine. He adored the situation with Maggie Brown and they talked of marriage. Despite the financial problems, Brown – a high earner as a model – saw a future with Dr Ward. She even made financial arrangements for them to take a four-bedroom house at 46, Chelsea Square, in north London, which would double as the alternative healing health centre he talked about starting.

Yet, Stephen Ward had two lives and he didn't want to give up either of them. His heart and mind may have played a romantic game but his gut made the rules for it. The plan and the relationship ruptured totally when Maggie Brown lost the huge £2,000 deposit on the property because her would-be husband did not follow through with the balance. The owner of the house, Hubert Parker, a judge at the Courts of Appeal, was annoyed at the nuisance the on-off sales caused him. Brown knew she couldn't be a successful model forever; she was offered film work in Hollywood and found a new life and marriage, in 1962, to the multimillionaire songwriter Jule Styne.

Dr Ward professed horror at this turn of events but he had his sketchpad and the pavements of London – and Spring Cottage. 'Every time I went to Cliveden, there were new faces, female faces. It was part of the attraction,' said Bobby McKew. 'Some were there for fun and sun but there was no question that some of the guests, the older guys, simply went there for a fuck. They might have played games and discussed the woes of the world, but they were there for a fuck.

'One weekend, I went into the kitchen and there was this grand man who talked with a plum in his voice having this girl: "Hello, Bobby – she always wanted to be fucked on the kitchen stove." I said: "Oh, really" and left them to it. Outside, people were walking around naked but getting laid wasn't essential.

'It was different from the ones Beecher Moore gave, where you went to screw. At Cliveden, people went off if they felt like it after a few drinks at lunchtime. At Beecher's, you could be talking to a naked girl and someone would come along and enquire about a fuck and the girl might say, "On you go, darling," and carry on talking to you. They wanted to appear sophisticated. Beecher Moore had the good orgies.

'He had a huge apartment, a penthouse in a building full of barristers' chambers in the Middle Temple, off the Embankment. He'd been there since 1940. He was an Air Raid Warden in the area and got the lease when chambers were easily available during the war and he remained a resident. After the war, he became a huge name in sailing. His partner Jack Holt designed hundreds of boats and won scores of races. He was born in New York, but came to London as a toddler.

'Beecher had one of the greatest collections of pornography in the world in the 1950s. When you went into his huge room he had a side lamp off the right, which was controlled by a wall switch. It had a big cream lampshade made of vellum. When you switched it on and it lighted up, there was the Royal Family standing around, sipping tea and talking. If you turned a hidden light switch, there was the Royal Family going at it.

'It was terribly funny. Everyone got to know about it because the maid who had been cleaning for them for years put it on extra power and saw it and wouldn't go back in the place again.

'Beecher and Bobbie his wife ran amazing parties. It was a magnificent flat, the only one in the Temple; the rest of the place was lawyers' offices. At night, he had the place to himself so they didn't disturb anyone! The same on Sundays, when they had their special lunches – you could be standing stark naked, talking and over in the other corner could see someone at it. A girl would come up and say: "Would you like me?" It really was like that.'

Beecher Moore married Bobbie Seal in 1954 and from the beginning of their marriage they hosted parties – conventional and less so. Bobby McKew was friends with the actor Michael Balfour and his girlfriend Katy Binder, daughter of Sir Bernhard Binder, the financier and adviser (appointed 1951) to Her Majesty's Treasury. The family knew Bobby McKew's parents in Dublin and Lady Binder would tell him not to keep her daughter out every night. The Binders lived at 11, Hyde Park Gardens, overlooking Kensington Park Gardens and opposite the Churchill home where Stephen Ward had treated Sir Winston. Bobby McKew has many memories: 'One night, I was asked to go over to the other house to help Churchill and old Sir Bernhard as they were both too pissed to get up the steps. I had to help them up, they were happy for it.

'Katy and Michael Balfour, who was always working, a great character actor, would go to Beecher's parties. Katy was a beautiful redhead and would take her clothes off at the drop of a hat. We were invited to a nice party down there and Beecher was having friends and relations in this huge room they had looking out over the Thames. We went there with Katy and a couple of other girls and everybody was dressed up smart, but they thought they'd gone to an orgy so they went into the bedroom and there were two or three of them in there and someone asked for cigarettes.

'In the big room, there were about 40 people, all drinking and politely chatting, and suddenly a stark-naked redhead comes out and says: "Excuse me, anybody got some cigarettes?" The conversation stopped. Somebody gave her the cigarettes and she said: "Thank you."

'Then she turned around, wiggled her backside, and strolled back to the bedroom.

'There was silence for a moment and then, typically British, everyone went back to talking as if nothing had happened. The conversation started and most of them didn't believe what they had seen.

'Bobbie Moore was another one who would take off her clothes without being asked – she really was crazy for it.'

Shirley Anne Field recalled Beecher's sexual tactics: 'I went to Sunday lunch with my friend Brian and it all started out quite normal, drinks and chat and so forth. During lunch, some guests said it was hot and took jackets off.

'Bobbie served the Sunday roast and she'd taken her skirt off and it was bizarre. Then, when she came in with the pudding, she'd taken her knickers off. She still had her bra on. I thought it was the wrong way round. I'd have taken off the top and left on the bottom but maybe her breasts had dropped after kids – I don't think Brian ever got over it. Then other people were taking their clothes off.

'They were all a good bit older than me, in their thirties and forties, and I thought it was a bit untidy after lunch, undignified to watch people carry on. If I'd been with my own age group... I said to Bobbie I wasn't keen and she smiled: "Don't worry, dear, take something off and sit over there on the couch." I was happy to do that. It was so quiet at the law offices on a Sunday. I don't know how I got exposed to all that. Did I go back? Every Sunday.

'Stephen slightly disapproved – he thought Beecher and company were nouveaus, not aristos and he was so hung up about the Establishment. I thought he disapproved of them. Maybe he didn't like them because the people weren't titled. The sex didn't bother him.'

Ward never saw any harm in granting desires if there was no coercion. Some people's sexual needs were keener than others. People lost their inhibitions with their clothes off; naked, they were trusting and that trust continued when they put their clothes back on: shared secrets was the key. Stephen had many of them with his sexual collaborator and faithful traveller in the outer limits of the sexual world, fellow keen voyeur Horace 'Hod' Chapman-Dibben, Battle of Britain hero and charmer of anarchists and prostitutes.

As co-host to some of the most notorious and popular sex parties in London, Dibben, an often dishevelled-looking character who seemed born as the long-lost uncle you'd be wary to see, has an infamous place in twentieth-century history, a strange bedfellow in perpetuity with Stephen Ward.

BOOK TWO
SEX, SPIES AND SECRETS

'NOBODY AT THE TIME DESCRIBED THE
ASSASSINATION OF ARCHDUKE FRANZ FERDINAND IN
SARAJEVO ON JUNE 28, 1914, AS "A SHOT HEARD AROUND
THE WORLD"; THAT TAG LINE ONLY WORKED WHEN
EVENTS HAD PLAYED AND THAT BECAME THE CATALYST
FOR WORLD WAR ONE.'

Harold Evans, *International Herald Tribune*, 11 March 2013

CHAPTER SEVEN

DOCTOR SUGDEN

'THE EVIDENCE IS OVERWHELMING THAT THE SOVIETS
INTEND TO USE NUCLEAR BLACKMAIL AS A MAJOR WEAPON
TO PROMOTE THEIR OBJECTIVES – NAMELY, TO SPREAD
COMMUNISM THROUGHOUT THE WORLD.'

Central Intelligence Agency (CIA) Director Allen Dulles, 19 August 1959

Horace Dibben was like a suspect scoutmaster: you never knew what he was going to shake. He had his hands in everything. He blamed the Plymouth Brethren and their stern beliefs but it's unlikely anything could have repressed his particular penchants.

In his early years, he frequented girls around the docks in his hometown of Southampton before marrying, but that was over by the start of the war when he went into the RAF and enjoyed a distinguished flying career. By then, pain had become his passion, sadomasochism a creed. Watching couples and groups have sex became part of his daily life.

'He had his strange ways,' recalled Bobby McKew. 'He had a tough war, all these men in the skies did. That sort of thing makes you want to get on with life quickly – Hod just did it at double time. For a Brethren boy, he certainly ran the most elaborate sex parties in London. You never knew who you might see there. Black magic and men in masks and peacocks wandering around was all at parties organised by Hod, not Stephen Ward. Stephen went to some of the parties but he wasn't organising them. For many of us, it was curiosity.

'They were going on all over town but Hod's were special, he had something for everybody.'

Dibben, like Stephen Ward, had twin lives. He'd been raised for prayers at 5am every day and the early-morning habit stayed with him. After leaving the RAF at the end of the war, he became useful in the antiques world and, as time went on, quite an expert in certain periods and a specialist in the Revolutionary France of the Marquis de Sade. In rare irritable moments, he told friends that Robespierre, and not the man from whose name the word sadism developed, was the most evil man – 'a bloody lawyer who guillotined people'. He advertised for an assistant and Patricia Johnson pranced into his life. She did not have an antiques world voice or name, so Dibben ran her through finishing school and her name changed to Patsy Morgan. As they grew closer, the more Chelsea and Mayfair user-friendly Patsy Morgan-Dibben emerged. Because of the age difference, it was presumed Patsy was his daughter – which added frisson when from his favourite, faded tan leather chair he watched her in action with other men. He would bring Patsy and friend(s) breakfast in bed, get into the bed with them and read the *Daily Express* aloud to them. It saved putting the fire on too early in the day or buying two newspapers.

'I don't think Patsy did wild parties in that she performed for people other than Hod,' said Kim Waterfield. 'She was very young but all the make-up, especially around the eyes, made her seem older. She certainly was sophisticated in her outlook. I think she was quite choosy about whom she bedded.'

Bobby McKew has a more lively view on Patsy Morgan's life in antiques: 'She had *lots and lots* of interesting people. In life with Hod there had to be parties and Patsy could turn on the charm. She called everyone "Sweetie".'

Even the local bobbies on the beat, who all knew her.

Police tolerance to the sexual activity of their betters had its antecedents in the 'Vault of Vice' trial shortly before the start of World War II. The authorities knew there were brothels operating in Mayfair and Belgravia and largely let them get on with it. When one keen inspector from the Flying Squad, the aptly named Ted Greeno, received reliable information that 'top-notch' people were frequenting a house of ill repute on Dover Street, he sped to his superiors.

Before he knew it, Scotland Yard's Assistant Commissioner, Sir Norman Kendall, found himself asking: what would be the consequences should 'top-notch' people be discovered? What if his officers caught 'a Cabinet Minister or something like that'? What indeed. Greeno raised himself to full height and pronounced, if it was the Prime Minister, he'd be nicked like anybody else. Sir Norman finally agreed to a raid on the premises but with caveats: the Flying Squad would go into action a little after 8pm when a Cabinet Minister or the like would be dining or at the House of Commons.

When Inspector Greeno and team hit Dover Street, they were amazed: on ringing the front door bell, they were greeted by Carmen Rosena, 40, a Jamaican and a little more than 6ft tall, and wearing only black thigh-high boots. Inside was one giant bedroom, the 'theatre'. Inspector Greeno didn't know where to look when he took Carmen and her staff – four well-spoken, upper-class girls and two good-looking young lads – to Cannon Row police station. Sir Norman wondered what might have been. Reporting restrictions were imposed and the public kept out of the 'Vault of Vice' trial at Bow Street Magistrates' Court in case some delicate names slipped out from the witness box on 5 April 1938.

Nearly two decades later, that remained something of the unofficial outlook but London's sex life had been undergoing changes. Kim Waterfield's contact Tommy Webb (under his 'Duncan Webb' byline) had produced a revelatory series of articles, 'Vice in London', for the five million circulation clever broadsheet the *Sunday People*.

The newspaper dossiers began a 1950s campaign and encouraged the ongoing switch in attitudes about sex on the streets of the capital but also behind some extremely smart closed doors. By the late 1950s, Webb had been 'slugged, kicked, lunged at with knives, shot at, knuckledusted and the target of a speeding car that raced on to the pavement of a narrow Soho street and tried to smash him against a building'. He survived and continued to hang out around the West End and 'in the public interest' place himself within such a corrupt culture.

A dedicated Catholic, Webb had something of the Kirk about him. He preached clean-up. He maintained that pimps – mainly the Maltese known as 'the Epsom Salts' – were making London 'a clearing house for foreign prostitutes'.

By then, Webb had an assistant, the Australian journalist Murray Sayle, who in 1952 had moved to London to pursue a romance with the entertainer Shirley Abicair, who had piqued the interest of a young MP, John Profumo. Now Sayle found himself pursuing street girls around the West End. The reporters were a formidable team and the always admirable and amiable Sayle created the most memorable sign-off line ever after prostitution exposés: 'I made my excuses and left...'

But, for the British Government, excuses about the laws governing the sex and gambling life of Britain were running out. Sociologists, politicians and the police were aware of the 'Wild West' image of London. The Clean Air Act (1956) had lessened the smell of sulphur from the air and opened up evening vision of the girls selling themselves on the streets. Something, as always, had to be done. The Sexual Offences Act (1956) had nudged working girls to be more discreet, to go to other places where everyone could find them, and brought into the courts more stringent strictures on brothel-keeping, procuring, living on the earnings of prostitutes and abortion offences.

As the talking went on, so did the action, though. Illegal chemin de fer, *chemmy*, games were a highlight of London gambling.

Games were held all around Mayfair and Belgravia. The insanely high-risk French card games were originally run by an exclusively underworld crowd but, one evening, the socialite-gambler John Aspinall, accompanied by Stephen Ward's young friend Dominick Elwes, witnessed the financial potential: that curious and supposed impossibility, a sure thing. If you ran the game as the 'bank', you controlled the *cagnotte*, the table slot into which went 5 per cent of every winning bank. The *cagnotte* could range from £100 to £500, whatever the bravado and the bankroll of the player who had called 'banco' would stand, many times that when Lord Derby once wagered the Stanley estates, which included most of Liverpool. As an evening progressed, the *cagnotte* steadily mounted and the bank was laughing all the way to itself.

On that Damascus evening for John Aspinall, Dominick Elwes' girlfriend Sarah Chester Beatty was there too, and she, as bad luck tactics required, provided the cash to pay off the two men's losses, which were purely an investment in the future. She could afford it – her father was Sir Alfred Chester Beatty, the Irish-American mining magnate known worldwide as the 'King of Copper'. Aspinall and his partner John Burke ran games mostly in friends' Mayfair or Belgravia homes. As insurance, regulars including the Marquess of Milford Haven and John Bingham, the future Lord Lucan, circulated around Belgravia to avoid police attention.

Billy Hill and Bobby McKew ran their own circuit of chemmy games and, as he did for Aspinall and Burke, Hod Dibben often provided the facilities. McKew explained: 'Hod did very well as an antiques dealer. He might have looked a little odd, with his mutton chop whiskers and those eyes, but he had money. At his parties people took a bottle and no money changed hands; the sex was free, for fun. All anybody ever paid for was a taxi or a packet of cigarettes. It was different at the chemmy evenings – he got money for that.

'Hod had a nice ground-floor apartment in Eaton Square and

we used that for chemmy games. Billy Hill and I went to the games and Gypsy would be there, she liked to gamble.'

Gypsy Riley, to all purposes, was Mrs Billy Hill, which gave her remarkable power. Gypsy was a rough diamond who, as Phyllis Riley, had fled east London, taken up with 'road' people and then been recruited by Maltese pimps ('Bill would fuck a snake if you held it down,' said Bobby McKew). Eaton Square was relatively grand and she was relaxed when she went to the bathroom one evening as the chemmy games went on at Hod Dibben's.

'There was this great shriek from the bathroom,' recounted McKew. 'Bill and I rushed over and Gypsy screamed: "Someone was peepin' at me taking a piss!"'

'Hod, of course – he had spy-holes all over the house. You couldn't get up to anything without Hod seeing. Even having a pee.'

Stephen Ward met up with Hod Dibben for regular dinners, usually around Knightsbridge. Often they would visit their friend Dr Teddy Sugden at his house in the centre of Belgravia. The doctor had a soft face – he looked the way a kindly GP who turned out to be the murderer in an Agatha Christie novel should. He also enjoyed sex games with reptiles.

Sugden kept snakes and other reptiles in cages at his home and enjoyed women simulating sex with the wriggly creatures, girls fondling snakes and pretending to fellate them. The girls couldn't tell if he was happy as he had a frozen face, which stopped him smiling. His features were locked into a benevolent frown.

Edward Charles Sugden was described by friends, including former *Dr Who* actor Jon Pertwee (and certainly by Hod Dibben and Stephen Ward) as being a 'nice fellow'. He might, at between £100 and £200 a time, perform more than 15 abortions a day. Unwanted pregnancy was a constant risk for sexually active women of the day. The accomplished social commentator Katharine Whitehorn lived through it: 'In war, standards completely go and people don't suddenly get moral simply because the war is over. People were more keen to experience things because they might not be able to tomorrow. Girls were more cagey about getting in trouble. There was contraception but not easy to get. You had to pretend you were married if you went to the Marie Stopes clinic. No one liked condoms. It could spell ruin if the girl got pregnant. There was no question of keeping the baby, so there were lots of adoptions. An illegitimate child was socially quite unacceptable.'

And abortion, or attempting to arrange one, was illegal.

Kindly-looking Dr Sugden's clients were actresses, showgirls and debutantes who had often got pregnant at his sex parties. Kim Waterfield knew girls who had to enlist his services: 'It was 150 guineas in those days. If convicted, they'd lose their licence to practise and they'd get seven years in jail. Teddy Sugden was one of the 150-guinea men and that was a hell of a lot of money, it really was. Hod Dibben had been something heavy in the war, a squadron leader in the RAF, as had Teddy Sugden, so that was their connection.'

Any question of Dr Sugden providing a social service is eradicated by his chief clients, the Messina brothers. They paid lavishly to get their girls 'sorted' and back to work. Immediately. After all, time was money.

Sugden ran his surgery from Half Moon Street, conveniently close to Shepherd Market, in a world estranged from literature's fictional residents: Bertie Wooster and his 'Gentleman's Gentleman' Jeeves. Dr Sugden was remarkably warm-spoken and quiet in demeanour when he appeared in court to testify for the Messinas and the women who worked for them. Jon Pertwee is on record as saying: 'He was weird, but a most loved man. His morals were not quite as people would expect them to be, but he was generous and nice.'

Pertwee also recalled that it was 'quite jolly' when he and others visited Sugden at his weekend playspot on the River Thames, near Bray. 'Everyone,' he said, 'used to go down and wander around in the nude in the sun.' There were always lots of girls and Dr Sugden never – well, he couldn't – lost that benevolent look. His wife allowed him to watch the action but not to participate.

At one nudist free-for-all, Stephen Ward arrived along the River Thames from Cliveden with a group of girls he had just met: three girls disrobed, the other one fled.

'Girls?' said Bobby McKew. 'Money could be in short supply but never girls. You couldn't turn around without seeing a new one. It didn't matter where you went, Cliveden or round the corner in Kinnerton Street. There were always orgies. I remember going to one with John Mills, and Alan Jay Lerner (lyricist of *My Fair Lady*) was wearing knee-length pantaloons and chasing a beauty queen who had enormous tits. She was one of Bob Hope's favourites. He and Bing Crosby liked the showgirl types. I never saw them both naked together but that would have been a picture. The Road to goodness knows where....'

Goodness had nothing to do with it for many of this crowd: the path was to Esmeralda's, a club established by Patsy Morgan-Dibben in a prime spot on Wilton Street in Knightsbridge, opposite the Berkeley Hotel. She was friends with Kim Waterfield, and Pietro Annigoni (whose 1956 portrait of HM the Queen had brought him international fame and commissions) created the interior design for the club.

At Esmeralda's, there were many famous guests, including Bill Astor, with his friend Stephen Ward, the usual Royals and Hollywood personalities mixed with indiscretions and vodka and heavy drugs, which were catching up with whisky and gin as the stimulant of choice while the Benzedrine spun the clock. With its discreetly owned multi-roomed properties, often taken by overseas embassies, Esmeralda's became a complement to the Eve Club. Five minutes from the American Embassy in Grosvenor Square, not much more from the Russian Embassy in Kensington Park Gardens, and a brief drive along the Embankment and a couple of lefts from Whitehall, it was convenient. As was the

Brompton Oratory, a monument to Catholic London on the Brompton Road next to the Victoria and Albert Museum.

MI5 kept a careful eye on the Brompton Oratory, a building that itself invites attention. The Oratory acted as an exchanged point of Intelligence between Soviet 'illegals' in Britain (secret agents operating with forged documents and identities) and their KGB hands-on controllers. MI5 decided it was better to know where the 'dead letter box drop' was (the organ loft, and six pews up from the altar, second statue to the right) than have them spread across London. If the spooks got jumpy, they'd scamper into Harrods with its multiple exits and stairways, and then stroll out the back into Hans Road and off around Sloane Street.

Alexander Nekrassov's father was a KGB colonel, as was his stepfather, and he spent his early life in the London Embassy. In 2013, the former Kremlin adviser and Soviet specialist told me: 'In the late 1950s, there were many, *many* Russian diplomats or researchers or whatevers attached to the Embassy.

'They all worked for the KGB. Why else were they there? It was the Cold War, it was frenetic – the world wasn't going to end tomorrow, it might end today. That was the environment they were working in.

'Every person who came to London from Moscow had a specific mission. It wasn't to learn to make tea.'

Which wasn't on offer at Esmeralda's. A good time and information were. Stephen Ward enjoyed trying out his French and German with 'our European cousins' and took to wearing his prescription dark glasses indoors, possibly after reading *La Nouvelle Vague*. He affected the louche Belmondo look in his forays into Notting Hill and the culture of hip and hemp.

By now, Ward had created an astonishing house of cards: his own amphitheatre at Cliveden, a social theatre within the homes of the great and the good, excursions into the world of sex games and debauchery, and these excessive needs were driving him further into the night. Though more careful with his kerb-crawling since the incident with Bloody Mary, he still took drives down Park Lane but more often now picked up girls on the Edgware Road or off the Bayswater Road. At Hod Dibben's, he had shown photographs of such girls posing in high-heeled shoes with bras on, but no panties. These were not artistic photographs – in the background were dirty ashtrays and empty coffee cups. When he had girls staying with him, he would bring prostitutes home and be heard having sex with them, including sadomasochistic games, the girls taking the pain. There was never any proof, despite the often fey manner he adopted, that his sexual requirements were ever anything but heterosexual. Of course it was suggested quietly throughout the 1950s; homosexual relations were against the law, as the talented Dr Ward plied his social medicine.

He was friendly with Toby Roe, who owned the Rockingham Club in Soho's Archer Street, where homosexual men would go to dance and drink and not be bothered. Quentin 'The Naked Civil Servant' Crisp remarked that it was the 'closet of closets' as famous faces were often seen there. Intrigued by the novelty, Princess Margaret and her set visited, but she is said to have felt her energies would be best served elsewhere. There was nothing seedy about the Rockingham, which, like its owner and his lush silk dressing gowns, was quite grand. Ward mixed with the artist Francis Bacon and the talented writer and grand photographer Daniel Farson, who was best before noon and around 8pm when the gin had worn off and he was starting again.

Painters Robert Colquhoun and Robert MacBryde, Scots who wore their kilts around Soho out of convenience, not patriotism or Kilmarnock memories, were part of that set and friends and partygoers with Dr Ward. It allowed more ambiguity about him, an aura he cultivated with his cigarette holder and suggestive voice. Still, there were moments when he too was taken aback by his own escapades. The vicar's son in him recoiled when confronted by a renowned and very butch lesbian.

Kim Waterfield took Stephen Ward for an afternoon drink at The Colony Club in Dean Street, Soho, opened by Muriel Blecher at Christmas 1948. A decade on, it was renowned for bad behaviour – especially from the owner, who sat at the bar with her legs over a couple of stools, her back to the wall and champagne glass, which members were expected to keep filled, always in her hand. She talked in homosexual slang, where all men were 'her' or 'she' – the *polari* of Kenneth Williams, who was establishing his career in *Carry On Sergeant*, the first *Carry On* movie, released in 1958.

Ward regarded himself as a libertine but was not prepared for the Colony, with its shared communal lavatory – or Muriel Blecher. Kim Waterfield knew what to expect: 'It was a haven for the great painters like Lucian Freud and Francis Bacon and all these characters. Vasco Lazzolo was a regular, people like that. I went in with Stephen and she looked at me and said: "Hello, cunty." I said: "Good afternoon to you, Muriel." She looked Stephen up and down and smiled: "Hello, precious cunt." Stephen didn't like it one bit. He insisted on leaving immediately. It was strange, for Muriel was mostly bark and people knew that.'

Ward liked a members-only life. He sought dignity in his deviance, not common depravity. Certainly, there were manners around Sir Gilbert Laithwaite, whom he regarded as a good friend (they had been introduced by Bill Astor's homosexual stepbrother, Billie Shaw). Dublin-born Sir Gilbert was a former Ambassador to Ireland and for the second half of the 1950s Under-Secretary of State for Commonwealth Relations. Dr Ward delivered Sir Gilbert, also a former British High Commissioner to Pakistan and friendly with the President, Field Marshal Ayub Khan, to several men-only parties. Through his social circles, Ward was able to help them meet convenient young men. It gave him contact, sometimes at Spring Cottage, with many influential men including Sir Gilbert's lover, the Reverend Monsignor Hugh Montgomery, an Oxford graduate and Foreign Office diplomat-turned-priest. It was an interesting cabal. Sir Gilbert, effortlessly superior, was a prominent member of the Travellers' Club, a home from Rome for diplomats, Foreign Office specialists and other overseas adventurers, at 106, Pall Mall. Dr Ward would lunch with him there in the dining room, known to members as the 'Coffee Room', and then they would sit and talk in the Smoking Room overlooking Carlton Gardens.

The conversations of the time at clubs like the Travellers' were dominated by espionage shenanigans, which made confusion out of what was a truly simple aftermath to the end of World War II. 'Uncle Joe' Stalin, a paranoid killer of millions, wanted to control and spread Communism around the globe. America, almost as paranoid, was eager to stop him. The two nations raced to develop nuclear weapons in preparation for a showdown like the one in President Eisenhower's favourite film, the 1952 Western *High Noon*. In the midst of this nuclear standoff was a Britain sidelined and hugely in debt to America. Who was faster on the draw? It mattered – nuclear missiles en route to Armageddon could cascade all over the British Isles.

When incoming missiles were first detected, there would be four minutes to panic before Britain vaporised.

Stephen Ward had studied a preview of the end of the world. At Cliveden and during drinks evenings in London, he would stir the conversation with talk of 'Ivy Mike', an apartment block of an atom bomb detonated in the Pacific, at Eniwetok Atoll, at half a second before 7.15am on 1 November 1952.

The blast punched out 10.4 megatons, power equal to 693 times more than the 'Little Boy' atom bomb dropped on Hiroshima from the Boeing B-29 Superfortress bomber *Enola Gay*, with tragicomic irony named after Enola Gay Tibbets, mother of the pilot Colonel Paul Tibbets, seven years earlier. The fireball that gave birth to this horror was nearly four miles wide; the cloud, that malevolent

Mr Confidence: Stephen Ward with visible baggage, cigarette and his trademark, but now slightly uncertain, smile at the start of one of the most inglorious trials in British legal history.

Left: Dr and Mrs Stephen Ward – the happy couple in 1949. His marriage to model Patricia Baines, like so many of his relationships, did not survive for long.

Below: The girl Stephen Ward wanted to make a Duchess – the beautiful Christine Keeler at Cannes before the Profumo scandal came out in the wash and reputations went down the drain.

Top left: The bright-as-paint teenager Mandy Rice-Davies who perkily aroused high society and indignation.

Author Collection

Top right: Dr Ward's original protégé, the suburban girl Vicki Martin, who enticed the world's richest and most powerful men.

Courtesy of Bobby McKew

Left: One of the first supermodels, the elegant Maggie Brown, who enchanted Dr Ward but could not tempt him away from his particular peccadilloes.

Author Collection

Above: Please raise a glass. Dr Ward's work went on display in July 1960 in London's West End when he was called 'the toast of artistic society.'   © *Getty Images*

Right: A specialist subject – Dr Ward's sketch of his friend and Moscow's spy in London, the ebullient Eugene Ivanov.

Above Left: Stephen Ward's painting of water ski champion (and former Mrs Bobby McKew) Anna Gerber.

Above Right: Stephen Ward's loving sketch of Vicki Martin, whom he said could smile into your heart with her eyes.

Below: Kim Caborn-Waterfield with his collection of art work by his friend, Stephen Ward.

© *Caroline Arber*

All artwork courtesy of Bobby McKew and Kim Caborn-Waterfield

Above Left: Real estate Mr Big – Peter Rachman – talking his way into the *Oxford English Dictionary* for his aggressive business approach: *Rachmanism.*   © *Mirrorpi*

Above Right: The host and hostess with the mostest – the deceptive Mariella Novotny, with the hat she kept on whatever she was doing, and her husband Hod Dibben, who wa never as innocent as he looked.   © *Courtesy of Bobby McKew*

Below: Starlet Audrey Hepburn in 1951, the year of her walk-on part in the film 'One Wild Oat', with (*Left to Right*) Kim Caborn-Waterfield, Pauline Rose (of the Susan Small fashion chain) and Bobby McKew at Les Ambassadeurs.   © *Courtesy of Bobby McKew*

Above: Spring Cottage on the Cliveden estate which was one of the delights of Dr Ward's life – and provided similar sensations for his friends.

© *Getty Images*

Below: The guests at Spring Cottage often got down to basics and, on a warm weekend by the Thames, clothes vanished along with inhibitions: it was 1960 and naturalism was the agenda for these titled ladies.

© *Courtesy of Bobby McKew*

Above: Where the players in the Stephen Ward story dived into trouble. The grand swimming pool at Cliveden, where opportunity met chance in 1961, and a world changed because of what Prime Minister Harold Macmillan called 'events, dear boy, events...'

© *Press Association Image*

Below Left: Bill Astor and second wife Bronwen Pugh with classical guitarist Andres Segovia and wife Emilia Sancho on the terrace of the magnificent Cliveden in July 1963.

© *Mirrorpi*

Below Right: Lord Astor's second wife, the model Bronwen Pugh, who always felt uncertain about her husband Bill Astor's close friendship with Dr Ward.

Author Collectio

mushroom, rose in its magnificent mayhem to 25 miles into the sky and then in neat numbers spread 100 miles, taking 100 million tons of radioactive material into the atmosphere.

Dr Ward would point out that 'Mike' – for megaton – the first experimental thermonuclear hydrogen explosion, made its debut on what the Catholic Liturgical Calendar noted was the Day of the Dead. It was enough to make anyone paranoid – and stop or start a discussion.

After the war, America had been generous with financial help but reluctant to release information that would help the UK develop its own atomic devices. Referring to the undergarments of the girls of London during the war, Billy Hill would note: 'One Yank and they're off!' Transatlantic relations had become a little like that, poodle politics. America needed Britain as a buffer to Stalin's ambitions and 'bribed' with billions of dollars. Rejected by the USA as a nuclear player and partner, Britain pumped the cash into developing its own programme, a nuclear submarine and sophisticated jets and bombers. The nuclear race was somewhat three-legged, and terrifying with the world so aware of the threat that it was halfway to oblivion. Stalin shrugged – he had his own atom bomb production line and cruel capability.

It had advanced with the help of Klaus Fuchs, who for years had fed nuclear secrets to Moscow. A fugitive from Hitler's Germany, he became a British citizen on 7 August 1942. Guy Burgess and Donald Maclean, recruited as Soviet spies, during their 1930s Cambridge University days, vanished in 1951. American and the British Intelligence officers knew they were in Moscow but nothing was said publicly about the secrets they'd stolen. They were Cambridge men, old school, pink gin alcoholics and, in the phrase that gained its place in language in the mid-1950s, 'the Establishment' mustered its ranks around them – and of course itself.

The American Security Services were utterly dismayed by what was going on in Britain. Spy scandals were like London buses, all arriving together. There were CIA agents all over the city and the US Embassy in Grosvenor Square was the only one in the world with FBI agents in permanent residence. At the Travellers', Sir Gilbert Laithwaite was fascinated by Burgess and Maclean, but not so much as he was by the other members of the Cambridge University-recruited espionage network, such as Sir Anthony Blunt. Sir Gilbert was certainly a confidant of such matters; he was friendly with Blunt, which was natural as his lover's brother Peter Montgomery was the lover of Blunt, surveyor of the Queen's Pictures and senior Intelligence operative for Moscow, instigator of 'The Cambridge Five'.

The Foreign Office, the Catholic Church, the Aristocracy and, now, 'The Famous Five' – the Cambridge crowd... It was quite a club to which Stephen Ward found he had access and got to know his way around. Of course, he'd sketched that other member of the Cambridge spy set, the Thursday Club guest Harold Adrian Russell Philby. Meticulous mole Philby was nicknamed 'Kim' after Rudyard Kipling by his Western Intelligence colleagues and known clandestinely as 'Stanley' by his controllers on the other side of the Iron Curtain. If only Ward had never opened the curtain.

He should have followed the lateral thinking of his famous patient Winston Churchill. When spotted by an aide not washing his hands after going to the lavatory, Churchill was admonished: 'At Eton, we were taught to wash our hands after going.'

To which Churchill replied: 'At Harrow, we were taught not to piss on our hands.'

CHAPTER EIGHT

DOCTOR ON CALL

'FASTEN YOUR SEAT BELTS. IT'S GOING
TO BE A BUMPY NIGHT.'
Bette Davis as Margo Channing, *All About Eve*, 1950

Harold Macmillan never finished Eton and he never washed his hands of anything. He came on like an Edwardian aunt, an appearance made more arresting by his vaudeville of a moustache. Time and tide might not wait for anyone, but somehow they did for this Prime Minister. He looked as though he should be dealing in gunboats, not atom bombs, and there was some comfort in that during the Cold War.

It never occurred that Mr Macmillan would *dash* into action. Yet, he was a ruthless man who coped with all manner of events. At a Conservative rally in Bedford on 20 July 1957, he told the flower-hatted faithful: 'Go around the country, go to the industrial towns, go to the farms and you will see a state of prosperity such as we have never had in my lifetime, nor indeed in the history of this country. Indeed, let us be frank about it, most of our people have never had it so good.'

What Macmillan wanted was to maintain growth and employment but keep prices steady. He advocated: 'What we need is restraint and common sense – restraint in the demands we make and common sense on how we spend our income.'

It was an economic message but restraint and common sense would have been useful in other areas too. Macmillan had intimate knowledge of human frailties. His wife Dorothy, the Duke of Devonshire's daughter whom he married in 1920, granted him immense social status – and desperation as a cuckold. His wife fell completely in love with her husband's MP colleague Bob Boothby. She wanted a divorce and said her youngest daughter Sarah's father was Lord Boothby, something he denied, telling Macmillan he was 'always careful' in his relations.

What began as a most conventional upper-class marriage with jolly-hockey sticks overtones emerged after a decade and four children as a melodrama: 'I never want to see my family again,' Dorothy Macmillan announced to the bemused Boothby. 'Why did you ever wake me?' she wailed. 'I never want to see any of my family again.'

Boothby, no novice in the self-interest stakes, would describe his lover as, 'on the whole, the most selfish and possessive woman I have ever known'.

The marriage stayed intact, glued by Macmillan's lawyer into a compromise enabled by having money, and a big house: Birch Grove in Sussex. Harold Macmillan was in one wing, his wife in the other. If they were in residence at the same time, they might take tea or dinner together and then follow their own pursuits. In politics, they played the married couple.

Macmillan was a stoic. And brave. During World War I, he was wounded five times: at The Battle of Loos and at the Somme. During the ferocious fighting at Delville (Devil's) Wood, he was shot in the thigh and pelvis. He rolled into a large shell-hole, where he stayed for ten hours, dosing himself up with morphine and reading the tragedies of the Greek playwright Aeschylus. He wrote home: 'The stench from the dead bodies which lie in heaps around is awful.'

During World War II, his plane crashed on take-off at Algiers and burst into flames. He fought through the emergency exit but then reversed back into the burning plane to rescue a French flag lieutenant, an act only ever recorded by others, and described by the US Assistant Secretary of War, John McCloy, who was there, as 'the most gallant thing I've ever seen'.

Macmillan was also daring on the home front. He told his colleagues and superiors when he thought they were wrong. And he was the only Conservative Minister to tell Churchill when it was time to go. Disliked by a great number in Parliament, he was hated too. 'He is his own worst enemy: he is too self-centred, too obviously cleverer than the rest of us,' Cuthbert Headlam MP wrote after a dinner with Macmillan. He followed with the haunting remark: 'He never will let the other man have his say, and he invariably knows everything better than the other man.'

There is, of course, *not hearing* as well as not listening, but as the most powerful man in the land neither creates good results. It was like his marriage, he appeared to forget there was a problem. The arrangement was no secret. Boothby, a bisexual known at Oxford as 'Palladium' as he was 'on twice nightly', bragged of his adventures with the Prime Minister's wife. His gambling was as wild as his sex life and he attended illegal chemmy games run by John Aspinall and John Burke. At Eaton Square games, the upmarket crowd nibbled on beluga and foie gras, and drank vintage Cristal and Delamain cognac, and when Boothby had enjoyed enough of everything he would make his other arrangements for the evening. 'We had the Duke of Devonshire and the Earl of Derby and someone who'd met the Queen earlier in the day playing with us and Bob Boothby would telephone 10, Downing Street and loudly announce that he was coming round to "fix the boiler",' confided John Burke.

Dorothy Macmillan never lost her fondness for her husband during their accepted arrangement. Politically, she was more in touch on the public forum, when meeting 'ordinary people'.

Stephen Ward's Cliveden neighbour Alan Brien was reporting on Mr and Mrs Macmillan's visit to the north-east of England in January 1959. It was very far north, Sunderland. When the Prime Minister walked around the North Sand shipyard to Joseph L. Thompson and Sons, Brien reported: 'There was Mr Macmillan, in a nest of girders, watching the workmen watching him. Then, the noon day hooter gave its bronchial blast. The motionless men sprang to life and poured past him in a hurrying, preoccupied flood. His eyebrows twitched in surprise and he muttered something to his wife. Lady Dorothy was quicker on the uptake. "When the whistle blows, they all go off for their luncheon." That evening was the debut of Tyne-Tees Television and Mr Macmillan graced them with an interview and commented on those he had encountered on his three-day tour of their broadcast area: "They are rather like fish, the further north you go, the better they get."'

He enthused about the co-operation of workers, adding: 'It has given me tremendous inspiration, even a few days like this. In London you really don't see what's going on.'

If so, it was only Britain that wasn't looking. Allen Dulles at the CIA had several personal wartime friends as agents and he deployed them to work within 'diplomatic' society in Britain. Ambassador Jock Whitney ran regular briefings with agents. At the same time, the FBI were following the commands of their director J. Edgar Hoover, who was battling to maintain his power base as the Eisenhower era was closing down. The anger in Washington over Burgess and Maclean's flight to Moscow was often engendered again by constant reference to them as 'British double agents' when the CIA had them clearly categorised as vital 'long-term Soviet penetration agents'. As such, they were XPD targets, to be eliminated with extreme prejudice.

The CIA's acute horror that Soviet agents were working within their own and their allies' Intelligence services resulted in crucial situations when no one knew who was spying on whom or, at times, who the real enemy was. They comprised a new paranoid class, like career criminals who will never take a drink unless they see the bottle opened, inside or outside jail. Who knew what information was poisoned? They suspected not just 'Kim' Philby but many others within what CIA specialists regarded as a sordid social climate in Britain, epitomised by the high life of London. Which, of course, was what Stephen Ward and his associates were enjoying.

Dr Ward had been making new friends. The weekends at Cliveden were becoming livelier. Bill Astor was still spending as much 'spanking good time' (he was now open about his penchant for caning girls on their backsides: 'like hunting, mustn't mind a little blood') at Spring Cottage and on sunny days in a little corner of the garden at what he called, with a snigger, his 'wench bench'.

John Profumo had moved upwards on the Government benches, appointed Minister of State for Foreign Affairs in January 1959. As such, he was often the 'minder' of foreign dignitaries on official visits to Britain and being entertained at Cliveden, the swimming-pool gatherings a welcome distraction from affairs of state.

Christine Keeler was an accomplished swimmer. As a teenager, she delighted in swimming in the muddy gravel pits near Wraysbury, Middlesex. She was proud of her skills and her body. Envious peers tried to bring her down by dubbing her 'Goddess of the Gravel Pits'. One childhood friend recalled: 'I remember Christine stepping from the water. Her homemade bikini of yellow jersey wool clung to her.'

For Kim Waterfield, Christine was indeed circean: 'She had the most tantalising silhouette. The first time I saw her she was topless. I saw this most beautiful girl. I thought her breasts were a little too far apart but only after looking for a long time.'

There were many others staring at Christine as she displayed herself on the stage of Murray's Club. Though still a teenager, her make-up and manner appeared older through the spotlights – it was her long legs that gave her the height. Stephen Ward said it was Christine's legs that first caught his attention. Her outfits, like all of those at Murray's, were feathers and nonsense and head-pieces that were for deportment lessons, not wearing. Clients at Murray's could gaze at what another couple of expensive drinks could bring.

Christine Keeler had always dreamed – it was easier than confronting the reality. She was born on 22 February 1942 to Julie Payne, who was 18 years old. Her father Colin Keeler, an adopted boy, had gone by 1949, working as a photographer at Butlin's in Clacton. A student who worked with him told me: 'He was a considerate man, but lost in himself.'

Christine learned to call Edward Huish 'Dad' when he took up with her mother in 1949. This new, nuclear-world family set up home in two converted railway carriages up from the River Thames on the dirt track known as Hythe End Road in Wraysbury, between Staines and Windsor Castle. There was no hot water, no mains electric power; no privacy. The scenic highlight was the gravel pits. Christine didn't need lessons about the birds and the bees long before the boys began looking her up and down. Her stepfather was possessive and when she caught him taking too much interest in her when she dressed and undressed, she began keeping a knife under her bed.

At 15, she had sexual intercourse with a student from Ghana. There were American GIs around and they too worked the magic Billy Hill remarked on. She became pregnant by a local boy called Jeff Perry but the baby (she called him Peter) died on 17 April 1959, at King Edward VII hospital in Old Windsor after a failed self-abortion attempt. It took six days for the child to die and the pain of that was carved into her. They say pain builds character but we cannot foresee what kind, especially with a disruptive and dark start to life; you harden yourself to the outside, to emotional equilibrium.

With her friend Pat, Christine fled Wraysbury and they got a room in St John's Wood. Christine in turn found jobs in shops and cafes and, like so many teenagers in London, was anxious 'to get into modelling' – it was the new black. Showbusiness grabbed her first.

Through a friend, Jenny Harvey, she met Maureen O'Connor, who worked at Murray's. 'Pops' Murray hired Christine – against much competition – after she walked around the room once. That was enough: he knew she'd be a star attraction, a sleek and sexy redhead.

When Stephen Ward first saw her, Christine was one of the topless showgirls posed behind the more fully dressed dancers going hell for motion in front of her. Between performances, the girls would be invited to join members and their guests for drinks. They could earn commission on the drinks, their 'scalps', and a smile and a flash of cleavage usually popped the champagne corks and UFOs, the 'unidentified fucking objects'.

Christine certainly popped John Profumo's cork. Murray's was where Profumo first saw her in nearly all her glory. He was still a regular at the Beak Street club and several habitués told me that they'd been there when Christine was on stage and Profumo was, as it were, in the audience. The film producer Harry Alan Towers told me: 'I saw Profumo at Murray's and other Government types while Christine was in the club, on stage and at table. I remember, for I was interested in her, but I had an arrangement with another girl at the time.' William Shepherd, a Conservative MP with links to MI5, said Murray's members would divide the girls up between those who did, and those who didn't. Harry Alan Towers paid close attention: 'I didn't miss much.'

Nor did Stephen Ward. Christine had been on display at Murray's for seven weeks when one evening she was invited to have a drink with Ahmed Manu, a young Arab with much money and hopes of a degree from the London School of Economics. She liked him and had 'scalped' him a few times previously. Young

Manu was with a good-looking ruby-haired girl called Claire Gordon, who in turn was, of course, with Dr Ward.

Christine sat down, smiled at the table; introductions were made, drinks ordered. For Ward, time froze – it was like meeting Valerie Mews, whom he transformed into Vicki Martin. He went into bedroom manner mode: he had seen Christine on stage, mesmerised. She was wonderful and would she honour him with a dance? Ward's false teeth clicked a little, and they did so on the word 'dance'. As they took to the floor, she wondered if 'dance' was the verb he meant as he held her close and tightly. Stephen offered to take her home but she politely declined. He persisted and, after smooth persuasion, had her telephone number neatly down in his worn brown leather notebook.

He telephoned her the next day, and the day after (he was good on the telephone, seductive) and she began to look forward to the calls. But she still refused to go out with him. She made excuses and, when he insisted, said she was visiting her mother at the weekend. Ward knew Wraysbury, just where her family lived, a lovely spot. The flannel needed to be rung out after that conversation. It was really no surprise when the white Jaguar appeared outside the converted railway carriages on a hot June afternoon in 1959. He charmed her mother, praised her stepfather, and, by the time he had invited her to Spring Cottage, they were all but packing Christine into Dr Ward's car and everlasting care. All the way to Cliveden, the glories of the place and his cottage remained his best material. On seeing the grounds, no one could fail to be impressed. Of course, after he had settled Christine into Spring Cottage for the day, his sketchpad appeared: he *had* to draw her.

She was, like so many before, overtaken by the ambience of Cliveden and the undoubted persuasive skills of Dr Ward. His London flat was by no means as grand as their present surroundings, he said, but she'd like it at Orme Square, just off the Bayswater Road (between proper accommodations he'd taken it as it afforded good light for sketches and painting). All afternoon, Ward showered 17-year-old Christine with talk of wealth and comfort and modelling, and Prince Philip and Winston Churchill and Bill Astor and all the fabulous parties at Cliveden, not to mention the glamorous guests. It was most civilised and, many hours later, he drove her home and did not invite himself in.

The next day, with Christine hardly knowing how or why, they were sitting at Dr Ward's favourite coffee shop on Marylebone High Street – and the day after that, and after that. He suggested she give up Murray's and go for a modelling career. She was, for goodness sake, beautiful and wonderful and super, super! It wasn't Mozart but it was the music that a teenager enjoyed, a subliminal seduction.

Platonically, they set up home together in the spotless top-floor studio flat in Orme Square, which was reached by an elevator. It was cramped but it had advantages for Christine, such as a bath and hot water to fill it. Off the bathroom was the bedsitting room with two single mattresses clamped together. It was cosy but platonic: they made strange bedfellows.

Dr Ward took Christine to a Maida Vale dinner party, introducing the hosts and the other couple as weekend regulars at Spring Cottage. It was the most elegant of places, tastefully furnished and the dining table glittered with crystal and Christofle, with a giant plastic penis as a centrepiece. As she had to leave for Murray's by 9.30pm, dinner finished early. The hostess appeared in a see-through grass skirt, the host went down on her, Dr Ward whipped her. The others watched or had sex on a sofabed. They were punctual. Christine left at 9.30pm with, as she walked to a taxi, the hostess shouting: 'See you again!'

Keeler always felt she had a back-up in her friend and sometimes lover Michael Lambton, whom she'd met at Murray's. He was besotted with her from the start, the one who did not treat her as a commodity. Of course, hard-to-get is better, even for a wealthy and superbly connected publisher like Lambton. His problem was drink: he adored it – even more it would seem than he did Christine. Yet, time and again, he would help her out with cash or accommodation at his flat in Onslow Gardens in South Kensington (Ava Gardner had the apartment below) – and usually both.

Towards the end of 1959, Dr Ward grew restless with the Orme Square flat. It had provided easy access to Notting Hill and the West Indian clubs, where he spent evenings sketching and experimenting with hemp. On these marijuana evenings, he was relaxed and would wander off and pick up girls; some he would talk to, others he'd take back to the flat and photograph, pictures he would share on his evenings with the antiques dealer Hod Dibben. He realised his erotic endeavours would benefit from a larger apartment and he felt 'a bit out of town' living in Bayswater. Through his friend Stephen Halsal (whom he had met at his offices in Paddington), he heard about a flat at Bryanston Mews West, nicely perched between the Edgware Road and Baker Street, behind Marble Arch. Arrangements were made for Dr Ward to meet the owner and view the flat. He took Christine with him, and the owner viewed her. After a moment or two, Peter Rachman rolled up his tongue, put it back in his mouth, and began explaining the disposition of the property.

Bryanston Mews West was one of a myriad of properties owned by Rachman, who had moved on from washing up in cafes and odd jobs at Jack Solomons' billiard hall. A decade on, he was one of the most notorious landlords in London and worth a great deal of money, much of which he kept under his mattress.

Born in Lvov, in south-eastern Poland and close to Nazi concentration camps, Rachman's parents died in 1940. Rachman fought and foraged, escaped to Russia and fought and foraged some more. Though he had eaten human waste to survive, he boasted: 'I never ate German shit.' He could never dispel the fear of hunger and hoarded stale bread wrapped in £20 notes. Nothing explained his need to have sex every afternoon as part of his business day, which was extremely busy. He'd realised in the

1950s, with soaring immigration, the prospects. He bought properties where statutory tenants were paying controlled rents. He'd then bring in troublemakers and, with racial bullying and strong-arm tactics (often brutal intimidation), force these tenants to leave and the value of the now unrestricted properties would soar. On top of that he would over-crowd buildings, 'sweat' them with West Indians, or rent them out for outrageous sums to club owners like Morrie Conley or to vice gangs for their girls. He confused the already confused housing regulations and company law; by what became 'Rachmanism' he created a slum empire. Yet, in a strange world, almost all who met him told me they found him generous, amusing and rather nice.

Rachman had the money to 'lobby' politicians, who provided him with insider trading information. He also had strong-arm teams, including psychopathic muscle like Michael de Freitas (later 'Michael X', executed in 1975 for the murder of Gale Benson, 27, daughter of one-time 5, Hamilton Place owner Leonard Plugge) and his favoured Serge Paplinski.

Ward was painfully pleasant but put out: 'I could see he was terribly taken by Christine and I couldn't get a word in about renting the place.'

Rachman's chief aide in his operations was Raymond Nash, who had already moved his girlfriend Sherry Danton into Bryanston Mews West. He told me in 2013 at his home in Marbella, Spain, how Rachman desperately wanted Christine Keeler: 'Peter wanted the best of everything – it was because of his background. We were very close. When he was told by the doctor that he had a heart condition, which could kill him, he told me and he said: "What do you think I should do?" I said: "Have the best time of your life. Enjoy every second and do the best for yourself, because you have enough money. Anything you want, you should buy, you can have."'

What Peter wanted that day was beautiful 17-year-old Keeler. He had an eye for her; he would undress her with his eyes as she walked by. She became his girlfriend and he bought her everything: high fashion, furs, nightgowns and jewels.

Not immediately; almost immediately. Sherry Danton, on Rachman's instruction, invited Christine for tea the next day. The teapot was still warm when Rachman arrived. He talked money and modelling: Sherry could help Christine in that world; he could help till she started earning. He gave her a white MG sports car (he liked white). She left Orme Square and Dr Ward for Bryanston Mews West and robotic sex ('like flossing his teeth') with Rachman and acquaintance with a two-way mirror, a legacy of the syphilitic voyeur Diana Dors' husband, Dennis Hamilton.

Dennis was a close friend of Hod Dibben, who supplied girls for orgies at Hamilton and Diana Dors' home, known as 'The Penthouse' in Maidenhead. He made cash from his 'home movies' (complete with soundtrack) of the action, taken through the mirror, centred on the ceiling of the master bedroom. Stephen Ward and Rachman were regulars, said Raymond Nash. As were a cast of household entertainment names, familiar faces in unfamiliar positions. Kim Waterfield told me: '"DD" was a darling and she was naughty and wild. For her, sex was a game that she loved to play. That was why she agreed to Hamilton's suggestion that they have a two-way mirror in their house and watch others making love. She loved to tell me about the well-known people in the mirror, going at it in the most bizarre ways.'

Some parties involved black magic hokum and young women, some teenagers, being playfully bound, gagged and whipped. Some guests were there for the tame sadomasochism (though not on the scale of Piccadilly's Red Kate), the rest for the group sex – the liberation of being 'swingers', part of showbiz. The pragmatic Rachman went for the high-stakes gambling sessions – and the anonymous sex.

When Dors finally divorced the relentless voyeur Hamilton in 1958, he transferred the special events mirror to Bryanston Mews, but he was dead, on 3 January 1959, before it was properly hooked up for Cinemascope: a victim of venereal disease. It was detail like this that bizarrely infuriated Stephen Ward. He'd wanted to make Christine Keeler a grand lady, to set her on the path of Maureen Swanson, into the aristocracy. And here she was actually slumming it, with a slum landlord *and* his horrid friends. In his fury, Dr Ward dismissed, without irony, Rachman (seven years his junior) as 'a dirty old man'.

It made Ward furious the more he thought of what Christine, young as she was, had done. Yet, her association with Rachman was under threat – *from Christine*. And her new lover: Rachman's lieutenant Serge Paplinski, who ran the property racket from Westbourne Grove. Paplinski had tried to resist Christine in over-the-top Lolita form but he was no match for her. As a young boy he'd fought with the Polish Resistance, shot and killed a female informer and lived wild in the forests of Europe and the streets of London until Rachman 'civilised' him. Paplinski had been trained to kill by the Resistance but Christine conquered him. Rachman knew she was seeing someone and put his minders on the case; Christine knew.

Stephen Ward received a phone call from her. Could they meet at the Kenco Coffee Bar, around the corner from the Devonshire Street surgery? Ward was intrigued and his normal, pleasant personality on the phone. As he walked to the coffee bar, his mood must have darkened for he accessorised his dark suit with one of Shakespeare's February faces, full of foreboding. He launched into his former flatmate: 'You have thrown yourself away on a man like Rachman, you are a silly girl!' And with disappointed fury he scolded: 'You could have been a *Duchess*!'

Christine fired up at what she saw as another lecture, another man trying to control her life. She went back to Rachman who, of course, was doing just that. Rachman's empire was prospering; he speculated with some ferocity, buying up much of west London's run-down areas, using other people's names. The Conservative Minister of Transport, Ernest Marples, who was a crony of

Rachman's, attended Dennis Hamilton and Hod Dibben's parties, and supplied Rachman with the route of the about-to-be-built M6 motorway so he could buy up property in its path and sell it back to the British Government at some remarkable profit.

Rachman seemed to scoot over rainbows with pots of gold at either end: he always got what he wanted. But, although he was having his daily sex with Christine, she always had to face away from him (she was romancing Paplinski in her own time). Rachman saw her as his, 24 hours a day. He attempted obvious displays of annoyance but had no passion for it: there were always more girls, but only one Paplinski.

It ended badly, but not violently. Paplinski was Rachman's and he kept him; Christine he locked out of Bryanston Mews. In early 1960, she found a home with her friend Jenny Harvey. Then, again, with Dr Ward who had moved into a house at 17, Wimpole Mews. He rented it for 21 guineas a week from the film studio 20th Century Fox. Behind the soothing grandeur of Harley Street, it was close to his surgery on Devonshire Street. A quiet little spot, it had good light for his painting.

CHAPTER NINE

DOCTOR AT RISK

'TO BE HONEST AS THE WORLD GOES IS TO BE
ONE MAN PICKED OUT OF TEN THOUSAND.'
Hamlet, Shakespeare

W hat was to set Stephen Ward's life off on a turbulent
trajectory was Hugh Leggatt's lumbago. Dr Ward cured it
in three treatment sessions and casually enquired of his patient,
who owned a London art gallery, if he could show him some of
his paintings and sketches. Leggatt, a prominent West End dealer,
had heard it all before from aspiring Picassos and the rest, but, as
his back was truly healed, he felt grateful and with some kindness
agreed. He was most pleasantly surprised when he saw Ward's
work. He dealt with old – and dead – masters but would stage a
one-man exhibition, commission-free, if Ward could present a
variety of work. The dealer explained: 'I did it because I liked him
as a person; partly because he was hopeless over money and
always forgot to charge you; and partly because he was good –
there are very few artists capable of catching a living likeness.'

Ward now had to deliver the goods. He called in the many he
had given to his famous friends and set about arranging to
persuade others to sit for him (it would take 30 minutes of their
time). A frugal man over everything, the world's richest, Paul

Getty, agreed the same day and was sketched at the Ritz. Getty's rival Nubar Gulbenkian, with his face foliage and monocle, made a startling addition; British Foreign Secretary Selwyn Lloyd, standing behind his FO desk, also posed for Ward; Rab Butler also did him the same honour at the Home Office. He drew the Opposition's Hugh Gaitskell, showing the failing health of the Labour leader. When he sketched the Prime Minister, catching that sometimes mischief in Macmillan's left eye, he had a political full house. Through his friend Peter Sellers, he reached Sophia Loren at Elstree Studios, where she was filming *The Millionairess*, and she became a prime subject in her own lunchtime.

As an artist, Ward appeared to work with little effort. He had a clear talent and his subjects all praised his work. Hugh Leggatt regarded the portrait of Lord Shawcross in his chambers as the best, but enthused: 'Ward was, at that time, the toast of what I call artistic society in the sense that he was creating something of which there was a serious vacuum in the London art scene. Everybody who was anybody approached me to arrange for them to have their portrait sketched by Ward.'

After a successful exhibition on 12 July 1960, the next day the acclaimed artist was called by Sir Bruce Ingram, editor of *The Illustrated London News*, offering a contract. The magazine wanted a series on famous people and then a run of Royal portraits. Sir Bruce had known King George V, the Queen's grandfather, which gave him strong leverage. Ward delivered Archbishop Makarios of Cyprus, who was visiting London, and a string of distinguished, mostly academic names. Then, his first Royal, Prince Philip, on canvas – 'The Prince had been to a party of mine at Cavendish Square before his marriage and he remembered me. "By Jove," he said. "You're the osteopath. I never connected you with this appointment." He was a wonderful sitter, still as a rock and yet relaxed.'

The Duke of Kent sat for him at Kensington Palace, and he drew the Duke's mother, Princess Marina, in a great drawing room.

Inexplicably to him, he found her difficult. Princess Margaret was up next. Dr Ward knew her from Les Ambassadeurs and he also knew her new husband, the late Baron's 'assistant', Antony Armstrong-Jones, whom she'd married only a couple of months earlier at Westminster Abbey, on 6 May 1960. Nothing was said about the Ward / Armstrong-Jones animosity.

There were more Royals, including the Duke and Duchess of Gloucester, and Hugh Leggatt was constantly sending customers his way.

He had a new friend, Noel Howard-Jones, who was helping him with gardening and maintenance at Cliveden. They met at the beginning of 1960 and Howard-Jones told me: 'I met Stephen when I was a student in London. I was working in the evenings in a place called the Brush and Palette in Bayswater – a bad restaurant and a place where people could sketch naked models. Now most of the visitors there were travelling businessmen, who were much more interested in staring at the naughty bits than actually sketching. It was quite surprising to see somebody come in – Stephen – who sat down and showed a great deal of competence, and in addition to that was only interested in sketching the face.

'I got talking to him and it turned out that he'd been a friend of my mother's in the West Country when they were both young and we became friends. He was delightful, full of anecdotes, an excellent speaker. And genuinely liked people. He had a way with women but I guess nowadays a bachelor with a Jaguar sports car, a house in the country and lots of friends in showbusiness and other glamour professions wouldn't find too much difficulty in finding attractive company. I think the girls got into society because of him, and not vice versa. He came from a comfortable background. And you know, once you're on familiar terms with Prince Philip, the lesser stars are not too much of a problem.

'I arrived in London in late 1960 and my life had certainly changed. I'd spent 12 years in English private boarding school, followed by two years in the Royal Marines. And London society when I got here as a student, at a time when the Pill had been invented and AIDS hadn't, and all of a sudden things became possible, which to a young man like me hadn't been possible before.

'Stephen had the cottage and, on Sundays in the summer, it was sort of open house. Anybody could bring a picnic and join the party and talk. And swim in the dams. People bring a friend, the circle would get larger and larger. I never saw Stephen out on the streets, prospecting for new friends. He was a good listener and you could go round to his flat in London at any time. He was never alone – I don't think he ever wanted to be alone. He loved talking, politics but also culture. What he really enjoyed was having people from totally contrasting backgrounds, a stuffy academic with some upper-class twit. Or a couple of people from showbusiness here, a journalist, a lawyer, and he would just act as a catalyst for the conversation.

'When I met him, he was friendly with Christine Keeler. Accommodation in London was expensive or relative to what people earned and, whenever she was on "skippers", she knew Stephen had a spare room. Quite often she would stay at his place between boyfriends. He liked her. And he had a sort of protective attitude towards her; he felt concerned.

'It might seem like a very odd relationship, a society osteopath and a showgirl, but he also befriended me, a penniless law student. And I certainly considered him as a friend. And he certainly treated me as a friend. On a couple of occasions when I was particularly broke, he lent me money and made it pretty clear that he didn't expect to get paid back. He'd been osteopath for Winston Churchill and a whole lot of other people. I knew nothing about his practice – at my age I had no requirement for osteopathy, and I didn't believe in it anyway.

'Although everybody I met, including Bill Astor, swore that they suffered agonising back pains and Stephen fixed them up in no time at all. I suppose it was temporary because he had to keep on doing it and that was of course the reason why he had the cottage – it was in full payment for the treatment he gave to Astor. The cottage was Stephen's pride and joy. And so when I saw him and Viscount Astor together they seemed to be on excellent terms as good friends.

'Astor used to regularly invite visitors, official visitors down for the weekend there, with some sort of junior minister as a babysitter. I gathered things became so paralysingly boring up at the big house on Sundays that quite often Astor would call in despair and say, "Stephen, have you got anybody interesting down there? Because if so, for God's sake, bring them up to the swimming pool!"

'Spring Cottage was pretty primitive, actually. Only half of it was even furnished. Stephen would go down there every weekend. On Sundays, it was open house and, if it was fine weather, people would be bathing in the Thames and sunbathing on the lawn. And if it was raining, well, we would all be inside, talking.

'I was a randy 20-year-old. It was very sociable. Bill Astor would invite us up to the swimming pool at the big house. It was a remarkable time: you could meet a girl, you hit it off together and what was more natural than you found yourselves in bed together? Christine Keeler was for a rather brief time my girlfriend. I couldn't take her to my place so we'd go to bed at Stephen's flat when he was working and I took her down to the cottage on my scooter. She was pretty, she was decorative, but, after a time if you're going to pursue a relationship with somebody, then you need a little bit more than that. I remained on very friendly terms with her afterwards but the relationship was short; it drifted away.

'On Saturdays, a rather small group of people would be invited and the routine on Saturday was one mainly of backbreaking work: Stephen's ambition was to build Britain's largest rock garden along the banks of the Thames there. So that a large part of

Saturday was spent in heaving rocks from a quarter of a mile further down to the rock garden site.

'Ivanov was a regular visitor. I was too. And a sort of shifting population of other people. Ivanov even christened this rock garden "the Russian Steppes" as part of his contribution in shifting stone to the site.'

Ivanov? Well, that would be Captain, second rank, Yevgeny (Eugene) Ivanov of the Soviet Union. He had arrived in London on 27 March 1960, with the papers of a naval attaché and the orders of an experienced espionage agent. Captain Ivanov was, like everyone else at 16, Kensington Palace Gardens, a Cold War spy. However, Ivanov was extra-special: he had a control outside the Russian Embassy, although for formality he filed weekly reports to the London *rezident*, General Alexander Pavlov. Ivanov (everywhere he went, they called him just that) was a trusted member of the Glavnoye Razvedyvatel'noye Upravleniye (GRU), the foreign military Intelligence organisation. His boss, General Ivan Serov, was the most powerful Intelligence officer in Russia and as head of the GRU answered only to President Nikita Khrushchev. Following Stalin's death on 5 March 1953, it took Khrushchev three years and the execution of many rivals, including Stalin's malicious secret police chief Lavrentiy Beria, before he took total power. Ivan Serov, a SMERSH agent in Poland during the war and one-time chairman of a man-of-four KGB control group, was his man.

Their plan, according to documents seen by 2013 Moscow-connected officials, was to further disrupt what they perceived as the already shaky Western political partnership of Britain and America. Ivanov was to be the Russian bull in the Western china shop, crash and bang around and break things up as much as possible. He was to put on a show, a carnival of distraction from more deep-penetration Soviet agents sent in to infiltrate the British trade union movement and, top to toe, the UK Labour Party. They had begun work about the same time as the agents from America's CIA. The Labour Party had more spies than policies.

'Ivanov would never have been able to operate the way he did without extremely specific instructions from the men running operations in Moscow,' Kremlin specialist Alexander Nekrassov said in 2013. Nekrassov went to great lengths to spell out the truth to me: 'In 1960, the world was on the edge and, in Moscow, they had teams of people preparing every mission – and every detail of every mission. There was purpose and intent in everything that was done. Of course, if opportunities presented themselves they were grasped – but only after Moscow had checked that the action would fit the final purpose. Ivanov was hand-picked.'

At a time when a suggestion of misdeed could induce greater paranoia and a clampdown on worldwide Intelligence, any stretching of allegiances was a victory. As would be information about the British and West German military and missile capabilities and an inside line on UK–US relations and NATO's strategic and operational thinking.

On that, Ivanov was tutored on the success of an 'illegal' in Britain: Konon Trofimovich Molody. Outside Russia, he became infamous as Gordon Lonsdale, mastermind of the spy ring that so successfully stole secrets from the British Admiralty Underwater Weapons Establishment at Portland in Hampshire, England. His team had captured great amounts of classified material, including details of Britain's first nuclear submarine, HMS *Dreadnought*. In Moscow, it was seen as one of the grandest coups of the Cold War. Lonsdale's main catch was a sad little Englishman called Harry Houghton. I saw him only once, in 1971, and mostly the back of his raincoat when he raced away from my questions about his decade in prison. With his flying legs and flapping raincoat, he looked like the clever British comedian Harry Worth. It was the modesty in Houghton's deviousness that got him recruited, in a long-firm-style operation, by the GRU.

In 1950, he was a Royal Naval clerk at the British Embassy in

Warsaw, and after two decades as a sailor liked the diplomatic good life, especially the gallons of cheap drink. One of Houghton's bar-room friends told him: 'If you don't make a pile here, you're a mug.' Houghton went into the coffee business, getting it supplied through diplomatic couriers, and moving his cheap supply at a good profit. Then, a tantalising new client appeared, Karytzia Grimrov, who had the cash for big shipments, long, dark hair and a body to commit crimes for. Harry did, but it took a little time. When his wife returned to Britain in 1951, his romance heated up. It was with some sadness a year later that he left Karytzia behind when, in a sensitive posting, he returned to the UK. He went to work at the Portland Underwater Weapons Research Establishment, lost a wife to divorce but became engaged to Ethel 'Bunty' Gee, a filing clerk and secretary at the Portland base. Like the life Houghton had created, she was built for comfort, not speed. They seemed to spend every weekend decorating their bungalow.

Harry Houghton was surrounded by new rolls of floral wallpaper when, in 1955, he answered the telephone to a heavily accented man. He had a message from Karytzia. Three days later, Houghton met the go-between at the Dulwich Art Gallery in south London. He put an emergency stop on any sentence Houghton had to offer. The Polish secret police knew of his affair and the black-market business with Karytzia, whom he said was 'politically unreliable'. Her former lover could save her by supplying secrets – and, the clincher for the lazy, self-centred Houghton, make some cash.

Missing out Karytzia, Houghton spun Bunty Gee a tale about the black-market problem and said he was being blackmailed by a CIA agent known to him from Warsaw: the Americans believed the British were withholding nuclear secrets. He would go to jail unless he gave them details of the research at Portland. With a man in her life for the first time, Bunty was in. The GRU were professional: Houghton got a Minox camera the size of a cigarette lighter – there was a bigger, sharper version he kept for documents he could take home – and the tradecraft for clandestine meetings and handovers was mundane. It was done by a code of pinpricks on life insurance brochures sent to him by Royal Mail. The material, about nuclear submarine development and anti-submarine weapons, was invaluable to the East. In turn, they kept Houghton happy with money, as well as 'protection' from his black-market past. He bought more than his fair round in pubs, drove a new car and the Sanderson wallpaper was top of the line. And he worked at a top-secret nuclear establishment at the height of the Cold War. A couple of people mentioned it as suspicious but for nearly four years Houghton (with the help of Bunty Gee) provided Gordon Lonsdale and the East with crackerjack material, better than all the more elaborate operators.

The grand theft from a British installation might have gone on and on, but to their delight the Americans cracked the case and the eggs all over Britain's face. The CIA got the break. Polish spy Michael Goleniewski (given one of those beloved CIA monikers, 'Sniper') offered up Houghton when he defected to Washington in 1959. Prime Minister Macmillan had to 'have a word' with the manager of a National Westminster Bank in Marylebone so that MI5 could take a secret peek in Lonsdale's safe deposit box and the smart attaché case inside with espionage equipment. Lonsdale had lifted secrets from the Holy Loch nuclear submarine base in Scotland and the priority now was information on Asdic, a sonar detection system by which warships can monitor enemy submarines.

Bunty Gee dealt with the Asdic files every day; she put seven green cover pamphlets of the secret material in a brown envelope and met Houghton in the car park, where she got a kiss on the cheek.

The rendezvous with Gordon Lonsdale on 6 January 1961 was outside the Old Vic Theatre, around from Waterloo station on the south side of London's Thames. As Lonsdale helped Bunty Gee with her shopping bag of secrets, a team of Special Branch officers arrested them. Cronies, aides and other agents were rounded up, but many escaped. The Labour Party's watchdog on all things military and security, Mr George Wigg MP, noted with much outrage: 'Heaven knows how many members of the Soviet gang took the tip and got out of England.'

Other espionage coups may have been more flamboyant but few were as effective. Even the arrest and trials of the participants was brilliant propaganda for Moscow. The point hammered home to Ivanov was that Lonsdale, working in deep undercover, had not achieved victory alone: he had recruited help. In the aftermath of the Portland victory, Ivanov had a dual role: make mischief, make friends, steal secrets.

If in doubt, get others to do the dirty work.

In 1960, the gregarious Ivanov, 37, was up for it all. He was just short of 6ft tall, had a boxer's nose, a gym chest and biceps, big shoulders, a touch of vodka and Mongolian ancestry around the eyes and a giant generosity of a grin. Fay Wray would have loved him; everybody else did. The Russians displayed that with their welcome, led by the Ambassador Alexander Soldatov and Ivanov's titular superior, Captain, first rank: Vlintov Zucherushkin. The warmth had nothing to do with Ivanov's superagent status; it was much more self-serving than that: Ivanov had connections, *big beluga*, through his family.

His wife Maya was the daughter of Alexander Gorkin, chairman of the Soviet Supreme Court. His brother-in-law was Colonel Konstantinov, head of the GRU *residentura* at Kensington Gardens. They had also been primed on Ivanov's rising star: talent-spotted in 1944, he had served in the Far East, the Black Sea and the Arctic, and received special Intelligence training by the GRU. Through diplomatic channels, Ivan Serov had made it known to the *rezident* that Ivanov was a social person – and was to be allowed to operate as he dictated. Which was outside the boundaries of espionage etiquette. It was acknowledged that a *second* naval attaché was a spook in that they were so lowly in rank that, if something went wrong, their Government could deny them and what they'd said or done. It worked both ways. So it was that MI5's counter-Intelligence 'D' Branch made a note of Ivanov's arrival and MI6 put him on their long list of Russian diplomats to monitor and, essentially, went to the pub.

Ivanov didn't appear a threat other than on the volleyball court behind 10, Kensington Palace Gardens. Yet, he was that most devilish of beings: a man of tremendous plausibility. He engaged with people at parties, he presented rather than punched the Soviet saviour stuff. Quick and bright, he was a sprightly conversationalist – a lot like Stephen Ward.

They met at that most theatrical of precious gathering places, in Covent Garden, at The Garrick Club. At the start of 1961, the stage was set for an epic turn of events.

It is expedient to say fate brought them together, for any other explanation, including premeditation, seems so impossible, involving, as it did, bad backs, bridge evenings, a flight to Mount Zion, the trial of the chief architect of the butchery of the Jews, former SS Colonel Adolf Eichmann, a monster in a glass-encased dock and a possible plan for Ward to sketch the Soviet Politburo. If it was a plot, it had talented scriptwriters.

Stephen Ward believed his future was assured. His connections were impeccable. The Editor of the *Daily Telegraph*, Sir Colin Coote, suffered from lumbago and his friend, Sir Godfrey Nicholson, MP, had recommended Dr Ward. The former Liberal MP, now editor, exclaimed: 'To my complete astonishment, the pain was tamed.'

Through the long series of treatments and card evenings at the Connaught Bridge Club, Dr Ward became increasingly intrigued by world affairs. He enjoyed having 'inside knowledge'. 'Stephen took on a certain grandeur in those days,' said Kim Waterfield, 'and why not? He knew pretty much everybody that mattered on first-name terms.'

It was a habit he continued with 'Eugene' Ivanov. Sir Colin Coote was impressed with his back doctor's artistic work and had suggested he might travel to Jerusalem in April 1961 to do reportage drawings for the *Daily Telegraph* on the trial of Adolf Eichmann. Ward was keen but he also suggested to the Editor that he'd like to do portraits of all of Russia's leaders. When a Russian delegation from the Embassy visited the offices of the *Telegraph*, the Editor hosted them for a drink. He was buttonholed by Ivanov in his mission to befriend the opinion makers of Britain. Sir Colin thought him a jolly fellow and, pondering on Dr Ward's interest in Russia, suggested lunch. At The Garrick, Ward sat down with Sir Colin, the newspaper's Soviet specialist, David Floyd, and Ivanov. The talk was intelligent, with Dr Ward listening and others displaying their grasp of the Cold War. Ivanov and Dr Ward nodded at each other constantly.

They connected like Siamese twins, almost immediately dependent on each other. Ward had found a man who was exotic and an outsider, just as he was. Ivanov would say that Ward had told him it was like getting another brother – it was just that this one preached the Soviet doctrine, and very convincingly. Still, it was the man, not the philosophy, that Stephen Ward, in a non-physical way, fell for. Here was a charming, witty and energetic and most intelligent fellow, one he could teach the manners and lifestyle of an English gentleman – and an aristocratic one at that.

Ivanov was not so bowled over. He regarded his lunch companion as 'a pet of the British upper class'. And blessed his luck – what a card to pull out of the pack. He played it well; he walked from The Garrick with his new friend who took him round to meet his other *great* friend, Jack Hylton, at Albany House. Within a couple of hours, the Soviet spy had, if not danced, shaken hands with two men who dined with the man who most certainly danced with HM the Queen. After Hylton treated them to a drink and a new song on the piano, they went to 38, Devonshire Street. Dr Ward settled Ivanov in an armchair in his office and – astonishingly – poured him a brandy, a small one. Ivanov said he received a monologue of Dr Ward's career, the sketching, the friends, the portraits, Churchill, ambassadors, Hollywood stars, academics, men of influence. Ivanov asked for another brandy. He said his head spun – from the number of names, not the drinks. Finally, the invitation came: 'You must come to Cliveden at the weekend, meet Bill...'

Ivanov knew that Dr Ward's friends could become his too. He hadn't just been dealt a good card: he had an *ace*.

Noel Howard-Jones liked him. He told me: 'Eugene Ivanov was central to it all. Officially, he was a Soviet Navy Commander. He was a true believer – you could talk politics for hours with him and he was an unshakable believer in the Soviet system. His wife, a history professor at Moscow University, would sometimes be here with him but she spent most of her time in Moscow, of course. And he was a nice guy. He looked like many Soviet military officers did, pretty much a shovel-faced peasant. Good guy – I used to play chess with him. And I liked him, really. I don't suppose he would have bothered with me if I hadn't been a friend of Stephen's. I learned that all Soviet military attachés were members of the GRU. And you know, so what? The appropriate circles in London certainly knew what he was up to.

'I think he was to some extent under the illusion that England was still a place run by Lords, and all that kind of thing. And I think perhaps part of his fascination, although there was certainly a genuine friendship between them, was the fact that he knew Stephen could introduce him to people like Lord Astor.'

'I had terrific times with Ivanov at Cliveden,' said Bobby McKew. 'He knew about boats and from my sailing days, smuggling out of Tangiers, we had the sea in common. His English was sharp, he caught slang words and he could swear when he'd had a drink. He never lost control as far as I could see. One Sunday he announced: "We must have lunch." And we did. We went to a little place on the Brompton Road, an Italian as I recall, near The Oratory. We talked about girls and parties and important stuff like that, nothing else – he was intrigued by the stories about the girls. He knew I was friendly with a great many people and maybe that was his interest. I didn't mind one bit – he bought lunch.'

There were moments when the vodka and his beliefs got the better of Ivanov – or seemed to. One evening at Wimpole Mews, he enjoyed a bottle of vodka with yet another of Dr Ward's redheads and then berated her for colouring her hair, something the great womenfolk of Russia would never do.

The girl stood up, stripped off and revealed she was a natural redhead. Ivanov responded with his bear's grin: 'A true Red!'

Unlike Marilyn 'Mandy' Rice-Davies, whom Christine Keeler would later describe as 'a true tart'.

But that was later.

Mandy Rice-Davies was a pushy teenager – blonde, brisk and full of it. Her parents were Welsh but had settled in Birmingham, her father a policeman, her mother forever distraught by an unrequited love of acting. Mandy looked angelic and, of course, she sang in the church choir and fought off the boys who tried to lure her into the vestry. She was a hard worker, earning enough from a newspaper round to be able to run a pony – an ambitious 15-year-old school leaver. Saturday mornings she worked at a local dress shop and that retail experience won her a full-time job at a department store, where she followed her mother's showbiz dreams.

Make Mine Mink was a Terry-Thomas film, a 1960 British comedy written, in another extraordinary happenstance, by Stephen Ward's friend Michael Pertwee (brother of Jon) who thought Dr Ward 'a social pimp'. Mandy was a social whirl. As part of a promotion for the Odeon screening in Birmingham, the producers had Thomas and Hattie Jacques in town. When they posed for the local newspaper, they did so with a heavily made-up and elaborately hair-styled Mandy. In an absurdity of coincidence, and how all manner of theories can begin, Thomas was a patient of Dr Ward.

Sixteen-year-old Mandy didn't care about that as she was taken home in a limousine as reward for her promotional efforts. She was a star and, after being offered a job modelling at the Earls Court Car Show, she was on her way to Fulham Broadway Tube station. She posed with a Mini, next to a Mini, behind a Mini, in front of one; she lunched with the car's designer, Alec Issigonis.

Having earned nearly £100, Mandy decided London was the place. She went home, her parents hit the roof, she ignored them, packed one cuddly toy and her underwear, a couple of dresses, a coat and she was out of the house while her parents were at work. Mandy was soon at work too, at Murray's. It had been a random thing, an advertisement for dancers in the London *Evening Standard*. Like Christine Keeler, she'd been an instant hire but, because of her age, she had to present a forged letter of permission from her parents. 'Pops' Murray didn't believe it for a moment, but he was legally covered – he had 'a letter'.

Mandy got a Red Indian squaw costume. The crowd liked her number, which she gave some oomph: Redskin Girl with Fire in Her Eyes, Bang! Bang! Bang! One Government minister (not Profumo) was said to have got into a fight over her.

She truly went on the warpath after she met her new friend, Christine Keeler.

CHAPTER TEN

DOCTOR FEELGOOD

'IT DOESN'T MEAN A DAMNED THING. IT'S JUST
LIKE WHEN HE WAS AWAY IN THE ARMY.'

Colonel Tom Parker, manager of Elvis Presley, on his client's demise
and future marketability, 1977

Stephen Ward went to bed and had sex with Mandy Rice-
Davies the first time he took her to Cliveden. It was his way
of making the point: he was in charge, the ringmaster. Dr Ward
believed he was juggling all the areas of his life as brilliantly, but
some of those around him had started to act independently of his
wise counsel. There is no doubt from those who knew him closely,
or as closely as anyone ever could, in 1961 that he was desperate
to stay in command of his circle in a world that was daily being
told it was about to be obliterated.

Approaching half a century in age, Ward's outlook on the end
of the world was much different to that of the teenaged Christine
Keeler and Mandy Rice-Davies. The two girls became friendly
and Christine often stayed over at Mandy's place, escaping Dr
Ward's all-seeing eyes. In time, they found a flat together in
Comeragh Road, way out on the District Line at Barons Court, for
£12 a week. Mandy had tried to do a runner on her previous flat,
but got caught. Christine, a little ashamedly, left a note at
Wimpole Mews. Dr Ward got a call from her a little later and they

made peace on the telephone. He made himself a regular visitor at Comeragh Road. Mandy found him charming but was convinced he was homosexual because of his precise way of speaking and smoking. In turn, Ward found Mandy difficult to read. Christine thought he was trying to tempt her back to Wimpole Mews. In fact, he invited them both to Spring Cottage. To complete the foursome, he invited his cousin, Tim Vigors, a Battle of Britain pilot and businessman.

That night, Dr Ward played prowler at the window and scared Mandy; indeed, frightened her into his bed. It was not an all-consuming passion for either of them. She said his sexual skills were good but it was the verdict of a young woman experienced in furtive couplings. The next morning, when Ward went off to Cliveden proper with his cousin to visit Bill Astor, the teenagers scarpered for London. The first car that saw them waving their thumbs stopped. As a duo, the girls had that effect – and they knew it.

Six days later, Ward and Astor appeared at Comeragh Road. Astor had his hands all over Mandy's bottom, while Ward handed a cheque to Christine; the girls' rent was due and Astor had written out a £200 cheque for it. The girls helped themselves too with a little casual, profitable, love-making with men like Douglas Fairbanks Junior, who enjoyed sex with both girls, a lively threesome, and especially Mandy licking his backside. Neither could watch *Sinbad the Sailor* on television again without having hysterics. They had Fairbanks Junior upstairs at the Twenty One Room in the West End, where Christine also met up with Major Jim Eynan, whom she saw regularly (they had sex at Comeragh Road and Wimpole Mews). He helped her financially.

But it wasn't all work. Dr Ward escorted the girls to a mammoth King's Road style party at Kim Waterfield's large and lavish Chelsea home (the only caveat on invitations was that all the single girls must be tall, slim and beautiful). Co-host of the evening, which provided hospitality for Peter Sellers, Bob Hope, the film exotic Linda Christian, Kim Waterfield's longtime friend Diana Dors and almost 200 others, was Jeremy Scott. His girlfriend's 16-year-old brother was at the party. He had left Harrow School the day before and by the next morning the badly dressed schoolboy had lost his virginity to Mandy in a roll around the floor, all for a laugh and a lark. It was fair enough – she was the same age.

The somewhat older Peter Rachman was going to have Mandy rolling in cash. Christine and Mandy were invited on a 'date' with visiting Americans: dinner at the Savoy (and coffee and men afterwards). The girls were returning from the lavatory when they cruised straight into Rachman and his blonde of the evening. Rachman kept the blonde, the girls ditched the Yanks – after a fine dinner in The Grill – and they all met back at Barons Court. Rachman knew the way – he owned much of the property en route.

The route took him through the formerly elegant and well-tended terraced houses, paint peeling off the upper windows (the ones that saw the sun), garbage spilling onto the streets. He bought cheap property and was not the only entrepreneur to benefit from the Church of England's lack of attachment to their worldly goods throughout the 1950s. His first deal involved a property with eight rooms, a house on the north side of the Harrow Road. Seven of the rooms were tenant-occupied, their rents controlled to pre-war prices – until they moved or died, the rents could never be increased as their statutory right. Rachman bought the house for £1,000 because of that. He rented the empty room to eight West Indians, whom he described as 'accomplished musicians', telling them to rehearse any time they wanted. Within 12 weeks, the seven other rooms were empty. He then squeezed as many West Indian families into the property and asked (and got) exorbitant rental prices.

With the building a going and profitable concern, Rachman sold it on for £5,000. He had the money to find good mortgage rates, dealers to get him the properties, thugs to evict the tenants and the brass neck to charge the Jamaicans, Trinidadians and Barbadians even higher rents. His pitch: other parts of London did not rent to 'coloureds'. It was true and he exploited that prejudice for himself, renting to all, take it or leave it.

Rachman parked at the end of his empire and went straight into the girls' Barons Court flat. He was disdainful of Christine – been there, done that. It was Mandy the cliché who entranced him, the bubbly blonde. Bright as paint, she was a gloss on his evening with her overwhelming energy, perky conversation and body, bouncing like a rubber ball all over the apartment. For him, it was convenience at first sight. She was in Rachman's pants and chocolate-coloured Rolls the next day.

When she turned 17, Mandy had her own car. Rachman gave her a white 3.2-litre Jaguar and, to save her the boredom of bureaucracy, a forged driver's licence in the name of Marilyn Rachman – he liked his stamp on everything he owned. Rachman had moved Mandy out of Comeragh Road but it had not distressed Christine, who was deeply involved with a wealthy Iranian student, an unpleasant lad called Manu. She still visited Mandy, who was now the lady of Bryanston Mews, receiving 'housekeeping' of £120 a week (a fortune in those days), a beautiful Arab stallion and the time to indulge herself. When Rachman wanted sex, it was the same deal as with Christine: a recurrence of need and habit.

Mandy found she could control Rachman, sometimes violently. The infamous Dennis Hamilton mirror covered a living-room wall with views of the bedroom through it. During one of their more chaotic rows, Mandy threw a hairbrush at Rachman; he ducked, it hit the mirror and for all concerned the bad luck, seven years or more, began. After that, Rachman made it up and presented Mandy with a necklace and matching diamond earrings.

Through Rachman's largesse, Mandy began to believe she

could walk on water. With that omnipotent mindset, there's a good chance of drowning.

Raymond Nash, married to a Korean princess and living in Spain in 2013, was happy for his friend Peter Rachman, whom he believed had safely settled down with his 'wife' Audrey (they had been together for 14 years but only legally married in 1960) and his mistress Mandy at Bryanston Mews, much as he had been with Sherry Danton: 'Peter was my godfather – he was the guy who taught me how to borrow 110 per cent from banks, and buy and buy. He was a very kind and gentle man, contrary to what everybody thought.'

Nash was the only man that Rachman allowed at the flat and he got on well with Mandy, as he had with Christine. He and Rachman owned the Condor Club, where Michael Caine and Terence Stamp would become regulars, but Rachman was very much the silent partner. Rock star Marty Wilde, earning £1 a night plus a bowl of spaghetti, was talent-spotted there by the entertainment agent Larry Parnes. Raymond Nash said: 'Peter was very good friends with Diana Dors and Dennis Hamilton, and went to their house a lot. He liked the fucking there. When Peter started spending all his time fucking and gambling, he more or less gave me the Condor Club.

'I gave Tommy Steele a job – we had cabaret at the Condor. I paid him £10 or £20 a week. I can't remember exactly, but I gave Matt Monro the same deal. Later, the Rolling Stones worked for me for a little while. The Beatles wanted six hundred a week. I said they would never make it – I said that nobody was worth that much in the world. The club was a huge success. And my property business was booming. I used to buy 20 properties at a time – I had nearly as many properties as Peter. Nearly.'

Mandy almost lost her looks, if not her life, playing hostess at the clubs. The gaming profits from El Condor tempted Rachman to open La Discotheque on Wardour Street, which billed itself as the first London disco in that it played only recorded music.

The front-door bouncer was Norbert Rondel, a colourful gangland operative who would knock people down just for being there. Rachman's main Polish protégé rent collector, he just had to turn up, smoke a cigar and tenants would pay an extra week simply to make him go away. 'Ronnie' Rondel was a fitness fanatic, incredibly strong and mostly uncontrollable. He found it difficult working with Christine Keeler's onetime lover Serge Paplinski, who was friendly with Stephen Ward, whom Ronnie quite liked. Rondel was born in Berlin in 1927, the roustabout son of a Jewish businessman who, when his mother died in 1934, left him behind in Germany while the rest of the family emigrated to Palestine.

Ronnie arrived in Britain as a ten-year-old through the Kindertransport system and was 'settled' in Manchester, where he learned to speak English and studied to be a rabbi at the Talmudical College. That didn't work out and in 1950 he became a professional wrestler, taking his mother's first married name and appearing as Vladimir Waldberg, 'The Polish Eagle' – or, if Rachman was in the audience, 'The White Eagle'.

Initially, he had a problem with the concept of professional wrestling: that it was a show. He believed you must at least maim, if not kill, your opponents. At La Discotheque, he was slightly more in control and a familiar, if fearsome, figure around Soho. If he wasn't trying to kill you, Rondel was easy enough to like – which is why the Kray Twins left him alone.

By 1960, Ronnie and Reggie Kray had made their way into London's West End and were taking protection money all over town. They'd go into La Discotheque, where there were too many people for too little dancefloor and the cigarette smoke and deodorant denial gave off its exclusive ambience.

Ronnie Kray, who was now sharing his love life and rent boys with Lord Bob Boothby, stagger-swaggered into La Discotheque. Mandy was behind the bar washing, again, and again, a glass for Rachman, who feared germs (which is why he disliked girls breathing in his face). She was still at work, aiming for hygienic perfection, when Ronnie asked for a drink.

'I'm not a barmaid.'

'Give me a drink, anyway.'

'No.'

'Look, get me a drink!'

'Get out of it, go away – don't bother me!'

Ronnie, who never swore when women were present, reached across the bar and grabbed Mandy by her silk blouse. Her hand, the one without the glass, came round and smacked him in the face, which turned purple with rage, not pain.

Rachman was swiftly at the bar and, at a couple of thousand pounds more than the price of a white Jaguar, Ronnie was persuaded that it had all been a bit of fun, which had turned into a little misunderstanding. Rachman was 'looking after' the Twins in return for protection of his general business interests. Ronnie Kray, who was drinking very heavily at that time, calmed down after he was given a couple of heavy-handed shots of booze. The danger wasn't just what was in his bloodstream: the haphazard contents of his mind could fatally switch his moods.

It was delight which made The Twins euphoric when they acquired Esmeralda's Club in Wilton Street from Rachman, who had bought it in a quiet deal. The Gaming Act came into force on 29 July 1960, changing all games of chance and London too. Gangsters like Billy Hill and his rival Jack Spot had generated much of their income from 'spielers', illegal gambling clubs. Parliament believed legalising gambling would drive away the criminal element when it would clearly do the opposite. With the new Gaming Act in force, gambling in clubs was now legal, and the Krays began to win at Esmeralda's. With its location and membership, people such as Bill Astor, Lord Derby, Teddy Sugden and Jon Pertwee, it would be like having their own bank, just down the road from Harrods and around the corner from Buckingham Palace. Some large cash arrangements were made and Esmeralda's became a success, one of the early Parliament-approved gangland establishments.

'I'd been away for a little time in Albany,' recalled Bobby McKew, 'and I went round to Esmeralda's to see what it was all about. Ronnie Kray, who I knew well from Tangier, was full of it, wanting to give me money from the till. "Give him what's in there," he told the barman. Ron had no idea how much cash was there, ten quid or ten thousand quid; he did give me what was there. For the Twins, the money was rolling in.'

Much as it was over at the Black Sheep Club along Piccadilly, on White Horse Street, run by Hod Dibben. Part-partner Mark Sykes knew most of the members, including Stephen Ward: 'I thought he was a very nice chap. He was always polite and always had lovely ladies with him. There wasn't much not to like about Stephen – he pursued his interests without any shame.'

As, of course, did Dr Ward's close friend Hod Dibben, who had three custom-made leather suits: two in black, one in a faded red. He said the leather intensified the pleasure when he was caned or, preferably, birched. It was so pleasant he didn't mind too much the chafing of the suits between his legs: 'not so bad, if you use lots of talc – Johnson's baby powder is best'.

The pink-bottomed Dibben was the charming raconteur of White Horse Street. He spoke highly of the teenager he married at Caxton Hall on 29 January 1960: 'She ties me to a chair in my leather suit, whips me and then makes me watch her screwing someone else.'

Exquisite excitement, he announced, adding: 'I'm showering her with gifts – nothing is too good for this wonderful girl.'

The only thing his bride (we'll call her Mariella, for brevity) never got up close and intimate with was the truth about herself. Stella Capes, aka Mariella Capes, aka Maria Novotny, aka Henrietta Chapman is up there as a wonder of the world. She had a name for all seasons, a kink for all takers, an explanation for everything.

'The only thing that was consistent about Mariella,' said Bobby McKew, who knew her well, 'was that she wore her hat at all times – she never took it off. Once I was having a drink with this rather upper-class chap, who told me he was meeting his new girlfriend, Henrietta Chapman. Would I like to meet her? I thought nothing of it and went with him and there was Mariella.

'I said: "Hello, Mariella."

'She smiles sweetly: "Oh, I'm so sorry. I'm Henrietta. You're he third person this week to make that mistake – we must look very alike."

'She was superb. She was sitting there smiling and wearing the hat she'd been wearing the night before when I saw her stark naked at an orgy. She was a one. She was certainly special – she was meant to be the President of somewhere's daughter but it was all bollocks, she was from Sheffield. But she turned everybody on, everybody upside down.'

Billy Hill's enforcer 'Italian' Albert Dimes, the model for the title character in Stanley Baker's 1960 film *Criminal*, also enjoyed Mariella, but with some caution according to Bobby McKew: 'Albert Dimes had her, but he was wary – he'd been told she put a needle through the window cleaner's bollocks when he tried to fuck her.'

The window cleaner, an associate of the British Security Services, admitted he thought it was worth the risk.

The man who would spend much time with Mariella, and have a daughter with her, was Agent Zigzag, Eddie Chapman, whose friend Bobby McKew often saw them together: 'Usually, they were in bed. Eddie saw a lot of her; Eddie liked to fuck her. Eddie would ask me to pick him up and they'd still be in bed having breakfast. Hod had served them – he'd be in bed with them or in his "viewing" chair, reading the paper. She'd have her hat on in bed. And then she has the cheek to whimper at me: "I'm Henrietta."'

The marriage (busy abortionist Teddy Sugden was the best

man) appeared a fair accommodation for all parties: everyone seemed to get what they wanted, Mariella possibly more than the others. Hod Dibben was nearly 40 years older than she when they married at Caxton Hall in London on 29 January 1960. Both presented varying stories of her background. She was a stripper to help her poor old mum; a dancer, trying to make it in showbusiness; a waitress, trying to establish herself in the catering trade; a relative of the President of (take your choice) Czechoslovakia, Hungary, Manchuria and somewhere no one can remember how to spell. Billy Hill bedded her and in return gave her an E-type Jaguar. Of all of the accounts of her attractions, Mark Sykes' is the most succinct: 'They all said she was terrific in bed.'

After the wedding-day champagne reception at the Black Sheep, Mariella met Stephen Ward again. 'Stephen was fascinated by Mariella,' said Nancy Gillespie, before adding: 'She was every fantasy except one – he could never make her a lady. Mariella had already marked out her life and no one was going to change that.' Gillespie, the onetime *Sunday Express* gossip columnist, lover of Mayfair, Hollywood stars and aristocrats (she married Christine Keeler's lover, Michael Lambton), told me: 'Stephen did try to fix up Mariella with Huntington Hartford (he thought that being an American, "Hunt" wouldn't mind the rougher edges). Hod was in on the idea with him.'

Stephen Ward knew all about the man he thought would give Mariella status and cash, if not the title he craved for all his female friends. As it was, George Huntington Hartford, one of the world's richest men and a fan of Hod Dibben's sex parties, found 18-year-old Mariella a little on the old side. Huntington Hartford was heir to the Great Atlantic and Pacific Tea Company, the American A&P, the largest supermarket chain in the world.

A pleasure seeker, he indulged his tastes in the Bahamas, where he created Paradise Island. It was all aesthetics, buildings painted strawberry ice-cream shades and many, many millions of dollars spent. In Huntington Hartford's home, some of the bedrooms were equipped with two-way mirrors. He created the island's Ocean Club, his own Xanadu, from monastic stones that William Randolph Hearst had been unable to use at his epic monument of himself, at San Simeon on the California coast, but lovingly stored in a Florida warehouse. He knew Barry Stonehill (whose family based themselves in Nassau), Salvador Dalí, the Duke and Duchess of Windsor and America's Vice-President Richard Nixon. He would spend time with heiresses Doris Duke and Barbara Hutton and movie stars – Marilyn Monroe ('too pushy, like a high-class hooker') and Lana Turner, despite saying the actress was 'past her prime' when he met her. The first of his four wives was Marjorie Steele, an aspiring actress. When they married in 1949, she was a teenager (Huntington Hartford liked prime).

Throughout the 1950s, employees would approach young women on the street on his behalf. In London, Stephen Ward, sketchpad in hand, did that for him. He also sketched a drawing of a girl being pleasured 'round the world' by a machine for Huntington Hartford, who gave it to a friend of Kim Waterfield.

The billionaire American liked girls in the flesh. As did the producer Harry Alan Towers, who was invited to a London party thrown by Huntington Hartford. There, with Stephen Ward and Hod Dibben, was Mariella. She was instantly invited for tea at Suite Twelve in Weymouth House. He personally came down and escorted her in the elevator; he promised to make Mariella a star. She didn't believe it for a moment but went around the next day, met Harry and his mother and went to bed with an American investor, who appeared to believe that was what she was there for (she never had tea). Instead, the wily Harry produced his battered typewriter and punched out a one-page contract, no typos. He bought her a Pan Am economy ticket for New York.

When I asked him about this, he said he had developed a relationship with Mariella in which they would enjoy sex together but, as he would be busy with film contacts in New York, she could enjoy shopping at Bloomingdale's (it being only ten days to

Christmas Day, 1960). Then he smiled: 'Hod did say she wanted to make a little money in New York, for expenses and such like, and I had no objections to that – it's what makes the world go round.'

Towers confirmed Mariella's story that she had sex for money while they were both staying at the Meurice Hotel, near Times Square, though he dismissed the suggestion that he had provided or encouraged clients for her. He said they had a nasty row when he moved to a rented apartment on West 56th Street and that Mariella said he would be deported as she had contacts in the US Government. A few days later, he was arrested by New York vice squad detectives, charged with living off the immoral earnings of Mariella. She had given him, on two occasions, $300 towards their living expenses.

'That looked terrible but it was simply that: when she had a little money, she pitched in – she was not a mean girl with anything.

'I know it sounds corny but I was typing up my TV shows when she was arrested by a policeman who was posing as a client. She was naked. I tried to stay out of the way, but they arrested me too.'

What Towers had missed was that Mariella was not alone in New York. Hod Dibben had followed her and, unbeknown to anyone, had taken an apartment in the Essex House, a familiar place to British visitors to New York. On Stephen Ward's suggestion, they had visited Douglas Fairbanks Junior at home 'for a merry time, just the three of us'. They also had four places taken in different names to run a prostitution service for 'party people' in New York: group sex parties, 'evening for swingers' and sadomasochist specialities, all of which interested British actor Peter Lawford, the brother-in-law of Senator John F. Kennedy.

Kennedy had been elected President of the United States only a couple of weeks before Mariella landed in New York. Lawford pimped for Kennedy, who said he got stressed if he didn't have sex regularly: he was a master of the 'quickie'. So much so that, if he did know a girl's name, then he didn't a few moments later.

Mariella said she had sex with Kennedy, before and after his inauguration as President of the Free World; that they played 'doctors and nurses' sex games with other prostitutes brought in by Peter Lawford; and she told Dibben that Kennedy had 'a nice haircut but a little cock'. Whatever, it kept busy.

At first, Towers could not raise his bail and was held in The Tombs, the Manhattan House of Detentions. With him were screaming and kicking prisoners, mostly drug addicts, and he said it was 'hell on earth'. With wired money from associates, he made his $10,000 bail and District Attorney Alfred Donati tried to get it raised to $25,000, pleading he would abscond – 'A large number of influential and wealthy persons involved in this case would like to see the defendant out of the country.'

Towers told me this was nonsense and it is true that the District Attorney, the prosecutor, is a political office and grandstanding in a high-profile case gets attention. Anyway, the judge didn't see Towers as a flight risk. He immediately jumped bail, drove into Canada, took a flight to Dublin, another to Copenhagen and then on to Moscow.

For J. Edgar Hoover, this was the final proof: Harry Alan Towers was a KGB agent, Mariella a Red Mata Hari and, along with Stephen Ward, they had all met Ivanov, who was the man from the GRU.

The problem for Hoover and his puritan policemen of the FBI was that this particular Mata Hari had supposedly screwed their President. And for another American official watching with a more penetrative eye – focused obsessively on any connection to the Red Menace – the psychotic patriot of the CIA, Frank Wisner. A master of covert action, Wisner was something of a rival to Allen Dulles, head of the CIA. He was also a superstar of propaganda, maybe one of the best ever.

In 1959, Wisner was appointed bureau chief of the CIA office in London; there he again met Kim Philby, whom he hadn't trusted in Washington – indeed, Wisner didn't even trust himself. He was prone to deep depressions but also, savant-like, to the details of espionage puzzles, information and events that didn't fit either a pattern or themselves. His total belief was in the right of America to do what was right – how could it do anything else? No questions asked.

Ivanov had only been a note on his desk when the 'Mariella in New York' information began to be fed via the FBI liaison at the Embassy in Grosvenor Square. Hoover had linked it to all manner of sexual and political twists and turns and switchbacks. There was a woman called Suzy Diamond (also known as 'Suzy Chang') who, like the Duchess of Windsor, was renowned for a magical sexual gimmick. She had worked with a Hungarian madam and the President was meant to have had her too. That Communist country link sent Hoover round to see the new Attorney General: the President's brother, Robert Kennedy. Now, Frank Wisner was sifting through the memos, including one stating, 'The President himself has expressed concern'. Another FBI memo noted the likelihood of 'an espionage-prostitution ring operating in England with American ramifications'.

For Wisner, the President and a hooker was no big revelation, whereas the President doing something about the Communists would be a story to tell. He and a Washington colleague dealt with Mariella first. She was contacted by a female CIA agent in New York and given a walk-on ticket for RMS *Queen Mary*, which was sailing for Southampton on 31 May (the pass was for friends and relatives to say goodbye to passengers before sailing). Mariella stayed on board and, by wonderful chance, a first-class cabin was available.

At the Captain's table, she told her various versions of events without uttering one word of truth. Wisner was delighted with reports from the CIA agent Jennifer S., who sailed with Mariella, but the FBI were not in on this and alerted the British authorities that Mariella had gone. Immigration were waiting at Southampton, but so too was Hod Dibben. Wisner had squared Mariella's arrival into Britain with the Security Services.

What the master of propaganda hadn't figured on was the wiles of Mariella and her husband, and their knowledge that greed could be rewarded in return for headlines. They sold their tale of high-level depravity and deviance at the height of American power to the *News of the World*. The crime reporter Peter Earle, a magnificent circus-master of such material, left liver spots all over the copy. On publication, it was about all that was left. The Security Services required the story to be 'edited' in such a way that it was a teenager's tame adventures in America: she didn't meet anyone or do anything interesting. Wisner kept the original copy in his desk file (the carbons were destroyed), detailing Mariella's revelations of Presidential naughtiness. It was only one of several carefully magenta-ink-notated folders. Wisner believed in direct Intelligence from his agents in the field, the analysis by politicians was usually misdirected. He argued with Allen Dulles about it and wrote disdainfully of 'the new Spirit of Moscow or whatever may be the sales slogan of the moment'.

Wisner was not a fan of Communists or of Stephen Ward, who he believed was being played as a dupe by Ivanov. Ambassador 'Jock' Whitney had met Ward at Cliveden and told Wisner he was 'a nice enough guy'. In turn, Wisner is said to have told him: 'It's the nice guys that get us all into trouble.'

Cynical and unstable, Wisner took everything personally but he was immensely powerful in and without the CIA, with its extraordinary budget and deep-penetration agents. He was also good at his job of spreading the American message: you don't stand on Superman's cape.

Frank Wisner's mission was to save the world from Communism. With 'Operation Mockingbird', he began to influence the American and international Press. One 'thinking' magazine in London, *Encounter*, was secretly funded by the CIA. It broadcast the views of, among others, Anthony Crosland, who had entered Parliament for the second time as MP for Grimsby in 1959. Along with Labour Party stalwarts Roy Jenkins and Denis

Healey, he was a friend and protégé of their leader, Hugh Gaitskell. They were seen as 'modernisers' and it was their lean to the right of the Labour Party that encouraged the CIA to entertain their thoughts. Jenkins, unsurprisingly, thought the magazine was funded by a kindly Cincinnati gin distiller; Crosland used it to promote his social democratic programme.

The CIA knew all about the MP, who, as Frank Wisner would point out, in theory they were paying. He had married Hilary Sarson in 1952, a marriage that had dissolved itself emotionally within a year and officially five years later. Crosland had girlfriends and one long-term romantic engagement with Shirley Anne Field (whom he met at a dinner party shortly after she'd been to Stephen Ward's cottage at Cliveden and had been invited to stay the night at the big house with Bill Astor). Field described her relationship with the politician: 'I was drawn to him not only because he was witty and confident but because he was committed politically. He told me all the policies he wished to instigate and, on some occasions, I went with him to his constituency in Grimsby. He was passionate about everything, not just his political beliefs. It's no wonder some politicians are in the headlines for private reasons as well as political ones.'

Frank Wisner didn't like coincidences, no matter how innocent. In the 1950s, he worked closely with Kim Philby and liked him, thought of him as a friend. He was aghast when he found evidence that made him suspect Philby was a traitor, a Soviet spy. Convinced but not convinced, he put his doubts to his boss, James Jesus Angleton, who after investigations expelled Philby from America. Philby went back to work for the SIS in London with some of those he'd gone to school with. Wisner never trusted Britain again.

With Kennedy in the White House, Wisner sat in his offices in London surrounded, it seemed, by spies, sex parties and secrets, and once again East–West tensions growing – the Cold War was driving him mad. And he didn't like having J. Edgar at his shoulder. The FBI in London had been ordered by Hoover to discover any 'dirty detail of possible significance' on the social scene in Britain, which, in reality, meant London.

Even when they grew out the crew cuts, FBI agents could never look like anything but FBI agents. It was the manner and the giveaway too heavy-soled shoes, which would never have walked out of Northampton. The Soviet spooks were walking around looking like Savile Row suits on the wrong hangers and the show went on: drops at the Brompton Oratory, drinks at the Bunch of Grapes in Knightsbridge afterwards. Ivanov was now buddy-buddy with Stephen Ward and the Americans were more aware than their British counterparts. The US game had ratcheted up. When the youngest man to be elected President of the United States was inaugurated in 1961, the contrast with his predecessor was vast. President John F. Kennedy, 43, said on his inauguration: 'Let the word go forth that the torch has been passed to a new generation of Americans.'

The Space Age President, JFK intended to boldly go where Eisenhower had been careful. Meanwhile, the nuclear cloud kept on growing. In 1956, Eisenhower said he'd been advised that a Russian nuclear attack on America would eradicate 65 per cent of the population: 'It will literally be a business of digging ourselves out of the ashes, starting again.' Then, in 1959, he declared: 'If nuclear war begins, you might as well go out and shoot everyone you see and then shoot yourself.'

Throughout all these edge-of-holocaust moments, behind the scenes, the American Joint Chiefs of Staff were set to blast away. Eisenhower resisted, there were no more skirmishes to be had; conflict was now an all-or-nothing option. And push-button technology is pugnacious. In Moscow, they did not regard as 'an idle gesture' the newly instigated US programme of building nuclear fall-out shelters in major cities. Inside the Kremlin, there was distrust and dismay: what if the Americans launched a pre-emptive nuclear attack? Khrushchev had much experience of Eisenhower but not the same comfort with Kennedy in the Oval Office.

JFK presented a more defiant posture when he took over as leader of the Western world. And the generals were whispering the question: 'What's the point of all this military if we can't use it?'

As the summer of 1961 approached, there was a telephone conversation recorded at the White House between the young President and Paul Fay, whom he knew well and who was serving as America's Secretary of State for the Navy.

'Have you got round to building that bomb shelter, yet?' JFK asked.

'No, I built a swimming pool instead.'

There was a pause on the telephone line.

'You made a mistake.'

CHAPTER ELEVEN

DOCTOR DOOM

'THE STRONG DO WHAT THEY CAN AND
THE WEAK SUFFER WHAT THEY MUST.'

Thucydides, 420 BC

On the first Christmas of the 1960s, Stephen Ward, Christine Keeler and Eugene Ivanov went to celebrate at the London townhouse of Lord and Lady Edham, heir to the Earl of Dudley and Maureen Swanson. From then on, for Ward and Ivanov, the holiday season was a carnival of parties and receptions. They popped into Paul Getty's at Sutton Place in Guildford, visited Cliveden and had a dinner and a tea with Bill Astor, visited Madame Furstova (the Soviet Minister of Culture, whom Ward sketched) and went on a vodka binge with Madame Tessiers, who would have been something within the Soviet Union if not for the Bolshevik Revolution. The doctor and the spy were running around like Charles Ryder and Sebastian Flyte in Waugh's *Brideshead Revisited* – it's just that the bear was Russian. And kept on the party circuit into 1961. Ward took the Russian as his 'plus-1' in spring that year to the wedding of his GP, Dr Frank Hughes. The bride, Caroline Hughes, recalled in November 2013: 'Stephen was my husband's National Health patient and wonderful friends with him. Frank turned out to treat Christine

Keeler for a cold. He'd always help Stephen. When we married he brought Ivanov along as his guest and they were terrific fun. Ivanov was very jolly.' Indeed, they were an entertaining double-act everywhere they went.

Ward was treated with great courtesy and warmth at receptions at the Russian Embassy, something that only increased his value to the other guests, the opinion makers and lords and ladies and the British Government, whom he had either sketched or played bridge with (and probably both). He also met diplomats from France and Germany, on whom he tried out his language skills. Meanwhile, he was not disguising his friendship with Ivanov nor his delight in it. If they talked politics, the end-of-the-world scenario, the top of the bill subject, the one thing Ivanov openly wondered about, was if and when nuclear weapons might be situated in West Germany.

Frank Wisner got more notes; J. Edgar Hoover received cables. The boys at MI5's D-Branch received something of a bollocking: they could not supply adequate answers to what Ivanov was up to, nor indeed the mysterious Dr Ward. Although the CIA knew what toothpaste Ivanov used, the British Security Services played a more conventional spying game. America was far advanced in satellites and signals, an irony in their battle with Communism. The Soviets relied on deep penetration, 'sleeper' agents and 'casuals' like Jack Jones, who was recruited when he was assistant general secretary of the Transport and General Workers' Union and a member of the National Executive Committee of the Labour Party. For cash, he passed on confidential information. He was only one of several believed by the CIA to be doing so.

Yet, the American agents were loath to share knowledge with the British Secret Services. Sir Dick White – long and lean, he moved like a Persian greyhound; an elegant, cadaverous character – had switched from running MI5 in 1956 to become chief of the Secret Intelligence Service, MI6. He could see every situation from every other party's self-interest. It seemed, at times, he could see around corners.

And get round them. He had a connection with the Americans, the new US Ambassador to the Court of St James's, a master of the punctilious world of international diplomacy, David K.E. Bruce, late of 'Wild Bill' Donovan's OSS. Bruce had served as the OSS director in London; he knew his way around a cocktail lounge and a Soviet set-up. He was Ambassador in Paris in the post-war years, and then Bonn before London. Earlier, in Washington, he had worked with Frank Wisner, and every Sunday evening at 3327 P Street in Georgetown had a potluck dinner at his friend's home. There was always a crowd of agents and it was said they formed American foreign policy over brandy. Well, the policy involving Russians and the Atom Bomb. These men liked to drink and they enjoyed women; twice-married Bruce had four children and enjoyed evenings at Les Ambassadeurs and at the Stork Room with visiting American celebrities.

Bruce was a Washington career insider but even he, in a report kept secret for 50 years by the US Government, had in the late 1950s questioned the extent of the CIA psychological warfare programme throughout the world, a programme involving mind-bending drugs. And he had seen some bizarre things as the right-hand man to 'Wild Bill'. He fondly recalled his time with Donovan: 'His imagination was unlimited. Ideas were his plaything, excitement made him snort like a racehorse. Woe to the officer who turned down a project, because, on its face, it seemed ridiculous, or at least, unusual. For painful weeks under his command, I tested the possibility of using bats taken in concentrations in Western caves to destroy Tokyo, dropping them into the sky with incendiary bombs strapped to their backs.'

The bat bombs didn't work out. After that, it is understandable that he told Sir Dick White that Dr Ward's particular peccadilloes were none too troubling to him. Ward was a man caught up in a world that had been hijacked – he had no idea where he was being taken. Ivanov was a mystery, a big-spending Russian, clearly a GRU agent but not a proven one, who appeared to stay within the diplomatic 25-mile radius of his Embassy. He drove his Austin Westminster on short jaunts, mostly to Cliveden and out to Barnes in west London. He was a puzzle at a puzzling time; neither David Bruce nor Dick White wanted any more upsets in their security worlds: they would play Ivanov and Dr Stephen Ward. Bruce cleverly saw Ward as above the humdrum: for such a long time Ward had felt protected, so intoxicated was he with his high place in the world. Others might have taken a moment to find some air; he did not.

Macmillan enjoyed taking time to ponder on interests rather than the end of the world. Because of his uneven marital status, he found solace in his London clubs, and he inhabited them constantly, which bred a distinct familiarity. He would be seen at the Athenaeum, Buck's, Guards, the Beefsteak, the Turf, the Carlton and Pratt's. Walking into Pratt's one evening, a member asked whether there was anyone in that night. He was told: 'Nobody at all, sir, only the Prime Minister.'

Here was a man who took pause and considered consequences before action. Or, possibly, if he took no action, the bother would take itself away.

Macmillan watched with some wry detachment the new President Kennedy's problems with Cuba. Where Eisenhower had waved a finger over Suez, Macmillan could raise an eyebrow over the 'spot of bother' in the Caribbean. It was, indeed, difficult to be fully sympathetic with the Americans.

On 10 March 1952, Fulgenico Batista y Zaldívar, the typist-clerk Army sergeant-turned-administration-usurper, brutally engaged his own enterprise, cancelled the upcoming elections and took over, with Army support, police and military commands and the radio and TV stations. He installed himself as provisional President of Cuba. Within 14 days, the USA acknowledged the legitimacy of Batista's leadership and he appointed a Minister of Gambling, with an annual stipend of US$25,000. Meyer Lansky, the most effective of all the American Mafia leaders, quietly accepted the non-Cabinet post. The US Administration was happy: they had a friend in power even if he was so open to corruption he wore his chicanery like medals. As were his troops, who were selling guns and ammunition to the young guerrilla leader Fidel Castro. America regarded Castro as a nuisance, a bedtime story for anarchists. Fulgenico Batista y Zaldívar was in control, with the assistance of the Mafia... until Castro took over in 1959.

Khrushchev had stated that a nuclear confrontation between East and West was not an option but America would lose the world through defeats in remote regions. Cuba was only 110 miles from the US mainland but that was remote enough for Kennedy. By 17 April 1961, a CIA-trained and funded invasion group made an abortive attempt to overthrow Castro but the Bay of Pigs, *Bahia De Cochinos*, was all over within three days. The public humiliation was severe, most so for the CIA. It followed the shooting down of CIA spy pilot Gary Powers' U-2 surveillance plane over Moscow almost a year earlier. Powers, the spy-in-the-sky, had one mission: to try to establish the nuclear missile capability of the Soviet Union, photographing installations from the air. Moscow was doing the same thing. All those involved wanted to balance the scales – who-had-what-and-could-do-what-to-whom? Khrushchev's chief concern was whether America planned to place nuclear warheads in Berlin's Western sector and, if so, when? The balance of power was all-important. Terrified about who could make the biggest bang, they were right to be alarmed.

Information, in itself, was not only a weapon; it was a dangerous one, dependent on interpretation and the intelligence of the mind analysing the Intelligence. Colonel Oleg Penkovsky had much of both. He was the man who identified, without doubt, Eugene Ivanov's work status in life: he was indeed who the other spies thought he was, a GRU agent. It was proof indeed for Ambassador Bruce, Frank Wisner and Dick White that they were correct in seeing his purpose in back-door diplomacy. The spies were wary of an 'illegal' operation, especially White, who had reluctantly moved over to MI6 in 1956 after the murder of Buster Crabb in Portsmouth Harbour by a Soviet 'barracuda', an assassin in a wet suit.

White had enjoyed Churchill but, when Anthony Eden replaced him as Prime Minister in April 1955, he kept his own counsel. Exactly a year later, the Soviet cruiser *Ordzhonikidze*, which had sophisticated submarine-detecting sensors, sailed Khrushchev and Prime Minister Bulganin into England for meetings with Eden and Cabinet ministers. The spies wanted to take a look at the bottom of the *Ordzhonikidze*, but Eden roared disapproval. He went red in the face saying no to a clandestine dip in the sea. So, when Lionel 'Buster' Crabb, 47, was secretly brought in to take a look underwater and was caught and killed, it was a political mess.

Crabb was placing a listening 'post' below the *Ordzhonikidze* when a Soviet sailor, patrolling underwater, spotted him, thought he was planting a mine and swam in, cutting Crabb's air supply and then his throat. When Crabb's headless and handless body was found on 9 June 1957 the propaganda was released that he had been caught in the cruiser's propellers – he had inadvertently drifted into them while testing secret diving equipment three miles from where the Soviet cruiser was anchored. There was no detail about 'Mr Smith', who had booked in with him to a Portsmouth hotel, paid the bills and took Crabb's small overnight case with him. Eden told the Commons that it would 'not be in the public interest' to disclose the circumstances of Crabb's death and took a swipe at the spooks: 'What was done was done without the authority or knowledge of Her Majesty's ministers.'

The vanishing of Buster Crabb remained a headline, with new theories every other week about his demise, when Dick White faced the enigma of Ivanov. They decided to play their own game.

Oleg Penkovsky had problems with the Soviet hierarchy as his father had fought for the White Russians during the civil war; he also hated Khrushchev. A highly placed official with the Soviet Military Intelligence, he was the optimum spy and prize when, in 1960, he began flirting with Western Intelligence agencies and initially made contact through the Canadians in Moscow. Penkovsky was the man who not only had the intelligence but also *understood* it. Secrets are useless unless you know what they mean and Penkovsky had been tutored by the correct professors. As a colonel in the GRU, he had access to defence data but had been trained by Ivan Serov and Sergei Varentsov, who was in charge of the nuclear missile programme, to know what was the most valuable information. Still, he had to convince the West he was not a plant. He did this by supplying, through the British Embassy in Paris, documents detailing his own status and also revealing Dick White's SIS secrets, which they could verify from other sources; this stamped his card.

Colonel Oleg Vladimirovich Penkovsky operated as a GRU officer under the guise of a protocol officer for the Soviet State Committee for Science and Technology. In 1961, he arrived in London as part of a Soviet trade delegation. He had persuaded MI6 agent Greville Wynne to secure him a meeting in London with both SIS and CIA agents (one of whom was Frank Wisner). It was during talks at the Mount Royal Hotel that SIS officers were told of Ivanov's role in London, though not his mission. He also identified the GRU operational head in the UK, Nicolai Karpekov. From then on, Penkovsky, who was given the file name 'Ironbark', was in contact through Wynne, who had built up a cover in Europe as a businessman; he became Penkovsky's chief courier. The Russian provided superb information on Soviet war plans, missile programmes and espionage tactics, and more than 10,000 pages of secret documents. He gave insights into Khrushchev's thinking and this was the real prize.

With the world on edge, anything that would stop the West falling over it was Intelligence gold; Western Intelligence officers were fascinated by tales of Soviet infighting, and how Khrushchev bought loyalty by promoting his military officers. Others, especially Beria's coterie, were simply not seen again. What was terrifying was his details of the division in the Soviet ranks about going to war over Berlin. One side was urging immediate confrontation, the other, possibly more aware of Russia's slack in military power, preferred a waiting game. The real frightener from Penkovsky: it was almost a 50–50 split. Yet, professionally, the British and American spies were beyond themselves with joy, only surpassed when their gold mine announced he would be in London for three weeks as part of a Moscow delegation. A safe house was prepared at Coleherne Court on the Old Brompton Road in Kensington. In July 1961, 'Ironbark' sang beautifully. Sir Dick White attended sessions, as did Frank Wisner. They made a fuss.

Penkovsky wanted to meet the Queen and pledge his loyalty but the spies hoped it was the vodka talking. Instead, they took photographs of him in the uniform of an American and a British colonel. He also asked for cognac – and sex. It was a tense, stressful time for Penkovsky; Mariella Novotny is believed to have helped relieve all that. Part of Mariella's deal with Frank Wisner on her return from New York was that she would be an informant, officially through Scotland Yard's Special Branch, in an arrangement he negotiated with the UK Security Services 'in our mutual interests'. Mariella was also 'on call' to service prized clients of the Security Services. She told her lover, war hero Eddie Chapman, that she had looked after a Russian at the time when Penkovsky was also being otherwise debriefed. While she lay back and thought of who knows what, Penkovsky's Intelligence only made the Western allies desperate for more of the same. The Colonel told them in 1961 – and was disbelieved or his information not acted on – that Khrushchev planned to place nuclear missiles in Cuba, America's backyard. He also alerted them to the planned Berlin Wall, but they soon saw that for themselves.

What excited them was Penkovsky's Intelligence that Khrushchev had made a direct and personal approach to the Russian Ambassador in London with one specific enquiry: how would Macmillan, the British Government, react to a confrontation over Berlin?

The resolution over the control and future of Berlin was to have been negotiated in May 1960, at a Paris summit between Russia, Britain, France and America but that negotiation was shot down, along with Gary Powers' U-2 spy plane on 1 May. It was a cruel moment for Macmillan. President Charles de Gaulle in France, whom Macmillan was wooing in regard to a British entry into the Common Market, didn't have time for any of his Berlin allies: he was soured by the Bay of Pigs and the Algerian Civil War in which he rightly believed the CIA had played a role. In turn, the Americans witnessed the KGB and GRU agents, as well as East German security, Intelligence and military experts acting as 'commercial advisers' in Cuba.

The occupational status of Berlin was the blue touchpaper of the Cold War. With nuclear fireworks possible, Khrushchev's question provoked another, this time from the spooks: was this an opportunity for backdoor diplomacy? Did Khrushchev want to talk? Was he bluffing? Dismayed by the Americans, was the Russian leader seeking friends? And did Penkovsky's revelations bring them any leverage in negotiations?

Already they had been round to have a word with Dr Stephen Ward. Now they would have to speak to him again about his chum, Mr Ivanov.

BOOK THREE
DEATH BY SNOBBERY

'FLEET STREET CAN SCENT THE POSSIBILITIES OF
SEX LIKE A TILE-TRIPPING TOMCAT; AND WHILE SEX –
BY WHICH WE MEAN, OF COURSE, EXTRAMARITAL OR
OTHERWISE NON-COMFORMIST SEX – IS NOT IN
ITSELF ENOUGH TO BURN A MINISTER AT THE STAKE,
IT MAKES EXCELLENT KINDLING.'

Julian Barnes, *Letters from London*, 1995

CHAPTER TWELVE

DOCTOR IN THE SWIM

'THERE MIGHT BE ONE FINGER ON THE
TRIGGER, BUT THERE WILL BE FIFTEEN FINGERS
ON THE SAFETY CATCH.'

Harold Macmillan, 1961

Stephen Ward's wonderful world began to unravel the way Hemingway said people go broke: gradually, then suddenly.

One moment, he was grinning contentedly and sitting by the swimming pool at Cliveden with Christine Keeler and John Profumo was taking their photograph (on the front cover of this book), the next all had slowly begun to change. The months that followed were fraught with fear and suspicion. He and the others in his circle became the subject of surveillance and inquiry by agents of Britain, America, France and the Soviet Union.

These were heavy-duty people. None believed hearts and minds were to be won: their business was treachery. Hearts and minds were for sale.

If you were unaware of what was afoot, you were at fault for being so. There is not much clarity in the clandestine world, which is why there's even more confusion with the innocent abroad, and the unreliability of the information squeezes the nerve ends. If no one is telling the truth, what *is* the truth? Something close to it can only be arrived at through studying all the circumstances with an open mind.

Especially when the espionage and political paranoia is racing in parallel with itself, and with events. Which is how it was that summer of 1961. Grand Soviet hero Yuri Alekseyevich Gagarin was the first human to successfully journey into outer space aboard his Vostok spacecraft on 12 April 1961. Following that triumph, he was on an international goodwill tour and he was in Britain that July, when Christine Keeler made a splash and they completed the architectural drawings for a wall across Berlin. If the war was cold, the swimming pool at Cliveden was warm, especially following one of the hottest days of the year, Saturday, 8 July. Which is why Keeler was naked when John Profumo first saw her at Cliveden.

President John F. Kennedy first saw Cliveden as a young man and, with his father Joseph Kennedy, as the US Ambassador, visited the grand house and Nancy Astor. JFK was familiar with the aristocratic families and the debutante scene. His visit to Britain on Sunday, 4 June 1961 was both business and pleasure. Macmillan joined him in an open-car drive through the streets of London before they had four hours of talks at Admiralty House. Kennedy briefed the British Prime Minister on his previous two days of talks with Khrushchev in Vienna. JFK said Khrushchev had told him that he would go in to East Germany 'within months' and secure the borders: out with Allied troops, in with the Soviet military. It was not good.

The next day, JFK and Jackie Kennedy attended the christening in Westminster Abbey of her sister Princess Lee Radziwill's son, Anthony. Later, he met informally with Macmillan when the elder politician said America should not shove Khrushchev too hard, round him into a corner where he had to react rather than act. Which would, of course, result in a nuclear world war. With this warning, Kennedy went back on *Air Force One* and his wife dined with her friend John Jacob 'Jakie' Astor, Bill Astor's young brother and another friend of Stephen Ward. Dr Ward had talked with

Kennedy – he'd worked on his aching back. The President had aggravated it in a tree-planting ceremony and the pain was excruciating. On the suggestion of Averell Harriman, who was advising The White House on Europe, Dr Ward made him comfortable for the flight home. Within Ward's circle, the contacts and interchanges were endless; he was indeed the man who knew everybody. Which is why an inspector called.

When 'Inspector Woods' first saw Stephen Ward, it was by prearranged appointment. They lunched on 8 June 1961, on Marylebone High Street, a comfortable walk from Ward's surgery. 'Woods' was Keith Wagstaffe, a counter-Intelligence agent for MI5, whose dark pinstripe suit and black bowler hat didn't conceal his years in the Army. Wagstaffe, who professed to be from the War Office, was out of uniform. Ward was no fool, reckless maybe, but no dupe. He correctly sensed 'Woods' was one of the 'funny people'.

The two men spoke of Eugene Ivanov and Ward explained that he believed his Russian chum was a good guy, a man who loved his country but wanted, if possible, to be friends with everyone. Ivanov might not turn on his own country, but he could mediate on behalf of another. The spy and the doctor got on well, officer class as they were, and Dr Ward invited the Inspector back to Wimpole Mews for tea. Christine Keeler poured. When Wagstaffe left, he gave Dr Ward MI5's 'cover' contact point in Curzon Street. Ward knew it well – a couple of rights and lefts from 'Bloody Mary' at The Dorchester. His world was shrinking fast.

On the record, Wagstaffe didn't rate Ward as much of an asset to MI5; that was the official report to his boss Roger Hollis, who followed Dick White as Director-General of MI5. Off record, Ward could be used several ways operationally: the glamour of the girls he lived with, his friendship with Ivanov. He had certainly played the plucky Brit, 'willing to help, old boy'. Keeler said she and Ward made up amusing scenarios around Wagstaffe's visit.

Neither of them took it in the least seriously. Ward wasn't concerned; why should he be? His life was for fun, not profit.

And it was certainly fun by the Cliveden swimming pool, the stone and the high walls containing the heat around him and Christine Keeler, as she splashed about and he lit yet another cigarette. Early that Saturday morning, he had driven down alone and was expecting Christine and Noel Howard-Jones to join him later, Ivanov the next day. Christine arrived late in the afternoon with her Persian friend, Leo Norell. On the drive down, they'd picked up a girl (she called herself 'Joy') at a bus stop. It was three for dinner at Spring Cottage. Howard-Jones, who Christine was mooning over, did not appear. After dinner (which, as always, Ward cooked), he and Christine went up to the swimming pool by the main house to cool off; it was unusually hot.

Christine didn't have her swimsuit but there was a clean one in the pool house. It was tight around the backside, a little uncomfortable. She complained to Ward, who told her to take it off – she'd be freer in her movement through the water. After leaving her swimsuit at the deep end, she swam around.

All the big house lights were sparkling. Bill Astor and his third wife, Bronwen Pugh (he had married the model and TV presenter in October 1960), were hosting a grand dinner party in a room once part of Louis XV's mistress Madame de Pompadour's hunting lodge. Guests included John and Valerie Profumo, a scattering of Tory MPs, Ayub Khan, the President of Pakistan, Lord and Lady Dalkeith, Lord Mountbatten, Sir Isaac and Lady Wolfson, Mr and Mrs Nubar Gulbenkian and Dr Ward's great friend from the Traveller's Club, Sir Gilbert Laithwaite.

With some good amount of refreshment taken, Profumo and his host went out into the gardens for a stroll over to the fountains, which were set off by the push of a button hidden in the magnolias. It was an escape from their wives, world affairs and Khrushchev's menacing words about Berlin. Hearing voices from the swimming pool, they kept walking past the rose garden.

Stephen Ward was watching Christine splashing about in the nude, content with only the sidelights of the pool. Next, jovial Profumo and then Bill Astor appeared through the guard door of the pool. Seeing them staring at Christine, who was wiping water from her eyes, Ward went into action. Grabbing her swimsuit, he threw it over a hedge as she made a dive for a small towel; it would only cover top or bottom. She got another towel, but by then the drunken men, egged on by Ward, were trying to grab the towel, which was providing minimal modesty. Astor was giggling and chasing Christine round the pool and Profumo joined in. She played the game, letting the towel slip now and again.

Astor turned on the floodlights. Whoops! The pregnant Lady Astor and Valerie Profumo, intrigued by the schoolyard screaming and yelping – that was the men – had arrived to investigate. With them in all their finery were the dinner guests, the pool water lapping up at the tails of the long gowns.

'May I introduce,' said Astor, cutting the discomfort from the moment, 'Stephen, you all know and this is his friend, Christine...'

Trying to cover herself up and dripping wet, pushing back her hair and dropping the towel in the process, Christine finally organised her dignity. She shook hands with Profumo and the other guests. With the wrinkles in the atmosphere smoothed and a glance towards his elegant wife for approval and a nod in return, Astor invited Christine and Dr Ward back to the house for a nightcap.

Profumo's bravado kicked up. He offered to escort his new friend Christine around Cliveden, to show her the grand house. Valerie Hobson raised an eyebrow; she knew only too well that her husband was always ready for a fling. There was talk in the theatrical and film communities, though not in the political arena, of 'Valerie's high sex drive'. Bobby McKew said the Profumos were known for being 'more discreet than most' in their wife-swapping activities.

Profumo's wife had complained of his treating attractive girls as fair game: 'You will stretch any manners, at any time, to do this – not quietly and discreetly, but laughing and showing off and behaving like an adolescent.' Certainly, the display around the Cliveden swimming pool confirmed this. Mrs Profumo got straight to the point when she had told him: 'Surely, there must be some way of concealing your penis.'

Well, not that evening. Profumo was soon running after Christine again. He displayed his knowledge of the paintings, identified those in the Astor family photographs, and had his hand all over her back and roaming across her backside. He asked for a kiss, started stroking her body. She laughingly said she required protection from him – and put on a suit of armour covering a corner of damp in a study. Already the centre of attention, Christine clanked back to the other guests. Bill Astor took the lead; it was all super fun. And there must be more fun with a Sunday picnic lunch by the swimming pool. Everyone was invited.

For Stephen Ward, it was a substantial social coup in his quest for consideration: his guests would be partying with Bill Astor's. This was a great achievement – the glamour, the Russian, the War Minister, Sir Gilbert, the President of Pakistan – what international politics, what gossip! For Profumo, of an upbringing and generation where sex was a hobby, like bridge, it would provide further opportunity to follow the scent of Christine. For him, it was part of his Great Game.

Early in the day, Sunday was truly hot when Noel Howard-Jones arrived. He enjoyed the warm: 'I was at Cliveden the weekend when Christine met Jack Profumo for the first time. It was one of those weekends where Astor invited Stephen's party up to the pool. We all met at the pool – it was good, clean fun. Even a swimming race, which Ivanov won – or, rather, *would* have won if Profumo had played by the rules. It was a race where you weren't supposed to use your legs. Profumo cheated and won the race. Ivanov was very direct and said he had cheated. And Profumo said: "That will teach you to trust a Minister of the

Crown." And that was the weekend when he met Christine. I didn't notice anything special going on – he must have slipped her his telephone number. They took it from there.'

John Profumo most certainly did. When Ward arrived from Spring Cottage with Christine, Ivanov, Howard-Jones and two girlfriends he'd invited for Sunday, Sally Norrie and Pauline Jones, the house party guests were already in the pool, with Bill Astor in charge of 'swimming events'. After the Minister of the Crown won a race by walking on the bottom of the pool, the next event was a 'jousting contest'. The men each got a lady on their shoulders and tried to push the others, splashing into the water. Although Ivanov had first offered, Christine clambered onto Profumo's shoulders; they were clearly rivals for her attention.

Despite the sun, the swimming and the drinks, Christine was still upset that her affection for Noel Howard-Jones was not reciprocated. By design, devilment or out of sheer convenience, she agreed to return to London and the redbrick mews flat with Ivanov (Ward stayed behind to treat Astor's back). Arriving at 17, Wimpole Mews, from the back seat of his Austin Westminster, Ivanov produced a bottle of vodka from the private reserve of the Soviet Embassy and invited himself in for a drink. Lubricated by alcohol, the human factor engaged gear. Between them, the bottle vanished. Ivanov, quite drunk, became angry because Christine put tonic in her drink – it wasn't Russian. She rather liked him aggressive. For the first and only time, they had sex. Ivanov said it happened twice, Christine said once, and later both agreed, it was once. Whatever the coupling count, it was an almighty fuck.

There would be several more in that category involving Christine. Ward gave her telephone number, WELbeck 6933, to John Profumo. The doctor knew it well – it was his number too. On 10 July 1961, the War Minister telephoned Keeler to ask if she would like to go for a drive. She would? Good.

That same day, Ward told Keith Wagstaffe of MI5 the detailed weekend happenings of Christine, Ivanov and John Profumo, the Minister of War. Available official records say Wagstaffe reported it to the Director-General of MI5, Sir Roger Hollis.

The weather was still hot, like John Profumo, that Monday. Christine was 19, he was the Minister of War, aged 46, and she knew absolutely what he wanted but showed some respect for his age, as he did for the circumstances that day. Profumo had been driven to 17, Wimpole Mews, said hello to Ward, and had taken Christine off down Downing Street from the War Office to show her where he worked. They drove around Regent's Park. There was no attempt at discretion – they were in a chauffeur-driven Government car, Union Jack fluttering on the bonnet. Like a cavalry charge, Profumo was going for a new conquest. A gentleman for the afternoon, he wanted to return to Wimpole Mews, preferably while Dr Ward was consulting. Later that week, he returned, driving his distinctive red Mini, and the Profumo Affair began agreeably enough on the sofa of Stephen Ward's front room.

On the late afternoon of 11 July, the Soviet Embassy hosted a fabulous reception for their space hero Yuri Gagarin. Stephen Ward was a VIP guest, courtesy of his friend Ivanov, and John Profumo and his wife Valerie were among the hundreds of others. Given that Gagarin was conqueror of space, it took about an hour to reach him through the reception crowd, where he stood resplendent atop a set of stairs. Ward made it through but, on his way back to the drinks, he met Harry Myers, who was the official photographer. He said he would have snapped Ward and Gagarin, had he seen them. No problem for Dr Ward; he went through the routine again and was presented to Gagarin for the second time: Myers got the photo, the spaceman got the laugh.

When Ward enquired why Gagarin and his interpreter were amused, the translator told him: 'Major Gagarin said: "Second time in orbit."'

That was memorable for Dr Ward but so too was the second

encounter within a few days of Britain's Minister of War and a Soviet spy.

John Profumo later said that he and his wife only met Ivanov for a moment on that second occasion, but Ivanov was seen going to the bar, where he had a vodka martini made for Mrs Profumo, before delivering it with great aplomb. The three then talked for a little time before Ivanov excused himself to go and greet other guests; it was all very cosy.

MI5 appeared bewildered. Frank Wisner's people were perplexed: through Penkovsky, they knew the main GRU agent in Britain was Nicolai Karpekov and wondered why he was not ramping up the situation. Simply, agent Karpekov was busy running a British spy named William John Christopher Vassall, a homosexual, which was an illegal sexual orientation in both Britain and Russia. Like Ward, he was a vicar's son, and he was known always as John Vassall. At the age of 29, he was distraught at having to contain his sexuality when posted by the Foreign Office as a junior clerk to the British Embassy in Moscow in 1954. Vetting did not seem prominent in the diplomatic vocabulary – the KGB had watchers all over the building, doormen to interpreters. Vetting was a chore. And Vassall scooted round the place like bait. As a junior clerk, the public schoolboys of the Diplomatic Service did not regard him as someone to invite to dinner – it was a push to permit him to do the teas on sports days. The parameters of the hierarchy were cemented: Embassy wives knew their place and which wife should walk into church first. Snobbery, like the collection plate, was on a rota.

Young Vassall's attempts at making friends were not so much resisted as never considered; he was snubbed by the class-conscious. But he had deeper reserves of character than anyone guessed. The KGB allowed him a year to settle into the routine of the Embassy, to be seen moving around different departments, to become a familiarity for when they might want access to the Registry... and the strong room and the sensitive files.

They gave him a friend – Embassy staff worker Sigmund Mikhailski – and he provided tickets for the Bolshoi Ballet and the opera, and to a social life, Moscow's homosexual underworld. Vassall was spying before the fat lady stopped singing. Not for sex – because he wanted to. It was during his second winter in Moscow that he was 'compromised' in a private apartment in the Hotel Berlin. Vassall's version was that he was fed enough wine and brandy to knock him out, undressed and then photographed with other naked men. Ten weeks later, so the story continued, he was picked up and taken to bed by an Army officer. The KGB walked in on them, showed Vassall previous incriminating photographs and made him an offer he didn't refuse: spy for us or be jailed in disgrace, in Moscow or London. Yet, he was a productive spy before that 'cover' story was established and became legend – and useful mitigation if his misdeeds were discovered. He took on the dirty jobs for the diplomats and they allowed him to go where and to do as he pleased. It got even better for his Soviet controllers in June 1956, when he was posted back to London as acting personal assistant to the deputy director of the Admiralty's Naval Intelligence Division. Nicolai Karpekov became his case officer.

While the CIA and MI5 pondered on Ivanov, Vassall had been, and was, feeding their enemies many thousands of classified documents including information on British radar, torpedoes and anti-submarine equipment. The Russian Navy benefited hugely from this and the KGB agents involved were honoured for their triumph. The Americans were the first to know of his treachery: KGB defector Anatoliy Golitsyn exposed Vassall as a KGB spy but there were ongoing doubts about Golitsyn's legitimacy. Karpekov, who Vassall knew as 'Gregory', avoided problems by keeping Vassall 'clean' for some months after Golitsyn defected in 1961. At the same time, Ivanov was closely following his master's voice. He knew of the running of other operations but never the details. With the Berlin Crisis ever present and the 'big *cojones*' contest between Kennedy and Khrushchev a daily threat to the world, his role was to be the 'friendly' Russian. Ivanov played a clown role: he adopted Stephen Ward's reverence for the aristocracy and indicated that he believed it was such people who led Britain. It put those he dealt with at their ease – he was a man trying to find his way in a foreign land, let's feel sorry for him. He's new, he's naive and he's foreign: simple but effective penetration. Off guard, the other side open the door. Ward was most certainly lured into this thinking: 'Ivanov and I took an immediate liking to each other. Ivanov had immense charm, wit, vitality and a measure of good looks. I believe I was closer to him than to anyone else in my life – the point about Ivanov was that he was wanted.

'It is more difficult to land a sputnik on the moon than to land in this group if you are not wanted; Ivanov was wanted. We are all curious about life behind the Iron Curtain.'

Given his information to Wagstaffe, Ward clearly saw a problem with Christine Keeler/John Profumo/Ivanov but he said: 'Even not sharing his belief, you were compelled to respect it. His politeness was the natural result of being thoughtful. He drove wildly but well. He had a considerable capacity for vodka, which seemed to produce no effect on him at all. He smoked American-type cigarettes and used an English lighter. One evening, I asked him to come to a party: "My collar isn't clean," he said. I looked in vain for marks. "It's as clean as mine," I remarked. "That, with respect, won't do," he told me. "You see, unless mine is absolutely spotless, people just say all Russians wear dirty shirts."'

No nation wants their dirty linen washed in public. Stephen Ward was desperate to sanction his exotic friend. He was an unreliable narrator. An avid reader of Ian Fleming from the publication of *Casino Royale* in 1953, his description of Ivanov is an askew mirror of the spy novelist's 007 hero. It appeared Ward didn't want to play, but to *be* Bond, enjoying as he did the girls and sadomasochist scenes, his mission to eradicate confusion.

Which is what the lack of clarity in the thinking around Ivanov produced. Wisner and Sir Dick White saw the point of him – a sounding post for the Soviets, and one listening to Moscow and London – but all around there was stumble and bumble from Sir Roger Hollis and his agents at MI5, their Special Branch associates, the Metropolitan Police and J. Edgar Hoover's FBI G-Men, who couldn't get anything right. Ivanov also fed rogue information to an FBI agent he met in a pub – The Lamb in Bloomsbury – much of which went into Hoover's archives as that fantastic oxymoron, informed hearsay, in the FBI's growing 'Operation Bowtie' files about Britain. And for Hoover possible advantage: he had his men watch and listen; every fraction of what they reported transformed from telegraphed information, sometimes planted nonsense, into official FBI 'Top Secret'/'Confidential' documents. It's not only repressed information that conceals what went on.

Jack Profumo's sex overdrive had cornered Dr Ward into an international mess, in which he had no reason to be present. Stephen Ward's lifelong mission to make friends and influence people had spun him into a vicious circle. He stayed calm, trusted in the security of his friends, but events were gathering round him like mushroom clouds, those terrifying signs of the atomic times.

CHAPTER THIRTEEN

DOCTOR STRANGELOVE

'I HATE THEIR GUTS. I ALWAYS HAVE,
AND I ALWAYS WILL.'

Labour MP George Wigg on the Conservative Party, 1959

W hat Stephen Ward confronted was unique in its bizarreness. The only normal action at 17, Wimpole Mews, in the high temperatures, was his regular watering of the window boxes. Otherwise, it would be tea with Ivanov, a Soviet spy, or a visit from Jack Profumo, the Minister of War, who would say hello and have sex with his house guest, Christine Keeler, who, unbeknown to Dr Ward, was also having sex regularly at the flat with Major Jim Eynan. The old soldier and the War Minister even met when Profumo, now entrenched in his affair, made a surprise visit to his new girlfriend: career soldier Eynan all but saluted Profumo. Luckily, he'd got his trousers on before the War Minister was taking his off – Brian Rix could have directed.

What appeared so Whitehall farcical was baffling to the spooks alerted to this extraordinary ménage and the goings-on behind the bright-blue door of Wimpole Mews; two bedrooms (master at the back, single alongside the living room) were separated by a spartan bathroom and the place was frugally furnished. It had to be very cold indeed for Dr Ward to light the fire seen as you walked in the front door. Green walls gave a dark aspect but the big kitchen was brighter. There were unpacked boxes in the basement; Dr Ward's status ornament, his white Jaguar, stayed outside the garage, which, like the fire, was never used for purpose except in severe conditions. The 14-inch black and white television set had to be twisted around to get good reception but there was never any good news to match it.

Though enchanted by Christine, Profumo was not so besotted that he didn't realise he should take more care – Dr Ward's flat was a little like Piccadilly Circus. He made the same offer as she had accepted from Peter Rachman: they would find a flat for her and he would pay for this love nest. Profumo had slept with Christine many times, sent her indiscreet notes and presents, and given her money. He was in for a long-running arrangement. It was not a casual affair and, with no privacy, it would soon be revealed.

At Cliveden, Profumo's interest had been clear. And in the Stephen Ward circle what they were up to was taken for granted. Noel Howard-Jones elaborated: 'I knew Christine and Profumo were having an affair. I didn't know the details. I'd bump into her now and again – she'd say she'd been out with Profumo.

'Stephen's attitude was that Christine's life was her own. I imagine he would have felt concern for Valerie Hobson, Profumo's wife, who he knew. And I think, you know, he wasn't much into people fooling around with married people. I never saw him say anything specific to Christine about it or, if he did, I don't remember.

'Profumo was only interested in her sexually – there wouldn't have been much conversation.'

Stephen Ward knew Profumo was proud of his conquest of the vibrant 19-year-old redhead. The Minister arranged to take her out in a Bentley owned by the Minister of Labour, Viscount Hare.

He had sex with her at his home, where he told her he entertained Royalty, including the Queen.

His behaviour was indicative of menopausal man, the onset a little early perhaps, but he was ardent in establishing his own esteem with her – and showing her off. He took her to meet his friend the Honourable George Ward, who, until October 1960, had been Harold Macmillan's Air Minister and was now Viscount Ward. After recounting the tale of their meeting at the Cliveden swimming pool, his friend saw the mirth rather than the perils. For Profumo, it was simply another sexual adventure, a bit of fun. Viscount Ward shared the amusement.

There wasn't much that George Wigg found funny. He was master of the long, sinister game, the particularly unattractive Witchfinder General of Her Majesty's Opposition. Wigg was not even as nice as he looked: he had made mischief with the lurid carnival involving Britain's espionage frolics but his passion was the Army and all those who served in it. He was elected Labour MP for Dudley, Staffordshire, in 1945, after 18 years in the Royal Tank Corps and wartime service as a Colonel with the Army Educational Corps. Colonel George Wigg would tell you not many MPs could polish his boots when it came to soldiering.

Unhappily, John Profumo tried to do just that only 11 days after he encountered the naked Christine Keeler. The House of Commons was told on 19 July 1961 that the previous month Army forces were sent to Kuwait, at the invitation of the Emir, to help defend a threatened attack by Iraq, which never occurred. But Colonel Wigg complained about the effectiveness of the troops' equipment and their general battle conditions. Tory backbencher Anthony Kershaw dubbed Wigg 'The Cassandra of the British Forces', adding: 'He is absolutely furious that in Kuwait everything has gone all right.'

Wigg, quite correctly, knew it had not and challenged the

Government version, saying it was a public relations exercise, not the truth.

Minister of War John Profumo rose solemnly to his feet and said: 'This is not a public relations exercise. It has been highly successful and very creditable to the Army.'

But the Army's great champion didn't like that: 'If the Right Honourable Gentleman is satisfied, is he aware that the troops went in without anti-aircraft cover, with ineffective anti-tank weapons, with no ground strike force, short of long-range fighters and without any effective longdistance freighters? If that satisfies him, well God help us if he had been disappointed!'

Profumo, clearly furious, was about to reply when the Speaker stopped the debate. The frustration only further reddened the remarkable visage of Colonel Wigg, who said Profumo had been evasive and, worst of all, harmful to the Army. The withering look the two men exchanged across the Commons was like an electrical charge. Wigg swore to several newspaper lobby correspondents that he would never accept Profumo's unsupported word ever again, would never trust him. Whatever George Wigg's reputation (and many MPs, including a majority of his fellow Labour Party members disliked him), he was a determined man and never gave up when he began a fight. Adept at compiling dossiers, he began one on what he regarded as the Kuwait debacle, filing it 'Wigg/Profumo'.

Stephen Ward had no co-star on his file, which in the summer of 1961 was copied through several Government departments and agencies. He also had no inkling, nor should he, of the simmering feud between Profumo and Colonel Wigg. Dr Ward had told Wagstaffe of MI5 that he was 'concerned about Jack Profumo'.

In turn, MI5 were increasingly intrigued by Ward.

The official Registry of the Metropolitan Police's Special Branch reveals that, on 31 July 1961, MI5 asked them to check their records on Stephen Ward. Special Branch reported back that Dr

Ward had no criminal record and his reputation was intact. In return, MI5 requested Ward be filed 'on alert' and any new information about him sent on. There was no specific instruction to Special Branch noted in the Registry for them to seek out damaging material on Dr Ward.

Officially, Ward was 'clean' as far as British Intelligence was concerned. The Americans didn't see it that way yet the FBI was no more sophisticated than the British. The International Security Services could understand the stealing of secrets, blackmailing of diplomats and scientists, turning of rival spies, but this was a purely British invention: a pantomime starring toffs, tarts – and traitors? A jigsaw with far too many pieces, nothing fitted.

Information now available indicates much disinformation was fed into the espionage equation, mainly who said what to whom and who knew what: the arrogance of politics, of all power, is to be seen to know all. And, if you don't, you pretend. Which is why an intoxicating mix of official and unofficial versions of events exists. The paper trail available under the Freedom of Information Act, 2000, also points up stark contradictions. There is an extraordinary sense of selective vision.

Whatever the detail, Stephen Ward was very much part of the game, something he enjoyed, but being centre stage makes for an easier target. Watching with him were some of the world's most powerful people and as such he was surrounded by hypocrisy, duplicity and stupidity. When mixed with the terror of the times, also a fear that provoked alarming actions. Indeed, so alarming they went into history as fantasy.

Unbeknown to Dr Ward, from that summer on, he began work on his own dénouement, casting himself as Sir Galahad but, instead of rescuing maidens from London's streets, he decided he would save the world. If there was something to take from the Profumo-Keeler-Ivanov firework, he was the person best placed to do so: he had made the introductions, as it were. For Stephen Ward, the instinctive squire of squalid society, there was a huge aspiration to matter, to belong, to accomplish – and be seen to accomplish. He dreamed of a permanent and rightful place at the top table; even chance encouraged him to play hero.

By the wonder of happenstance, reality and fantasy were about to collide. One of his longtime friends and a visitor to Spring Cottage, the exotic Zena Marshall, was to star in the film version of Ian Fleming's 1958 novel *Dr. No*. She secured the role of Miss Taro, a glamorous opponent and sex partner for Sean Connery's James Bond. As further evidence of the small world of the times, Marshall was the former wife of Paul Adam, bandleader at Les Ambassadeurs. It is also at the Le Cercle casino of Les Ambassadeurs where the early scenes of *Dr. No* were filmed.

Zena Marshall was also friendly with Harry Alan Towers for several years, before the world witnessed her wrapped around Bond in 1962. He told of how they had enjoyed themselves in the roof bar of a New York hotel with grand views of the East River. After every drink (and there were a few), Marshall tossed her empty glass into the air high above Manhattan. She was also an active player in Stephen Ward's world, but Towers' favourite story was the one she told herself: she was on show at a film festival in Buenos Aires when there was a caller at her hotel bedroom door: 'I am Carlos and I am your escort. Use me.' And she did, telling Towers she did not want to offend her Argentinean hosts.

The difficulty for the British Government was that they did not wish to offend anyone, including Khrushchev and Kennedy – and, officially, Macmillan and his Cabinet had no knowledge of the complicated triangle of Profumo-Keeler-Ivanov. But the spooks did: they had operated independently of Government approval when they sent Buster Crabb into the waters of Portsmouth Harbour to study the hull of the *Ordzhonikidze*. That had been Dick White's call, now Roger Hollis was in charge of the game. The idea that MI5 might have attempted to entrap Ivanov, turn him through a sexual indiscretion, is greeted with some dismay by many, including Alexander Nekrassov, expert in all things Russian. He said: 'If Ivanov's antics hadn't had absolute Kremlin approval, he would have been hauled back to Moscow almost as quickly as he arrived in Britain.'

Ivanov's role was to play the society spy; his Moscow puppet masters controlled his movement. His wife and family were deep inside the Soviet system. In the circumstances, his mission was to encourage indiscretion and not worry about compromising himself. The most obvious of all were not sexual adventures but his *Boy's Own* partnership with Stephen Ward.

Indeed, Roger Hollis at MI5 knew his agency's mission rules: the private lives of politicians or anyone else were only important if they were subversive, a threat to the Realm. He did not tell Macmillan in their regular consultations about John Profumo's relationship with Christine Keeler. In 2013, Dame Stella Rimington, the first female and the first publicly named Director of MI5, told me that Hollis behaved impeccably. According to her, his behaviour was a guideline for all chief spooks and noted: 'It is not the responsibility of the Director-General of MI5 to seek to protect the Government of the day from embarrassment – that is the job of the Whips. The DG should only pass on anything about behaviour if it could adversely affect security in any way.'

Still, it seemed, Hollis wanted to alert Profumo to steer clear of Ivanov and, in theory, as well as in practice, that also meant limiting contact with Stephen Ward. Possibly the Director-General was giving Profumo a friendly nudge-nudge on the extra-marital front. He did it through the offices of Cabinet Secretary Sir Norman Brook, prince of intrigue, who knew (and could fix) the plumbing of Government. Brook saw Profumo on 9 August 1961, and warned him off Ivanov. Nothing was ever recorded as being said about Christine. And, despite much speculation, Profumo's plain paper note to her the next day, postponing a date, was written for just that, not in a panic. In sloping, shorthand scrawl, it read:

9/8/61

Darling,

In great haste & because I can get no reply from your phone
– Alas something's blown up tomorrow night & I can't
therefore make it. I'm terribly sorry especially as I leave the
next day for various trips & then a holiday so won't be able
to see you again until some time in September. Blast it. Please
take great care of yourself & don't run away.

Love J

I'm writing this 'cos I know you're off for the day tomorrow
& I want you to know before you go if I still can't reach you .
by phone.

Those are not the words of a panicked man or a distressed and
discovered lover. They are the words of a man who wants more.
Christine put the letter in a bureau drawer. Her affair with
Profumo did not end after five weeks but six months later,
including a session in his red Mini.

While the Minister of War was distracted, Dr Ward worked on
how to save the world, a mission in which he enlisted Bill Astor's
help. He persuaded Lord Astor to write on 2 September 1961 to
the British Foreign Office offering his friend Dr Stephen Ward,
who had become friendly with Ivanov, as a means of passing
information to Moscow, which would give them an accurate
picture of Western intentions. Ward could provide the
information directly, or Ivanov could take a meeting with the
Foreign Office. Like Batman and Robin on the international stage,
Ward and Ivanov would be vigilantes for world peace. Indeed,
Ivanov often boasted, 'Anything important you tell me can be on
Khrushchev's desk in 20 minutes.'

The Foreign Office were bemused (international political chit-
chat was their game) but sufficiently tempted to interview Dr

Ward on 18 September 1961. Ward offered the full story of his thinking and friendship with Ivanov; he wanted it to be of use to his country, to help towards nuclear disarmament. Thanks, but no thanks, said the Foreign Office. Ward then recruited his friend and patient Conservative MP Sir Godfrey Nicholson, who agreed to meet Ivanov for dinner at the House of Commons. Sir Godfrey was impressed by the Russian and was his own man.

Yes, he would see what could be done about British intentions over Berlin. Sir Godfrey consulted the Foreign Office and, in time, the Foreign Secretary, Lord (Alec) Home. He also wrote *three* letters to Ivanov, vetted by the Foreign Office. Sir Godfrey gave all the letters for delivery to Dr Ward: the first two he handed to Ivanov and the third, as Ivanov was then in Moscow, he delivered to the Soviet Ambassador at the Embassy in Kensington Gardens. Sir Godfrey, then a Conservative MP for more than 30 years, had created an astonishing situation.

Stephen Ward was the link between the British Foreign Office and the GRU and the Soviet Ambassador, who were in direct, round-the-clock contact with the Kremlin. Much more important than James Bond in a world crisis, Dr Ward was licensed to negotiate.

It was an incredible situation. From any viewpoint, Ward was an eccentric character. There were nuclear missiles pointing at each other across the Atlantic. Britain was the nation in the middle – represented, even if by remote proxy, by Stephen Ward. This was not a scenario the Whitehall mandarins would like screaming across the front pages, or on cables to Washington. It would make the high-stakes, poker-playing Pentagon freak… much more than Aloysius 'Lucky' Gordon, though he gave pause for thought. Stephen Ward met him through his own relentless pursuit of pleasure. He had taken to hosting bridge games when, after the cards were stacked, girls would fan out around the table and strip off. Gentlemen players would then take turns in whipping the girls and having them whichever way they found most enjoyable.

One evening in October 1961, the bridge game was cancelled. Instead, Dr Ward went out on the prowl.

He had taken to driving Christine around Paddington to sight-see prostitutes on Westbourne Park Road and into Notting Hill late in the night, where he would stop at West Indian cafes. His sketchbook opening doors for him, he became friendly with many residents. To all who would listen, he would rave that this was truly life in the raw. He had picked up many of the West Indian girls – he told Christine he was fascinated with sketching and having sex with them. Thirty-one-year-old Gordon felt similarly about Christine, just not the sketching.

Ward and Christine Keeler met 'Lucky' (his parents won the Lottery the day he was born) Gordon at the El Rio café in Notting Hill in October 1961, as the autumn days were truly closing in. Then, Notting Hill was a wicked carnival every weekend: a parade of pimps and prostitutes, with jukebox parties as the background: Portobello Road, Talbot Road, Ledbury Road, Powis Square and Colville Terrace were noisy with loud cars, shouts, screams and arguments and sometimes eerie with the stillness of violence, the moment time stops. It wasn't racial tension; this was 24-hour tension. Stephen Ward adored it, and Frank Crichlow's El Rio cafe at 127, Westbourne Park was action HQ. Home to hustlers, like Lucky Gordon and Michael de Freitas (Michael X), it attracted those whom Crichlow described as 'rebellious and a bit smart, those with street intelligence, those for whom the factory was not their speed'.

The Fiesta One cafe had become Ward's favoured haunt but on this evening it was quiet – 'quite dull', he told Christine and his friend Vasco Lazzolo, whom he'd invited out to see the action. Instead, Dr Ward escorted them to the El Rio cafe, where life was all dope and dancing – and the dominating Lucky Gordon. He was bad news. After arriving in Britain in 1948, he soon found trouble in the British Army (which ejected him for punching out an officer) and with the police as he angrily fought his way into several convictions for assault. Wiry and aggressively short, with a Cagney swagger and a thug's attitude, he sported a beret and dressed in black, which matched his attitude. Ward thought he was interesting, as was the drifting marijuana aroma. He gave Christine a ten-shilling note and asked her to buy some pot for them. Dr Ward also wanted a 'sister'. Lucky stepped into the scene and promised to keep everyone happy. Within two days of their meeting, he telephoned Wimpole Mews with news of more dope and a 'sister' if they returned to the El Rio.

They did, and the wild times began with Lucky Gordon becoming obsessed with and possessive of Christine, and she and Ward indulging in marijuana. Christine was held at knifepoint by Lucky and raped; on other occasions, she slept with him voluntarily, but Gordon became increasingly jealous. He stalked Christine, turned up at Wimpole Mews, telephoned throughout the night. She was naturally disturbed by the violence of the attention. Ward witnessed some of this and Christine began to resent his concern, was suspicious of its intent. Suddenly, she heard from Mandy Rice-Davies in November 1961: for Christine, it was a freedom route, escape from Lucky Gordon.

Mandy had tired of Peter Rachman – there were only so many fur coats, so many necklaces – and had found a flat in Dolphin Square, on the Embankment at Pimlico. Christine moved in and, with the help of Rachman's seed money, they planned to embark on a modelling career. Like the cash, Mandy's independence from Rachman didn't last and soon Christine had the Dolphin Square apartment to herself. She couldn't stay far from spies. Unbeknown to her, John Vassall, the Admiralty cipher clerk and KGB spy, was a neighbour. They did not encounter each other; she never attended any of his grand parties.

Still, she had a good time, according to Lucky Gordon who later said she was visited by several MPs and lawyers, many of whom lived part-time in Dolphin Square, with its easy access to

Westminster and the High Court. Within the CIA (who were monitoring Ivanov), they believed she saw members of the US diplomatic corps. Yet, Lucky Gordon had had his motives, the CIA their own disinformation agenda. Certainly, Christine was content at this time and relished running her own life. She continued seeing Stephen Ward, the then constant in her life, although she was wary of his control. In turn, Dr Ward was rightly concerned about the events, not of their making, invading their lives: 'Lucky' Gordon was turning out to be anything but. Meanwhile, Ward maintained his faith in Christine and they socialised frequently. He introduced her to Paul Mann, whom he'd met at the Connaught Bridge Club. Together with Paula Hamilton-Marshall, one of Ward's regular sex partners, and her flatmate, Kim Proctor, photographer from the Stork Club, they'd go out on the town.

On one marijuana-scented evening, they headed for the All Nighter club, a heaving, loud venue in the West End's Wardour Street. Lucky Gordon all but greeted them at the entrance. He was all smiles and beatitudes: everything that had gone before was history, forgotten. Lucky was so convincing he was invited back to Dolphin Square to continue the good times. There, his conviviality vanished. He tore a fire-axe from the back of the front door and went on the rampage as the dulcet tones of Johnny Mathis spun from the record player. Christine's guests vanished as fast as they could.

She and one other girl were left and for 48 hours they were terrorised by Lucky Gordon. Christine was badly bruised and beaten by Gordon, who finally left them to go and buy cigarettes and they rang the police. On his return with two packs of Kensitas, the cops were waiting. They had a clear case and he was duly arrested and charged with assault. Two surprising things happened: Stephen Ward stood bail for Gordon, who had become his de facto drug dealer, and Christine Keeler, much to her everlasting dismay, was persuaded by Gordon's brother to drop the assault charges. For Ward, concerned with his other 'high-level' dealings with Ivanov and Sir Godfrey Nicholson, it was for the best: he wanted to avoid any high-publicity court case. Still, for both him and Christine, Lucky Gordon became a phantom in their lives. So terrified was Christine she bought an under-the-counter German automatic pistol, a Luger with two magazines of bullets. Ironically, it didn't protect her, instead inflicting more damage on her and Stephen Ward – it blasted Britain about, too.

Strangely, given all the politics and nuclear paranoia, it would be the world and not this particular group of players that would remain intact.

We have hindsight; they had a party.

CHAPTER FOURTEEN

DOCTOR IN DOUBT

'IN THE MIDDLE OF DIFFICULTY
LIES OPPORTUNITY.'

Albert Einstein, 1939

It was not a man in a mask but the aristocrat with two peeled tangerines in his mouth, a noose around his neck and a somewhat ludicrous contraption on his penis who was the star of Mariella Novotny's 1961 Christmas party at Hyde Park Square. A solo sex act with accessories got the evening going. When the applause ended, guests' hands were grappling with their clothes or other, more intimate, parts of their person.

Mariella wore her trademark hat and a dominatrix leather ensemble with spikes in her burgundy boots. Hod Dibben had on a new suit, which looked like his old one. Stephen Ward had taken a bus over from Devonshire Street after a late appointment. Astonishingly, he had brought a bottle of French burgundy. He told Dibben that he wanted to celebrate the arrival of what he hoped would be a positive and peaceful New Year.

By the time he got there, Bobbie Moore had, as usual, the bottom half of her clothes off and her husband Beecher was naked and discussing yachting plans for 1962. Someone asked if he minded if he had 'a little playtime' with Bobbie and was told:

'That's why we're here.' But, before they could get to it, Mariella announced that, as they had nine courses, dinner was being served early. She had gone to much trouble for 'The Feast of the Peacocks', stuffing the birds (apparently quite inedible), and, with the tail feathers replaced, they were the centrepiece. Spread along and across the antique dining table, which seated 22, were plates of traditional Christmas fare; with each place setting were sets of plastic handcuffs. Some guests sat at the table wearing only the paper hats from the Christmas crackers. Mariella had hired six girls ('fluffers') for the evening and their assignment was to provide 'stimulation' for the men, to ensure their excitement stayed intact. She herself would do the proper servicing.

One man spent the evening crawling around the floor and under the dining table: a shy, small City businessman, he was a Mariella regular. He wore a mask – a tight, rubber affair, which made his breathing heavy – for pleasure, which he also took from being verbally abused and lightly beaten by Mariella. Gossip, with a little help from Stephen Ward, identified the Man in the Mask as Ernest Marples MP, the Minister of Transport. He *was* there, though not in a mask. For much of the evening he was attached to his regular prostitute, a girl called Sheryl whom he had been seeing for 18 months.

Marples was a sex addict and, as such, being a Government minister, a severe security risk, which Lord Denning himself pointed out to Macmillan in a clandestine report. Daily outings with prostitutes also distracted him, as Minister of Transport, from spotting the flaws in the Beeching proposals for Britain's rail system: his ultimate sin.

The Man in the Mask became legendary through tales from Mandy Rice-Davies (who wasn't present) and the jottings of Mariella herself. She maintained the masked man 'was strapped between wood pillars, a flail or whip was in front of his naked figure. As each guest arrived, they gave him one stroke and then left the man to join the party. When he was released before dining,

he was ordered to remain beneath the long table, out of sight.'
Hod Dibben told friends that several of the men at their parties
were regulars, there because they craved involvement in
sadomasochistic orgies; several were masked, for thrills not
disguise. He enjoyed that himself before the extra pleasure of
watching more conventional, if group, sexplay. Also present was
a barrister who enjoyed severe pain and humiliation. He too
sported a mask (in black leather), with evil little penknife cuts for
eyes and fastened up the back with red shoelaces. It was worn
with a white lace apron to 'protect his modesty'.

The behaviour was all happily accepted and Mariella vocally
rejected those who called her parties rather upsetting. She
entertained all manner of foreign visitors, including, according to
Eddie Chapman, Ivanov. He had insisted on straightforward sex
but ended up being turned over and playfully spanked by
Mariella (she told the Russian it was good for him). Stephen Ward
was an enthusiast, an early believer in the recuperative physical
and emotional powers of free love. He attended, usually only as a
voyeur, parties themed along black magic rituals – naked girls and
men in hoods, that sort of thing – which mostly involved the
women demeaning themselves before their men; it was sex as
conquest. Other times, it was more of a coupling show, with
enthusiastic lovers putting on a display and then the aroused
audiences choosing their own partners.

Stephen Ward viewed: it gave him enormous pleasure to watch
someone he liked being happily brought to orgasm. Psychologists
say this is common; a husband observing his wife having sex with
others is known to stimulate. One of Dr Ward's early Mayfair
circuit partners said: 'I think it gave him immense excitement and
satisfaction to watch someone else making love to a girl of whom
he was fond. And the more passionate or violent the sex act, the
more it seemed to satisfy him. I got the feeling that Stephen used
to identify himself with the girl he liked as she lay in someone
else's arms. He used to take me to a club on the way to a sex party,

and pick out a man he thought would make an interesting partner for me that afternoon or night.'

Indeed, Ward was quoted in a 1963 magazine article about parties where marijuana and uppers and downers were used to encourage the fun, the crowd an eclectic mix of debutantes and prostitutes, businessmen and street hustlers: 'No money ever passed at any of these sessions. The girls came because they wanted to. If someone brought them along for the first time, and they didn't like what went on, they could leave. I never saw anyone, excepting sometimes the person who had brought them, press them to stay. If they showed any real inhibitions of disgust at what was happening, they were encouraged to leave.'

Ward said he first attended one of the Mayfair parties in 1955: 'I was attracted by curiosity, but I remained because I was fascinated and, after a few visits to parties like it, I sometimes used to take along a girl that I knew. But I never did so unless the girl revealed, without prompting, that she had a genuine desire for this sort of experience. Most of my girl friends were just friends. Man has made a prison of sex. Many people need this extra sexual stimulus. Give it to them, and they will live happy, married lives. No more than that.'

That particular evening, the happily married Hod Dibben, along with his friend Stephen Ward, was viewing his wife in tumultuous action. It was like a Windmill Theatre tableaux with moving parts, many moving parts.

There were to be many versions of that 'Man in the Mask' evening. Christine Keeler went to the party but only to collect Stephen Ward, whose car was in for repair. Mandy Rice-Davies was with her but remained in the car while Christine went to find Ward. She discovered him in a room with Hod Dibben, where they were both intently watching Mariella, breasts bouncing, legs akimbo, frolicking with several naked men, who all wanted to mount her front and back. Astonishingly, she could get them all going at once. As Bobby McKew told me: 'She was known as

Mariella the magician – she could make an erection appear from nowhere. And then make it vanish delightfully.'

It must have been a relief – and a rest – for the participants to enter 1962 without so much fanfare.

Stephen Ward took it most confidently. He continued to seek out glamour, high social times and influence over everyone he met and, although he could be schoolboyish in his sexual adventures, he took his present role most seriously. He fervently believed he could stop the bomb in this era of the hair-trigger. Those who knew him said he was relaxed. Ward could compartmentalise his life: the elegant guest at Cliveden high society receptions, the habitué of west London dope dens, enthusiast at black magic sex parties, negotiator between world powers... he was the talented Dr Ward.

'Stephen never seemed to change,' said Shirley Anne Field, who was by then a famous young actress, co-starring with Albert Finney in *Saturday Night and Sunday Morning* (1960), Laurence Olivier in *The Entertainer* (1960) and with Steve McQueen and Robert Wagner in *The War Lover* (1962). She hadn't, as Ward wanted, become a titled lady – she was a huge movie star, just as she wanted. 'We stayed in touch – almost everyone who *really* knew him did that. He always wanted to help.'

He was also busy sketching and painting, including a grand portrait of Mrs Bobby McKew. Water-ski champion Anna Gerber married McKew in 1958 at Hampstead Register Office. In 2013, Gerber said at her home in Tangier: 'Stephen didn't seem to have a care in the world. He was most relaxed when he painted my portrait – it was all very pleasant. The painting found its way into our garage and stayed there for years. Stephen didn't push himself forward nor was he difficult: he was good company, good fun.'

Ronnie Sommerby, a hugely successful clothes retailer, was friendly with Dr Ward and, in 2013, recalled at his Yorkshire home: 'There was always so much going on in Stephen's life – it was hectic all the time but he never behaved in a troubled way. He felt secure in his circumstances. He knew everybody – he was a good man.'

Meanwhile, Christine Keeler was finding life with Dr Ward claustrophobic, especially with the cordons they created to keep Lucky Gordon at bay. She was mightily interested when Mandy Rice-Davies, during another bout of Rachman-phobia, suggested they head for Hollywood to try modelling, maybe acting. Christine was living at Wimpole Mews and also with Michael Lambton, who was willing to bankroll the American trip if the girls went to New York first, where he would join them, and then on to California. Ward didn't interfere: he was deeply involved in negotiations between Moscow and London, something he could apparently box off from the rest of his life.

Encouraged by the MP Sir Godfrey Nicholson's previous interventions, he suggested they try to make contact with the leaders at the Foreign Office, particularly the Permanent Under-Secretary of State, Sir Harold Caccia. On 5 April 1962, Stephen Ward lunched with the top man and Sir Godfrey. He made his case to the Foreign Office mandarin, one of despair that not enough was being done to prevent a nuclear showdown between East and West: Britain, the nation in the middle, should mediate. He suggested a meeting between Sir Harold and Ivanov. Officially, Sir Harold rejected the offer but took away the sentiment. Internal information suggests the diplomats believed Russia was making so much noise, wearing a big hat, to disguise lesser capabilities. Mr Wagstaffe had three meetings with Dr Ward over the early summer months.

With rockets galore threatening the world, Christine Keeler and Mandy Rice-Davies sailed into the sunset. It took some weeks to arrange but, on 5 July 1962, they left Southampton on the Dutch cruise liner *Niew Amsterdam* and, after a string of high-seas romances, arrived in New York. It began as fun and ended rather miserably when the money ran out. All Mandy had left of value was her mink from Rachman, a little too much for the sweltering New York summer. For a few days, they camped out in a double room in the Hotel Bedford on East 40th Street, then went for the weekend (unknowingly) to America's major homosexual resort, Fire Island, where the only action they got was from the sun – both burned badly.

Back in New York City, they appealed for funds: Christine from Michael Lambton, Mandy from Peter Rachman. BOAC flight 506 took them back to Britain on 18 July 1962. We have an accurate record of such travel details, thanks to the Director of the FBI, J. Edgar Hoover himself. When the Profumo Affair hit the fan, Hoover wrote to the US Attorney General Robert Kennedy and half a dozen senior agents spelling out what they knew of the girls' activities in America. 'They thought they'd fucked President Kennedy – they'd fucked everybody else that mattered,' was the reaction, unofficially, from Hoover's rival, the CIA.

When Christine and Mandy landed back in London, the oncoming hurricane of scandal that had been simmering for months began to ferment. Many players involved themselves in forthcoming events, few, if any, with much distinction. One MP or another said that George Wigg, the Labour Party's moral general, 'scented carrion'. In the patois of the times, what went on from now was all *pretty rotten*. And sad, for Stephen Ward, who believed he could save the world, had so much less chance of saving himself.

Christine returned to London and to Wimpole Mews: she felt safer there. Ward was sympathetic towards Paula Hamilton-Marshall, whom he'd met on Devonshire Street, close to his surgery. Always willing to help the wounded, Christine got on with Paula, who was trying to cope with her drug-addict brother John and her pregnancy, courtesy of a black American airman who had flown quickly back to the USA. Social work, it seemed, was simply another part of Dr Ward's services. That late July

1962, he and Christine visited Hamilton-Marshall at her flat in Devonshire Street. At the flat was Peter Rachman's young helper from years gone by: Johnny Edgecombe, who paraded around London as 'The Edge'. He was overflowing with bravado. Christine sat nervously in the flat, couldn't really sit still. Her new friend, 'The Edge', asked what was wrong and the tale of Lucky Gordon, in all its violent glory, was told. Edgecombe said it was not a problem – he knew Lucky Gordon, *he* would resolve the problem.

For Ward and Christine, still on a knife-edge, that was positive news. Which wasn't the case for them or John Profumo when the August edition of the society magazine *Queen* was published on 31 July. On the gossip pages was a snippet from Robin Douglas-Home, former romantic partner of Princess Margaret, nephew of the Foreign Secretary, Lord Home, and an assistant editor at the magazine. 'Sentences I'd Like to Hear the End Of' ran the headline. It was the blind item of the gossip columnist insufficiently certain of the facts to risk blatant expression. The pertinent sentence went: 'called in MI5 because every time the chauffeur-driven Zis drew up at her front door, out of the back door into a chauffeur-driven Humber slipped...' The Humber was UK Government issue, the Russian car could be nothing but an Embassy vehicle.

What flummoxed all the watchers, spooks and Fleet Street, the CIA, the KGB, MI5 and the FBI was the remarkable relationship between Stephen Ward and Eugene Ivanov. Yes, Jack Profumo was visiting Christine – and still was, well into 1962 – but Ivanov was going to see Dr Ward. The conspiracy theory brigade could understand the sex triangle but, given Ivanov's single encounter with Christine, that had been overtaken by an altogether different and more complex geometry.

And Stephen Ward was the imponderable in the equation. He, it seemed, was the part of the puzzle to most fear, the natural apprehension of the unknown. There is, however, a huge

Daily Mirror

If MPs say it again 'in the open'..

PROFUMO'S WARNING—I'LL SUE!

Daily Mirror

PROFUMO THE UNANSWERED QUESTIONS

Political Crisis Commentary by VICTOR KNIGHT

His visit to the Palace 'an affront,' says MP

I WARNED THEM, SAYS WARD

Premier orders a security check

Daily Mirror

Three-hour interview at Cliveden

POLICE SEE LORD ASTOR AND PROFUMO

THE PROFUMO SCANDAL AND THE PRESS

'Death threats' to Christine

CHARLES DID BUY THAT DRINK

READ ALL ABOUT IT:
Fleet Street was chasing headlines, not footnotes, and the minutiae of the Stephen Ward story initially got lost in typographical shrieks.

© *Mirrorpix*

Above: Smiling through the media frenzy, an apparently carefree Stephen Ward with the equally delighted looking Julie Gulliver, the final young girl in his life. The smiles would fade as his Old Bailey trial progressed.

© *Popperfoto/Getty Images*

Right: Never mind the protocol: Eugene Ivanov warms up the Cold War, snuggling into Nancy Murphy, wife of Captain Thomas Murphy, the assistant Naval Attaché with the U.S. Navy in London.

© *Courtesy of Bobby McKew*

Above: The First Couple, Jack and Jackie Kennedy, visit Harold Macmillan in London on 4 June 1961, the summer in which 'events' began stacking up for the British Prime Minister. © *Mirrorpix*

Left: Medals jangling, the British Minister of War, John Profumo, and his actress wife, the glamorous movie and theatrical star Valerie Hobson. © *Mirrorpix*

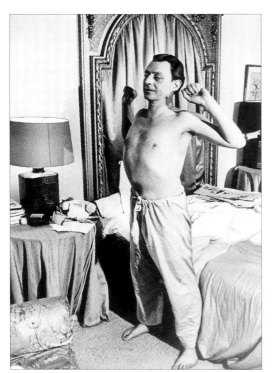

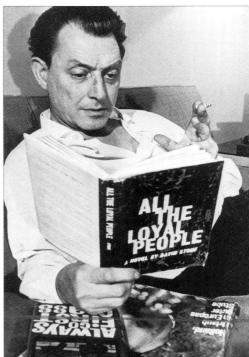

Above Left: Rise and shine: Stephen Ward prepares for another day in court – still confident that he would be 'looked after' by his friends.

© *Mirrorpi*

Above Right: Stephen Ward engrossed in the ironically titled 1960 crime novel *All the Loyal People*.

© *Mirrorpi*

Below: The name's Ward, Stephen Ward. In true 007 style, the osteopath climbs from his stylish drop-head white Jaguar en route to Spring Cottage.

© *Mirrorpi*

Above: Harold 'Kim' Philby, the great British traitor and spy, tells a press conference that he's a good, loyal Englishman as Alan Whicker, the television globetrotter who died in 2013, takes notes.

© *Mirrorpix*

Below: The much derided Home Secretary Henry Brooke, dubbed on television 'the most hated man in Britain' by David Frost's *That Was The Week That Was*. He was the last Home Secretary to allow the death penalty.

© *Mirrorpix*

Above Left: His Master's Voice and the picture of a vanishing Britain: the bowler-hatted Lord Denning, who applied the past to the present, protected some and condemned others on the same testimony. © *Press Association Image*

Above Right: America's great diplomat and superspy, the suave Ambassador David Bruce – who used his great mind and privilege to pursue his nation's interests no matter what – in London with his second wife Evangeline. © *Press Association Image*

Below Left: Hello, hello, hello: a London bobby keeps a wary eye on Aloysius 'Lucky' Gordon, with his lawyer Ellis Lincoln in neat moustache and bowler hat directly behind him, during a break in his trial for attacking Christine Keeler. © *Press Association Image*

Below Right: A grim time for the man who fired the bullets at Stephen Ward's flat. Johnny Edgecombe is on his way to trial for the Gunplay at Wimpole Mews, after firing the shots that ricocheted throughout British society. © *Mirrorpi*

Left: Stephen Ward's tired face tells the story, the loose shirt collar testifies to his jail-time weight loss, as does the stubble to that incarceration. Still, though, there remains a flicker of defiance. © *Mirrorpix*

Below: Faces in a crowd – 'the witnesses had to walk through a vast leer, a huge concupiscent exposure of cheap dentures' – as the world wants a glimpse of Christine Keeler and Mandy Rice Davies. © *Mirrorpix*

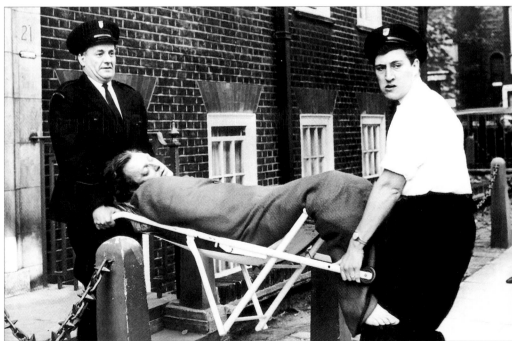

Above: The 'Naughty Sisters', Christine Keeler and Mandy Rice-Davies, who became the leading ladies of the trial of Stephen Ward – a sensation then and now. Few books on the history of the 20th Century do not contain an image of Christine Keeler.   © *Mirrorp*

Below: The last image: being lifted on a stretcher, a red hospital blanket over him; his head rests limply to one side. It was the end of the beginning of the story of Dr Stephen Ward – an eternal headline.   © *Mirrorpi*

argument that he was doing more than some to help in what came to be known as 'The Cuban Missile Crisis'. And, to others, the feeling you might not see the next day. Some were so terrified they turned it into denial. That anyone kept a clear head in the frenetic, final days of October 1962 is in itself remarkable. Crisis collided into crisis. The Macmillan Government was spinning, the Kennedy Administration panicking and, most important of all, Khrushchev was bluffing, a game dismaying even Moscow.

For playing a 'blind' can be the most dangerous gamble of all if you don't have a good hand, if you don't have the luck. And the Soviets didn't. Much of the mess was the work of the spies on both sides, East and West; espionage the prompt of paranoia, induced by the scaremongering. These were operatives who didn't trust themselves. Would they play fair? Few were willing to do so at all levels in an ongoing turmoil of greed, conspiracy and intolerance.

In London, Harold Macmillan was wary of how President Kennedy and his new White House advisers would react to the increasing military connection between Moscow and Havana. In July of that year, the CIA reported 65 Soviet ships sailing to Cuba, and infrared photography suggested ten of them carried sophisticated weapons. On 2 September 1962, Khrushchev announced weapons would be included in a new trade agreement with Cuba, totally at odds with the information fed to US Attorney General Robert Kennedy. It was widely mooted in Western spy society that the President's brother had met with high-ranking Soviet spies to circumvent just what was now happening. There is circumstantial material to suggest it did, but no positive proof.

Within the next 16 days, shipments of medium range SS-4 Sandal nuclear missiles appeared on the island. Preparations were also being made to accommodate SS-5 Skean rockets – which could strike a bullseye anywhere in America. There were 40 launchers and 80 warheads – enough to knock out nearly 90 per cent of American nuclear weaponry in a pre-strike – being readied on Cuba. A U-2 spy-in-the-sky plane photographed the Sandal missiles on 14 October. They also took aerial views of nuclear bases being prepared; areas for storing nuclear warheads, others for rocket launching sites – 80 miles from Florida.

President Kennedy was presented with breakfast and this news on 16 October 1962. Secretly, he convened an emergency meeting of his senior military, political and diplomatic advisers to discuss the doomsday development: 'ExCom' (Executive Committee). After rejecting a surgical air strike against the missile sites, ExCom decided on a naval blockade and a demand that the Soviet installations, under construction but nearing completion, be dismantled and missiles removed. What the President was not told was that Russia had fewer than 50 Intercontinental Ballistic Missiles (ICBMs) capable of hitting the USA and were terrified of being wiped out in a pre-emptive strike. Both sides had spook information, but not all they required. Kennedy's men then found from new reconnaissance the true extent of the Soviet ICBMs. They advised the President that, if it came to a shoot-out, they would fare best; there was no 'missile gap', they had the advantage.

It was of little comfort to Britain and the rest of Europe. Russia had many, many nuclear missiles capable of annihilating that part of the world. America set up a naval blockade to prevent Soviet missiles being installed on Castro's island. Kennedy stated Cuba was now 'quarantined': if the Russian freighters did not turn back, the US Navy would board them. On 22 October 1962, JFK gave a television broadcast to that effect. He had an end-of-the-world demeanour, eyes closed, as he made grave remarks about the 'clandestine, reckless and provocative threat to world peace'. Ominously, he threatened he could not rule out military action to prevent the Soviet weaponry reaching Cuba.

Brinkmanship began, as did the jail term for the colourful spy John Vassall. That same Monday at the Old Bailey in London, he was given 18 years for 'selling his country for lust and greed'. Vassall was convicted after a trial held partly in secret. He got away with his dubious story that he had been compromised by the KGB into spying. A lurid tale and much endorsed by the Establishment – and Fleet Street, who loved the chase of 'pinko gays' – once again it also revealed the snobbery in the ranks of British society. It was an ominous early opening for the fate of Stephen Ward. Macmillan was running a grandee Government, a place where 'one Balliol man to another would negotiate the future of the nation'.

The Vassall story highlighted and mocked all that simultaneously. He operated in a world where, if you spoke and behaved in a certain way, your actions were unlikely to be questioned. Even if you were of low ranking in the Civil Service, a powerful mentor eased the working days. Vassall, an assistant private secretary to the Honourable Thomas Galbraith, a junior minister at the Admiralty, was vastly overspending, much of it along Savile Row, buying from the most exclusive stores to present himself as a gentleman.

This man, happily despatching classified material to Moscow, was living in a lavish Dolphin Square flat and was better dressed than the Duke of Windsor himself. But no one noticed: he was a clerical-grade civil servant, earning £750 a year. When he was arrested on 12 September 1962, Special Branch officers searching his apartment found 36 suits (almost all bespoke), 3 unwrapped cashmere overcoats, 29 pairs of custom, hand-lasted shoes, custom-designed silk shirts, bespoke silk pyjamas and underwear. For his collection of Burberry mackintoshes, he had a specially designed clothes stand. He also had two drawers of beachwear, used on Caribbean holidays.

On arrest, it appeared that he had some sort of private income – no one at the Admiralty had noticed other than that John Vassall 'always looked smart'. This explained why some of his trial was held 'in camera' – it wasn't the spy stuff the spooks wanted hidden, it was Vassall's fashion secrets. For this spotlighted how useless they had been and, given the horror over Cuba, something they wanted to keep from Washington. Strange, but the other material quickly became public.

When Section DI of SIS listed an inventory of Vassall's Dolphin Square flat, it comprised a Praktina document – copying camera, a Minox and exposed 35mm cassettes recording 176 classified Admiralty and NATO documents. These were hidden in the secret drawer of a fake antique bureau. The contents of his wardrobe were clearly more embarrassing. As were the endorsements given about him by Galbraith and other superiors, who enthusiastically praised his piety and impeccable character. They did not say that he was known around the office as 'Vera, the Admiralty Queen'. This led to a junior witch hunt on the Honourable Thomas Galbraith, heir to the barony of Strathclyde. There was never a homosexual relationship between him and Vassall but there might just as well have been, given the implied innuendo, gossip and many, many newspaper stories. Yet, in 1963, two reporters were jailed for contempt of court for refusing to reveal their sources about Vassall's style and life. Given the details of the Vassall wardrobe and his gentlemanly aspirations, if they employed any rat-like cunning in the affair, the chain-smoking Brendan Mulholland of the *Daily Mail* and the affable Reg Foster of the *Daily Sketch* were not far off the mark. Indeed, a former Special Branch officer, James Francke, said in November 2006 that a colleague of his was the much-maligned reporters' 'Deep Throat'.

Their problem was that their normally inoffensive 'colour' and detail was thoroughly damning of the Security Services and their masters, the Macmillan Government. Vassall was strutting like a peacock at one of Mariella's parties and no one saw any difficulty. Maybe they were wearing masks.

What hurt Macmillan and his Government, what garnered a grudge, was that Galbraith, guilty of no more than gullibility, was hounded from office.

The Establishment attitude to Vassall was gathered concisely in the words of Harold Macmillan, when his spy chief, Roger Hollis of MI5, announced the traitor's arrest: 'When my gamekeeper shoots a fox, he doesn't go and hang it up outside the Master of Foxhounds' drawing room, he buries it out of sight.'

Reviewing the remark, one academic suggested Hollis 'might legitimately have replied that some gamekeepers had the sense to hang the vermin they had shot on the nearest fence to warn off other predators'.

Of which there were many on the trail of Stephen Ward.

CHAPTER FIFTEEN

DOCTOR OF DIPLOMACY

'CLEARLY, OUR SECURITY ARRANGEMENTS
HAVE BEEN UNSATISFACTORY.'

British Postmaster General Reginald Bevins
(following the Great Train Robbery), 8 August 1963

Blithely unaware, Stephen Ward was working in cahoots with the CIA, or at least pursuing the same objectives. Britain had been aghast at President Kennedy's television announcement of the Soviet missile cache being established in Cuba. Some were downright sceptical, others described the reaction as Yankee warmongering.

America, unlike Britain, wasn't a target point for a nuclear missile shower. It was understandable that many agreed with that Tuesday morning's *Daily Mail* leader: 'President Kennedy may have been led more by popular emotion than by calm statesmanship. He has gone too far.'

The *Daily Telegraph* was dismayed by the naval blockade rather than the possible onslaught of a nuclear holocaust: 'In Cuba, the Monroe Doctrine appears to conflict with another and still more venerable principle of American diplomacy – the freedom of the seas'.

Publicly angrier were the 3,000 seemingly professional pacifists who massed outside the American Embassy in Grosvenor Square and struggled with the police. The philosopher Bertrand Russell (at 90, he retained a robust voice as a social critic) cabled America, telling President Kennedy:

YOUR ACTION DESPERATE.
THREAT TO HUMAN SURVIVAL.
NO CONCEIVABLE JUSTIFICATION.
CIVILIZED MAN CONDEMNS IT.
WE WILL NOT HAVE MASS MURDER.
END THIS MADNESS.

President Kennedy was a little less hectic in his response: 'I think your attention might well be directed to the burglars rather than to those who have caught the burglars.'

While this exchange was happening, an American Air Force Boeing was bumping its way across the wintry skies of the Atlantic en route for RAF Greenham Common in Berkshire, almost 50 miles west of London. As a Cold War base for the US Strategic Air Command (SAC), it had command and control of American land-based strategic bomber planes' aircraft and land-based ICBMs.

An appropriate rendezvous.

That afternoon, a dull one in Grosvenor Square with low cloud and the peace protesters having been removed, Ambassador David Bruce took a call from Washington: he was to meet the aircraft and retrieve an urgent package for Harold Macmillan. Advised to arm himself, he took his Service revolver with him. On reaching Greenham Common, he was greeted by a courier, a group of CIA agents and armed aircrew. He was given a parcel containing photographic evidence of the Russian missile build-up on Cuba. He then had talks with the plane's chief passenger, America's former Secretary of State Dean Acheson, one of those central to the establishment of NATO. Kennedy's unofficial adviser's mission was to garner support for the naval blockade from President Charles de Gaulle in Paris and Chancellor Konrad Adenauer in West Germany, but he told Ambassador Bruce that, most importantly, he must persuade Macmillan of the necessity.

With both photographs and a personal letter from Kennedy, it was not hard to convince Macmillan, who had a warm attitude towards the US President, that a threat to the peace of the West was well advanced in the Caribbean. Yet, he had to be careful: the general feeling in the country, and within his Cabinet, was that Moscow would not have pushed its luck so far, been quite so audacious. The official statement was that the Soviet missile build-up was 'a shock to the whole civilised world'. UK Foreign Secretary Lord Home placed Britain, if not quite shoulder to shoulder, nevertheless with America: 'The Communists must not be allowed to filch away free territory from free men. But I've always insisted that, so long as Communist policy is double faced, our response must be double handed. It is our duty to search for areas of agreement.'

In Paris, Dean Acheson talked for an hour in de Gaulle's tapestried office in the Elysee Palace, and the French President said officially: 'We understand your position and we approve the measures you have taken in self-defence.'

At NATO's Paris headquarters, Acheson consulted with ambassadors of all the other 14 NATO nations. They listened without comment, except for an occasional grumble about America not consulting them in advance; they agreed the decision to take drastic steps against Cuba was fully justified. From Paris, Acheson moved on to Bonn, where the veteran Adenauer at first suspected that Kennedy's crisis about Cuba had more to do with the election than with the progress of the Cold War with Russia, and he rather liked the idea; it was the kind of tactic he enjoyed. Defence Minister Franz Josef Strauss saw a cynical deal trading off bases between the USA and Russia, which would weaken his own long-range goal to obtain nuclear missiles for West Germany, a question that had regularly engaged Stephen Ward and Eugene Ivanov.

But, when Strauss and Adenauer studied the photographs of the Russian installations in Cuba, they knew it was all for real, much too real. Adenauer gave President Kennedy his endorsement in a national television broadcast. In West Berlin, part of the city that had suffered so much, households were sufficiently shaken to stock up on food. In Washington, Soviet diplomats were shredding and burning sensitive files. The White House had a list of those who would be allowed into the President's special 'nuke bunker'.

In London, the reaction continued to be careful, and with good reason. Archive documents show tension had been stretching since 25 September, when the Government and Armed Services had been presented with the Joint Intelligence Committee's (JIC) review of Soviet defence policy. The information came from the secret world, from code signals and spies working behind the Iron Curtain. Khrushchev's faction in Moscow, the hawks, were flapping, put on guard by Kennedy's urging of his nation to build nuclear shelters in their backyards: fall-out shelters in major cities were not perceived as idle gestures. Also, like London, in Russia, General Eisenhower was seen as a cool hand, able to control his military machine (young Kennedy hadn't created that sort of credit).

The British group led by Sir Hugh Stephenson, Deputy Under-Secretary at the Foreign Office and Chairman of the JIC, also saw from the JIC review that Russia was swiftly building up its military potential, both nuclear and conventional, especially at sea – a consequence, they supposed, of Kennedy and America's swagger. Yet, Khrushchev's blustering was all mouth and no missiles. He did not have the capability to take out the USA – and many in the Kremlin didn't want him to even try. But – and it was a big but – handing over all of that.

What also cramped the hand of the British was the embarrassment in the days leading up to the discovery of Soviet nuclear plans in Cuba of a UK Intelligence team in Washington. It included Sir Hugh Stephenson, Sir Burke Trend (Macmillan's upcoming Cabinet Secretary) and General Kenneth Strong, the man responsible for the Joint Intelligence Bureau's atomic and missile Intelligence gathering. Throughout their visit, they feverishly maintained the Soviets would never put missiles in Cuba. On 19 October, with a wry grin, Ray Cline, the CIA's Deputy Director for Intelligence, showed them the evidence.

An extraordinary series of moves began. Two super-powers were playing gamesmanship with the planet – gambling, if you like, with mankind. And in the midst of all this was a 50-year-old osteopath with a penchant for young women, for photographing them, for watching them have sex with other men and women, and for attending often quite bizarre sex parties. Also an acquaintance of some world leaders, a friend to others and their entourages, he had sketched the British Royal Family and many famous faces, and walked the red carpet at film and theatre premieres. He had played bridge with luminaries, including the Chancellor of the Exchequer, and smoked dope and caroused in the West Indian clubs of Notting Hill. J. Edgar Hoover of the FBI was on his trail, Frank Wisner of the CIA was watching him, MI5 had interviewed him and, on the morning the Cuban Missile Crisis began, he was gardening at his cottage at Cliveden, one of the most renowned stately homes in England.

Stephen Ward had a remarkable CV but was it enough to prevent the world from being blown up? It seems so ludicrous, fanciful, but for a time he, rather than any celestial power, was part of the juggling act, the powerbrokers with the whole world in their hands. As Soviet ships followed Khrushchev's commands and sailed for Cuba, Ivanov, the Russian voice in London, contacted Ward on 19 October 1962. It is thanks to the diligence of the late Warwick Charlton, the accomplished writer to whom Dr

Ward talked, that we have Ward's first-hand version of the timetable. That Friday, Ivanov invited him to the Soviet Embassy:

At this time Russian ships were on their way to Cuba. A confrontation with American ships seemed inevitable to us all. Eugene said: 'There's something we can do.' He then asked me to convey privately to the British Government a Russian offer to end the threat of war. I did this through Bill Astor who, in turn, put us on to the Earl of Arran and we went over to his place to discuss the matter. Sir Godfrey Nicholson was a party to all this, so I naturally assumed our discussions had some relevance to events. The guts of Eugene's argument was that Khrushchev was prepared to come to London to talk to Macmillan about the crisis. This certainly was important enough to me, and I did my best to get the Foreign Office and the Government to take some notice. Eugene also said that under certain conditions the Russians would be prepared to withdraw their missiles. I at once told all this to the Foreign Office. By the following day we had received no word from the Foreign Office so I took steps to get the information through to Mr Macmillan direct. Ivanov told me that, from what he had heard at his Embassy, the man who was blocking the way was Lord Home who, said Eugene, ran the Foreign Office with an iron hand. I didn't regard my part in this as that of a Russian agent. That would have been nonsensical. I was simply a loyal citizen who happened to have a very good Russian friend who was obviously desperately anxious that East and West should not begin to blow each other up. To me that seemed an entirely sensible desire and I wanted to help in every way I could. Why nobody ever gives me any credit for this I really can't understand. I thought I was being very patriotic.

But this, again, was in a world that didn't trust itself, in an atmosphere where perception was more valued than truth. However, in the charge towards nuclear war and extinction, Stephen Ward played a preventive role: he opened up communications between Moscow and London. Others saw it play out differently to how he described it but the eventful episodes remain the same, despite elaborate and demeaning propaganda over Dr Ward's role, fifth-column stuff that would distort history and severely damage its victim. As details have emerged, so has the extent of the subversion. It is established that Ward believed the British Government was key to breaking the Cuban deadlock. If his actions were tinged with *Boy's Own* hero aspiration, so be it, but he went for it. And he was most certainly entertained by the British Foreign Office, who made time for him and carefully listened to and noted down what he had to say. There was never, ever any official suggestion that he was a time-waster. The opposite, it appeared. He had what Ivanov had worked for: a way to the powerful, access to the decision-makers.

On 24 October, Dr Ward talked to the Foreign Office and explained that Lord Astor had said he should contact Sir Harold Caccia to arrange a peace summit. The duty officer took the call and agreed to relay the message. The next day, Ivanov convened an 'urgent' meeting at Dr Ward's consulting rooms to which Sir Godfrey Nicholson was invited. In *An Affair of State* (1987), Phillip Knightley and Caroline Kennedy reveal a recording of Ward's account of that meeting:

> We listened to Ivanov with growing amazement as he unfolded his suggestion. He said he was empowered by his ambassador to speak for the Soviet Government. There is no doubt at all that this was so. No one from the Soviet Embassy would dare to say this unless it was true. The Soviet Government wished to suggest that a summit conference should be called in London. The British Prime Minister, Harold Macmillan, might or might not attend as he saw fit.

Once the calling of the conference had been agreed, Moscow would stop their ships, at that moment sailing on a collision course with the U.S. Navy.

Sir Godfrey Nicholson took a taxi from Devonshire Street to the Foreign Office with that news, which he gave to his friend and fellow Old Boy (the unofficial network remained effective) of Winchester School, Sir Hugh Stephenson. That positive was countered, as far as Ivanov told Dr Ward, by Lord Home, who had rebuffed Russian approaches that the UK should step in and mediate in the crisis, stop the impending nuclear war. There was a mutual distaste between Lord Home and Ivanov; Home saw Moscow as trying to breach the 'special relationship' between London and Washington. He seems to have been lost about Britain's vulnerability to Soviet missiles and American invincibility – simply, Russian weaponry could not hit the United States, it did not have the range. Far more horrifying was if America, with a nuclear power of 20–1 over Russia, launched a pre-emptive strike.

Much frustrated, Ivanov urged his well-connected friend to aim higher, to 10, Downing Street. Which, with some light relief in such perilous circumstances, brought in the Earl of Arran, an eccentric Old Etonian peer who wrote columns for the *London Evening News* and kept in touch with friends from his diplomatic service.

Dr Ward returned to his home county of Hertfordshire to visit Lord Arran at his country home near Kings Langley. He drove Ivanov, who brought a bottle of vodka. Arran provided rosé wine for Dr Ward and himself; Ivanov stuck to the homegrown.

While they talked for nearly two hours on Saturday, 27 October, the nuclear confrontation on the high seas was storming to a final confrontation: the 'quarantine' of Cuba began on 23 October but Kennedy decided to give Khrushchev more time to consider by pulling the quarantine line back 500 miles. By 24 October, Soviet ships en route to Cuba capable of carrying military cargoes appeared to have slowed down, altered or reversed their course as they approached the quarantine, with the exception of one ship: the tanker *Bucharest*. At the request of more than 40 non-aligned nations, UN Secretary-General U Thant sent private appeals to Kennedy and Khrushchev, urging their Governments to 'refrain from any action that may aggravate the situation and bring with it the risk of war'.

At the direction of the Joint Chiefs of Staff, US military forces went to DEFCON 2, the highest military alert reached post-war, as the commanders prepared for full-scale battle with the Soviet Union.

That day, 24 October, Khrushchev sent a telegraphic message to President Kennedy encouraging Ivanov and Dr Ward's suggestion that a super-power summit meeting be held, the one they were canvassing should be organised in London. The White House reply was an agreement, if the missiles went from Cuba. It was crucial stuff.

On 25 October, the aircraft carrier USS *Essex* and the destroyer USS *Gearing* attempted to intercept the Soviet tanker *Bucharest* as it crossed over the US quarantine of Cuba. The Soviet ship failed to co-operate, but the US Navy deemed it unlikely that the tanker was carrying offensive weapons. On 26 October, Kennedy learned that work on the missile bases was proceeding without interruption, and ExCom considered a US invasion of Cuba. The same day, the Soviets offered a proposal for ending the crisis: the missile bases would be removed in exchange for a US pledge not to invade Cuba. In London, Sir Godfrey Nicholson briefed the Prime Minister on the Ivanov–Ward initiative, something Macmillan noted in his diary.

The next day, as Dr Ward's crisis-summit took place in Hertfordshire, Khrushchev bet heavily by publicly calling for the dismantling of US missile bases in Turkey as part of any peace deal. While Kennedy and his advisers considered this, a U-2 spy plane was shot down over Cuba, and its pilot, Major Rudolf Anderson, killed. The Pentagon wanted to blast Cuba 'off the face of the earth' but the President stopped any military retaliation – unless any more spy planes were attacked. To calm the deadly crisis, Kennedy agreed to dismantle the US missile sites in Turkey at an agreed date, something that appeased Turkey, a key NATO member.

That Saturday night, there was no guarantee of a Sunday morning but the world woke up on 28 October to Khrushchev announcing the Russian intent to dismantle and remove all offensive Soviet weapons in Cuba. With the airing of the public message on Radio Moscow, the USSR confirmed its willingness to engage with the solution secretly proposed by the Americans the day before. In the afternoon, Soviet technicians started taking down the nuclear weaponry while an angry Fidel Castro complained to Moscow.

For the previous, tense days, Moscow had been desperate to get this message, this approach to appeasement, to the masters of world affairs and Stephen Ward had played his role. But the authorities were uncomfortable with it. The backtracking by the Security Services and Government began, which was to be inflamed by the other central figures in the Profumo Affair.

That momentous Saturday/Sunday of the missile crisis was less violent than Christine Keeler's same weekend encounters with Lucky Gordon. Once again, he had stalked her in the street, but this time he knocked her about, punching her on the body and arms, throwing her onto the pavement. Christine complained to Johnny Edgecombe, who saw confrontation as the answer. On the Saturday night, he and Christine visited Lucky's regular haunt, the All Nighter club in Wardour Street. It kicked off immediately. Seeing them, Lucky grabbed a chair and wielded it like a lion tamer at Christine. Edgecombe went for him and all three were rampaging through the club. Lucky tried for the stairs but that getaway was blocked by club bouncers; he turned, cornered, and Edgecombe flicked a knife open and took the blade down Lucky's face, from forehead to chin, deep and painful. The blood spurted through Lucky's fingers, now clamped to his wounds.

As Lucky screamed, 'You'll go inside!', Christine was dragged off into the night by Edgecombe. When they stopped to get his clothes (and Christine's Luger), she phoned Stephen Ward late that night and told him what had happened. Still, Edgecombe forced her to escape with him to a friend's apartment in Brentford, near the Hammersmith flyover.

She had switched one violent lover for another.

It was an increasingly tricky time for Ward. He wanted to help Christine but she was bringing trouble to his door. The political encounters over Cuba had made him more aware of the set-up of Jack Profumo, Christine and Ivanov. Of course, none of them was much good at keeping a low profile. Christine thought she might have her old room back at Wimpole Mews, but Dr Ward had rented it out for £25 a week to an Indian doctor. Anyway, Mandy was using it on and off, as she was on yet another break from Peter Rachman. Ward would see if he could find a flat for her and his friend Rosemary to share. He also arranged for Christine to meet Michael Eddowes, a successful lawyer and businessman who owned the Bistro Vino restaurants, one near South Kensington underground station (he thought Eddowes might have a flat available above one of his restaurants).

Eddowes, 59, had a little more than that in mind and, although Christine did not entertain him in that way, they got on. As she did in a third-floor apartment at 63, Great Cumberland Place, around the corner from Dr Ward, with her new flatmate Rosemary. When she'd left the Brentford flat, she couldn't find her gun – she'd left it under the mattress – but did not make a fuss. She didn't want Edgecombe to know she was going.

Now, all seemed, for this group, relatively calm. Then Lucky

Gordon made a delivery to Wimpole Mews – 17 tiny pieces of gut, the stitches from the wound Edgecombe had scarred across his face.

A nasty punctuation in the events, some of the players believe it was an omen. Nothing did go right from then on.

CHAPTER SIXTEEN

DOCTOR SAVUNDRA

CHRISTINE'S FALLEN OUT WITH LUCKY
JOHNNY'S GOT A GUN
PLEASE PLEASE ME'S NUMBER ONE...
'NOTHING HAS BEEN PROVED', DUSTY SPRINGFIELD AND
THE PET SHOP BOYS, 1989

'Fuck the Cabinet!'
'Fuck Macmillan!'
'I want to play chemmy – Banco!'

Lord Robert Boothby, lover of Lady Macmillan and toy boys supplied by Ronnie Kray, was also a lover of gambling. He and three other members of Harold Macmillan's Government were regulars at the chemmy games organised by society gamblers John Aspinall and John Burke. When the Clermont Club opened on 5 November 1962, he was a guest along with his colleagues, Churchill's son-in-law Christopher Soames, the Duke of Devonshire and Richard Stanley. Boothby did not repeat his cry of an earlier session, when at 8am two of that trio, the Duke and Stanley, were sober and sensible – they were expected at 10, Downing Street to meet the Prime Minister at 10am.

Exuberant and not totally sober, Boothby was clearly enjoying himself. When his Cabinet colleagues tried to induce him to come away with them, he banged the table and shouted: 'Fuck the Cabinet! Fuck Macmillan! I want to play chemmy – Banco!' It was a familiar cry, but he restrained himself as the great and the not-so-good arrived to pay their respects to Aspinall and Burke's remarkable enterprise. The Clermont was something else, rich and fanciful, like much of the clientele, and a monument to perfidy.

Stephen Ward was there, as was his friend Charles Clore, who with Lord Samuel ran a company called Samuel Properties, the owners of the Clermont Club building (they had agreed to lease it to Aspinall for £12,500 a year over two decades). There were many mutual friends around: the buccaneer businessmen James Goldsmith, Gordon White and James Hanson, Lord Bingham (who would become the 7th Earl of Lucan in 1964), 'Lucky' Lucan, playing for the house, Mark Birley, the Duke of Atholl, banker Jocelyn Hambro and champion horse trainer Bernard van Cutsem. John Burke recalled that, as always, the main topic was the gambling, the odds, who was winning or losing. For those there for the glamour not the gaming, there was political chatter – and gossip.

'I knew Christine from Paddy Kennedy's,' Burke told me. 'She would often be in The Star, everybody was. There was certainly talk that evening about her – and Profumo. It didn't seem much of a surprise to anyone that he'd been having an affair. He was known for it; he and his wife were often on the town. It wasn't whispered about like some great secret and I just presumed it was common knowledge, at least around the Commons. It was at the gaming tables, and at the Clermont, that evening. Stephen Ward was at the dinner and the party but spent most of his time talking to an American diplomat.'

That, according to other sources, was Alfred Wells, who acted as secretary to the American Ambassador, David Bruce. Wells is reported to have enquired as to his antecedents but he should have known of him – CIA footage existed (on the orders of Frank Wisner, who had been recalled to Washington). Some of the photographs were shown to a newspaper group executive, John Matthew, according to his son Tom, who told me: 'My father was told that publication of some other pictures which were said to be in circulation would be against national interest. I presume other newspapers got the same information – and warning.'

Although some gossiped about Profumo's affair with Christine, there was said to be one remarkable exchange, one that showed the affair *was* known to MPs. As they strolled up architect William Kent's stunning staircase to the Clermont's Salle Privée, off a landing between the first and second floor at 44, Berkeley Square, Christopher Soames heard the names Keeler and Profumo in the same sentence.

'So what?' he bellowed.

'At least it's a girl.'

'You too could have her for five pounds a go.'

Now, as a former Minister of War, John Profumo had taken over his job when Soames became Minister of Agriculture, Fisheries and Food in 1960, and, as a Privy Council member, Soames was not an idle purveyor of gossip. He knew what was going on. Of course, there is no way to determine for certain how many others did too. He would also be acutely aware of the mundane material handled by the War Minister.

With whom, George Wigg was now obsessed. Six days after the Clermont opening night was Armistice Sunday and Colonel Wigg attended services at Stourbridge, Worcestershire, that 11 November. He was with his constituency party agent, Tommy Friend, and on their return he was told he had received a phone call. No one but his wife Minnie knew of his whereabouts. A bemused Wigg checked and no one had called his home. The phone rang again and an unidentified male voice told him: 'Forget about the Vassall case – look at Profumo.'

Creep? Crank? Or vital information? And ammunition? Colonel Wigg wasn't sure, but he was hopeful.

Fleet Street was also on the alert that something was about to make headlines, but, after the Vassall business, they were hesitant to push their luck – or their lawyers – without hard evidence. They didn't spot Charles Clore leaving the Clermont that evening and, rather than returning to his home at 22, Park Street, going to Wimpole Mews to enjoy an evening of sex with Christine Keeler.

In time, an as-true-as-possible version of events would arrive, along with some intriguing personalities. One of them was Stephen Ward's friend Tom Corbally, an American who was familiar with the Grosvenor Square diplomats and the gaming tables. That November, John Aspinall asked John Burke, who ran the money side of the Clermont, to give money – £3,000 in cash – to Corbally. Burke was puzzled: 'I had no idea what the money was for. John's story was that he had foolishly joined a poker game, but had soon realised that it was not a game in which he would be allowed to win anything. He had wisely left the table, promising to pay what he had already lost. It didn't make a lot of sense – John would have usually asked for a revenge match and fixed the game. Possibly, he was paying off Corbally for someone else. It wasn't a great deal of money in our world.'

Corbally, a former and then freelance CIA employee, knew about Christine, Profumo and the Ivanov spanner in the works. Now released American archive material says he informed Alfred Wells, David Bruce's secretary, and also told the Parliamentary Private Secretary to the Air Minister Hugh Fraser, who had taken over from Profumo's chum Georgie Ward. The documents also indicate Corbally said Macmillan was aware of Profumo's affair with Christine – he had been informed by David Bruce, for whom Corbally had carried out his investigations. His 17-page statement reporting the result of his enquiries is lodged in a Washington vault; most of it, in 2014, remained classified.

Tom Corbally was the loud American. That disguised much of his personality and his quiet activities. He said he knew or could know anyone who mattered – *and* their secrets. J. Edgar Hoover didn't care for him. He was a spook's spook but his own man. Corbally lived a Park Lane lifestyle with no visible signs of income. He was friendly with Stephen Ward (he had spent time at

Spring Cottage) and through him had met Christine Keeler and Mandy Rice-Davies.

Corbally cast a long shadow and there is no definitive on who knew what when, but the circumstantial evidence that November–December in 1962 suggests the Profumo Affair was well known some months before Macmillan and co were 'surprised' by the revelations.

Not much surprised Mandy Rice-Davies but Peter Rachman's death did. He had told her he was dying but she'd ignored him. She was in Paris 'trying her luck' when Rachman succumbed to a giant heart attack on 29 November 1962. Mandy returned from Paris with a stuffed toy for her lover. Stephen Ward met her and gave her the news. She collapsed in a heap of wails and tears. According to Dr Ward, she then asked: 'Did he leave a will?' It was a good line and could easily have come from Mandy.

But doubtful, given what happened next. Distraught, Mandy took about 30 sleeping pills and collapsed on her bed at Wimpole Mews. Christine found her and had her taken to hospital, where the pills and much of her energy were pumped out of her. Christine didn't take Mandy's actions too seriously but, then, neither did Mandy. She kept an eye on her when they returned to Dr Ward's flat but Mandy remained listless and depressed.

Christine tried to cheer her up and together they went to the Kenya Coffee Shop on Marylebone High Street. There, they met Bobby McKew and his friend and business partner, Michael Marion Emil Anacletus Pierre Savundranayagam.

Emil Savundra was a socially and morally depraved fraudster, who was happy to use other people's money to buy sex and sainthood. His girls were just as happy to accept, as was the Roman Catholic Church: it was only the girls who delivered.

McKew was involved in a motor insurance business with Savundra and, in late 1962, financed their offices in Crawford Street, Marylebone – a central point of Stephen Ward's life.

McKew introduced Savundra to Ward and they became friendly, with Savundra also consulting the osteopath after hurting his back in a boating incident. Savundra was a silver-haired chancer, a giant fraudster, but flawed by his own pomposity and self-regard. In Ceylon – Sri Lanka – he had learned the ropes with strange arms deals and even stranger shipping movements. He was jailed in Belgium in 1954 over a cargo of rice for which he was paid, but which never found its way to Antwerp. He then turned up in Ghana four years later as an 'economic adviser' to the poor: his advice was not appreciated, he was deported. He moved on to India, China and a coffee-bean swindle in Costa Rica.

In London, he had cash and plans: car insurance was a booming business, with more cars and improved roads, including motorways. By law, all drivers need minimum insurance, but even that expense was too high for many. Savundra's ploy, picked up from a similar operation in Leicester, offered low-cost policies that, in reality, were worthless; he did not have the resources to meet the claims. But thousands of new drivers wanted to drive, and the little pieces of paper from Savundra's company allowed them to do just that. It was a gold mine dug from others' aspirations and dreams – all Savundra dreamed about was girls.

'He knew every place for a screw in London. We would go out walking and he'd say: "Bobby, have a coffee, wait for me for a minute." With that, he'd be into a doorway, have a fuck, and be back 20 minutes later, talking about his new secretary. He took me to my first brothel, just off Sloane Square. I was with him dozens and dozens of times all over London and most times he popped in somewhere for a fuck. If I asked him if he enjoyed himself, he just put on this silly grin.

'All the time the business [Fire, Auto and Marine finally collapsed in 1966, with 400,000 UK motorists losing out] was building and building. He was a good Catholic – he gave 10 per cent of what he stole to the Church. When he was in jail in Belgium, the Catholic Church put so much pressure on the Belgian

Government that they released him. He looked after the Church; they looked after him.'

Savundra regularly met Stephen Ward at the local coffee shop and that's where he first encountered Christine Keeler and Mandy Rice-Davies.

'I knew the girls,' said Bobby McKew. 'Savundra liked girls' company and I asked them over to join us – a bubbly blonde was always going to make Emil's day. After that he was giving Mandy one for a tenner a pop round at Stephen's.'

The arrangement between Savundra and Rice-Davies has rarely been put so concisely. Those arrangements (with the price raised for some reason) were pivotal to the hidden pressure now building on Stephen Ward. He said he had rented the single room at Wimpole Mews to Savundra for £25 a week, it being a convenient and discreet place for his tenant to indulge himself. The financial arrangement he had with Mandy was that she would contribute £6 a week towards the rent and share the cost of food and the utilities. Ward had no interest in any other cash transaction, although both Christine and Mandy said they would all borrow two or three pounds at a time from each other when they were short and pay it back. It was a flatmate thing, like making sure there was milk for tea in the morning.

And Christine, although not living at Wimpole Mews, was around there much of the time. On 14 December 1962, she went to collect Mandy to go Christmas shopping. Suddenly, with Mandy doing her make-up, there was a ringing: someone was calling WELbeck 6933. Reluctantly, Christine answered. It was Johnny Edgecombe; he wanted to see her. She said she was only there for a minute, visiting Mandy, not living there. They argued. The phone crashed down. Not many minutes later, Joe Winton drove his red mini-cab up Wimpole Mews. His passenger got out and rang the bell of number 17. Mandy opened the door to Edgecombe, told him Christine had gone and slammed the door in his face. He turned but while walking towards the mini-cab he heard a noise at an upper window. Turning again, he saw Christine at the window.

Bedlam bounced between them and then Edgecombe produced a pistol, Christine's Luger, and fired seven bullets: three at the front door and four at the upper window, at Christine. Two shots did superficial damage to the window ledge of next door but no one was injured.

Seconds later, the gun magazine empty, Edgecombe leapt into the car. On being told 'Drive!' Joe Winton crashed into gear and, being in third, bumped off before hitting the right gear and the accelerator. 'The Edge' didn't quite live up to his nickname: although he made it to Brentford, he was arrested there and charged with the Wimpole Mews shooting and the wounding of Lucky Gordon.

Christine, now 20, was perplexed. She took Mandy off to her flat in Great Cumberland Place (Rosemary happily vacated her bed and found another flat). After an initial round of police interviews, they were told that further enquiries would continue in the New Year. It was Christmas time in London, though not a happy time for Johnny Edgecombe.

The next day, the shooting made the front page of the *Daily Telegraph*. Christine looked grand, tall and slim, with the photographers catching her high cheekbones; Mandy looked fun. Edgecombe looked smart when he appeared, the same day as the headlines, at Marlborough Street Magistrates' Court in a dark-blue overcoat, suit and winklepicker black suede shoes. He was accused of shooting at Christine Keeler with intent to murder. Detective Chief Inspector Sidney Bedford said, when charged, Edgecombe told him: 'I understand, sir. I love the girl – I was sick in the stomach over her. I went to see her and, when she came to the window, she would not listen to me and told me to go away. My sickness in the stomach overcame me and I started firing the gun. I am bound to plead guilty.'

He returned to jail on remand and stayed there. The detectives looking into the shooting kept hearing familiar names being associated with Christine and Mandy and Stephen Ward. And, as was the fashion, they would pass on their thoughts at the watering holes around Scotland Yard and the alcoholic ferret run through Fleet Street.

Peter Earle of the *News of the World* and Roy East at *The People* had the thickest chequebooks and would flip them open on the bar of the Magpie and Stump pub, opposite the Old Bailey. Another player, if a little cagier, in chequebook journalism was the *Sunday Pictorial*, about to be retitled the *Sunday Mirror* in 1963, which had a forthright and fun editor, Reg Payne. Such newspapers and editors were not of Stephen Ward's world but his world fascinated them all. With Christine paraded across the news pages following Johnny Edgecombe's gunplay, it heightened the stories of her sleeping with a Government Minister.

An affair she had confessed in detail to Michael Eddowes. When they first met, the wily lawyer had warned that Christine's affairs entangling both Lucky Gordon and Johnny Edgecombe would end with one of them trying to kill her. Lucky used an axe, Edgecombe had shot at her, and that night she telephoned Eddowes for advice. He arranged a meeting with her and, while he served sympathy, Christine poured out the Profumo-Keeler-Ivanov triangle, including highlights of being asked to find out from the Minister of War when America would supply nuclear warheads to West Germany. After her deadly encounters, Christine found it cathartic to discuss her tormented adventures of the previous months. She also confided in Stephen Ward's racing driver friend Paul Mann, and to the remarkably shadowy figure Nina Gadd, who said she was a freelance journalist and could help Christine profit from her story.

Christine believed, correctly, that Ward was distancing himself from her. Ivanov was not around, no one had seen him. On 17 January 1963, the *Guardian* noted in its 'London Letter': 'Commander Eugene Ivanov, the assistant naval attaché at the

Soviet Embassy, quietly left England to return to Russia and how much all his English friends would miss him'. The day that was published, Edgecombe was committed for trial at the Old Bailey on four counts: shooting with intent to kill, shooting with intent to cause grievous bodily harm and two charges involving the possession of a firearm. Keeler appeared as a witness in the committal proceedings and was bound over, on a recognisance of £40, to appear at the trial. It was becoming claustrophobic.

Isolated, Christine and Mandy went to the offices of what was still, just, the *Sunday Pictorial*. The professional Cockney newspaper editor Derek Jameson was picture editor and was with Reg Payne when there was a call to the Editor's office: there were 'two young birds' in the front hall and they would speak only to the Editor.

'Young birds' proved the open sesame. Christine and Mandy appeared in front of Reg Payne. Christine told all, and Jameson reported: 'Reg said: "All very interesting, but where's the proof?"'

'At that, Christine tips the contents of her handbag on to his desk – purse, make-up, keys, the lot – and a letter from John Profumo.

'The first word, "Darling", was enough to ruin him.'

Payne needed little convincing that for 'a young bird' Christine had led a newsworthy life and had a story to tell. She said she was prepared to sell, at a price that almost stopped the interest. But the letter, beginning 'Darling' and signed 'J', kept the chequebook open.

Christine talked about Profumo and Ivanov, and Payne talked to his bosses about the exclusive of the year – 'of the fucking century!' It was good stuff, yet the Radcliffe Tribunal (established in November 1962 by Macmillan to investigate the reporting of the Vassall case) had not just convicted two reporters but also hung a shroud over scoop journalism. Was it worth the risk? Christine might be lying and the letter could be a forgery; the damages for libel that Profumo could collect would be astronomical. Nevertheless, she was paid an advance of £200 against a publication fee of £1,000 and it gave a hint of the possible financial security her story could bring.

Stephen Ward learned about the *Sunday Pictorial* negotiations from Peter Earle, who was attempting a 'spoiler' with Ward's version of events. Fleet Street had the story; it was only a matter of cost, and risk.

Ward recruited lawyer friends and others to prevent publication but all avenues had flaws, the high risk of exposure of the relationships they were attempting to conceal, and he feared for his friends Bill Astor and Profumo, as they feared for themselves. When Ward asked William Rees-Davies – the one-armed lawyer whom Peter Rachman had hired to lobby on the Gambling Act – to act, a legal game of charades began. Representatives of Astor and Profumo, MI5, the Attorney General and three legal firms became involved in what amounted to nothing. The *Sunday Pictorial* did not publish Christine's story – they would print Stephen Ward's 'The Real Christine Keeler' at the conclusion of the Edgecombe trial.

Ward had contacted Reg Payne directly and, while pointing out errors in Christine's account, had offered his own. It provided low risk, high sales and served the purposes of Cecil King, chairman of the newspaper's owners, the International Publishing Corporation (IPC). King was cultivating his new friend Harold Wilson, leader of the Labour Party, following the sudden death of Ward's patient, the respected Hugh Gaitskell, on 18 January 1963. Wilson was seen as 'dry, diligent and devious'. The new Leader of Her Majesty's Opposition was heavily supported by one particular MP: Colonel George Wigg, who had his own friends in Special Branch. Wigg wanted Profumo's scalp, and Payne's scoop was still readily available, begging to be published.

As scalps and scoops tempted, the gallows, if being built slowly, were getting high. On Thursday, 7 February, Commander Evan Jones of Special Branch made direct contact with Sir Roger Hollis. He told the MI5 Director-General that Christine Keeler had made some extraordinary statements on 26 January to officers at Marylebone Lane police station.

The Special Branch Registry accounts, in a laboured way, that 'Christine Keeler said she had once had an affair with the Secretary of State for War, John Profumo, and she had been asked by the Soviet Naval Attaché, with whom she had also been friendly, to obtain details of any deliveries of atomic weapons to West Germany.'

For Sergeant John Burrows, it had been the most surprising result from a routine task. Christine had liked him and volunteered her story, which he hastily handed on, with his notes, to his immediate boss, Detective Inspector Anning. In that report, edited in the Special Branch files, Christine is quoted as talking about 'gentlemen in high places' and sex contacts.

The unedited notes, now available, read: 'She said that Dr Ward was a procurer of women for gentlemen in high places and was sexually perverted; that he had a country cottage at Cliveden to which some of these women were taken to meet important men – the cottage was on the estate of Lord Astor.'

Inspector Anning contacted Detective Inspector Morgan of Special Branch. They arranged a joint interview with Christine on 1 February 1963 – a Friday. But Commander Evan Jones, after discussions within Special Branch, stopped the interview; he knew of the *Sunday Pictorial* debacle and had no interest in Special Branch being inveigled in a political mess.

At Marylebone, the detectives understood this to mean to leave Christine and her stories alone. Detective Sergeant Burrows telephoned Keeler and, without elaborating, said that he would not be visiting her that Friday. Commander Jones had created a security mess. Somewhere, possibly, someone was sensitive for 'gentlemen in high places'.

Special Branch had, after MI5's instructions in 1961, supplied information to the Security Service in regard to Stephen Ward's activities, especially being seen at Russian diplomatic parties. Routinely, they had messaged Curzon Street after the Edgecombe shooting at Wimpole Mews, which Ward had left. To escape the press and other distractions such as Lucky Gordon, he had moved into the Bryanston Mews flat, which he and Christine had been shown round by Peter Rachman when life had been altogether simpler.

What persuaded Commander Jones to tail round to MI5 was direct action by Dr Ward. He had presented himself on 5 February 1963 at Marylebone Lane police station, reporting a journalist had stolen some of his photographs, including one of John Profumo with Christine Keeler. Two days later, Scotland Yard and Evan Jones of Special Branch saw the report. Jones arranged to see Hollis and gave him the police report summarising Ward's allegations. He asked if there was anything MI5 knew that might influence the CID's inquiry. Hollis denied there was any security or Intelligence aspect to the case and told Jones that Profumo was already well aware of the situation. Back at Scotland Yard, Commander Jones compiled a memorandum. Given all that was afoot, it is quite a document:

The facts given in the police report on Ward were already known to MI5 in broad outline. Their principal interest is, of course, the Russian diplomat, whose identity is known to them and in whose activities they are taking an interest. Officially they are not concerned with the Profumo aspect, but they do know that Profumo is aware of the position and that such action as is possible is being taken by his solicitors with the newspaper. They believe it to be true that Profumo has told the Prime Minister of the matter but they do not know that for certain. I think it wise for us to stay out of this business and MI5 agree.

So, Special Branch stayed away; the cops thought they were meant to stay away. A strange affair was becoming even stranger. The purpose of the Special Branch is to enquire into sensitive affairs of state. It had sent on information about Stephen Ward at Soviet cocktail parties – but not Christine's allegations of spying, which Inspector Morgan reported as a possible 'security breach'. This was, at the very least, a serious allegation of espionage against Ward, but the Branch sat on the information for almost a week and then commanded Detective Inspector Morgan to back off, so as not to attract the newspapers. There was much more gossip at the Branch about MI5 than usual, most of it unpleasant. It didn't, and still doesn't, make sense.

Unless you believe that behind the scenes the Establishment puppet-masters were busily taking precautions.

Harold Macmillan was enduring much upset: it was turning into a difficult year. Macmillan was not sentimental. The previous July, he had dismissed seven of his Cabinet in the 'Night of the Long Knives'. Liberal MP Jeremy Thorpe noted Macmillan's ruthlessness: 'Greater love hath no man than to lay down his friends for his life.' Strong as he could be, Macmillan held back on a Profumo witch hunt, although Westminster was wallpapering offices with the story. What his advisers did not know (nor indeed did anyone for decades) was that he had been informed of a potential security risk because of Minister of Transport Ernest Marples' love of prostitutes, and also with 39-year-old Denzil Freeth, MP for Basingstoke and a Parliamentary Secretary at the Ministry of Science, and his indulgence in 'homosexual activities'. Both were open to blackmail and a threat to national security.

It was because of this, and not their sex lives, that MI5 had informed the Prime Minister. You have to think he may have turned over a few pages of *Aeschylus*. Through his inaction, he wasn't being kind to Profumo, he was being careful, pursuing what all politicians crave: survival.

In Edinburgh, the divorce case of the Duke and Duchess of Argyll was progressing slowly through the Court of Session

240

before the brittle, dry and cootish Lord Wheatley. Margaret, Duchess of Argyll, said that most people believed Wheatley 'must have lived an extraordinarily sheltered life'. He might have done so but there were others surprised at one highlight of the divorce hearing, which involved a photo of the ever-frisky Duchess, wearing only a string of pearls and performing oral sex on a man whose head is not visible in the pictures. Later, in a devastating 40,000-word denunciation of the Duchess and moral standards, Lord Wheatley found for Ian, Duke of Argyll. But who was the headless man? It was all anyone wanted to know. Douglas Fairbanks Junior always denied it, even if he went redder in the face than the Duchess. The snag was that she enjoyed performing fellatio and there were other suspects known only to her and themselves. One was the sexual adventurer Duncan Sandys, habitué of Hod Dibben and Mariella 'functions', son-in-law of Churchill; it was difficult for Macmillan when Sandys offered to show him his penis to prove he was not the headless man. That examination was left to a doctor, the exasperation to Macmillan.

Things were not going well.

On 23 January 1963, Harold Kim Philby, longtime suspect superspy and *bon vivant* of the Cambridge Five, vanished from Beirut and his freelance journalist duties, after being presented with new evidence of his treason by SIS agent Nick Elliott. His vanishing act was hidden by the Information Policy Department in London but newspapers kept pressing the Foreign Office for answers. Edward Heath, Lord Privy Seal to the House of Commons, said, on 20 February, that Philby had left the Foreign Service in 1951 and since then had no access to official information. Macmillan and his Cabinet were aware, if not certain, that Philby was with his true masters in Moscow. The reporters in the Vassall case had just gone to jail. And there was another imminent spy problem, one that got somewhat lost in events.

MI5 were on the trail of Dr Giuseppe Martelli, an atomic physicist working for the Atomic Energy Research Authority at

Culham, Berkshire. He was a Russian spy and the Security Services had instructed Special Branch to detain him on nine breaches of the Official Secrets Act.

Another Old Bailey trial and tales of spies and toffs, and quite soon.

While Ted Heath hummed and hawed in the Commons about Philby, the Macmillan troops were deep in despair about one of their own: Jack Profumo, a favoured wartime son of the Prime Minister. Few who knew him or of him, of his style and his reputation, were in any doubt that he had enjoyed a dalliance with Christine Keeler. Profumo was charming with a confident demeanour that belied his political power for he was never going to be the first batsman, somewhere around number seven or eight. But he would be first with the *bon mot*, the opening of the door for a lady, the pulling out of a chair, the turning down of a bedspread.

Which makes it so difficult to explain the apparent ease, the downright sexual naivety, with which Chief Whip Martin Redmayne, Attorney General John Hobson and Solicitor General Peter Rawlinson accepted the War Minister's denial of any hanky panky.

When the story was overwhelming Whitehall, Sir John Hobson invited Profumo to see him and told him what was being said, urging on him the vital importance of 'complete frankness and of telling the whole truth about the matter'. Profumo told the Attorney General the almost endless story: he and his wife had met Miss Keeler, he said, and he had seen her several times at Dr Ward's flat at parties but she was not his mistress, he had not committed adultery with her and no impropriety of any kind had taken place. Sir John said that, if his story was true, then he would have to take proceedings against anyone who repeated any of the rumours. He advised Profumo to get the best legal advice.

Profumo duly enlisted Derek Clogg, senior partner of Theodore Goddard and Company, experts in libel, divorce and cases in which truth and perception, fact and lies often go walkabout.

Clogg was an old-fashioned character and Profumo told him: 'I implore you to believe me because I know how difficult it is going to be to persuade you.' What someone dubbed this 'simulated sincerity', as well as Profumo's undeniable skill at maintaining the same story and threatening all who might print such lies, convinced Clogg, something he told the Attorney General, John Hobson. Putting cream on this pudding of nonsense, Profumo gave instructions to Theodore Goddard and Company that they were to take proceedings for an injunction against any newspaper that planned any story by Christine Keeler claiming any impropriety by him. Interestingly, Solicitor General Rawlinson checked with Theodore Goddard that he had, indeed, done that. Profumo's brazenness wasn't as convincing as he thought.

It was said that Profumo lied from the outset because he feared the wrath of his wife – Valerie Hobson had put him on 'last orders' about his philandering. Yet, he was a man born to believe he could walk on water, could escape any trouble. And Redmayne, according to then Conservative MP Ian Gilmour (Baron Gilmour of Craigmillar), was a dud: 'Profumo asked if he should resign. Probably every other Conservative Whip since the war would have said, "Yes". With his usual lack of judgement, Redmayne said "No".'

Macmillan had made, it seemed, a positive pact with himself to allow 'people of his own age' to quiz Profumo. The Prime Minister knew trouble was on the horizon, but did nothing. A note from his aide John Wyndham provoked dread within Macmillan's Cabinet, the rumour and salacious gossip was like a bunch of vultures. It also concerned the Cabinet so much that Stephen Ward was singled out as *the* person of interest. Released documents show that he – not Profumo, not Christine, nor Lord Astor – was picked as the culprit for all that was wrong. Within a week of the beginning of February 1963, Lord Dilhorne, the Lord Chancellor, had completed an urgent report labelled 'Top Secret' and headed 'The Stephen Ward Case'.

Cabinet minutes show rumours that other senior politicians were involved in bouts of orgiastic sex-and-spying preoccupied high-level discussion at Cabinet meetings. Ministers were nervous of talk of Profumo and Soviet spies, of good-time girls and secrets for sale. Macmillan, it would seem, was out somewhere grazing with the ostriches.

John Wyndham was friendly with Mark Chapman Walker, general manager of the *News of the World* and a former research director at the Conservative Central Office, who gave him information, crafted from memos from his crime man, Peter Earle. From which Wyndham wrote the following memo to the Prime Minister, dated 1 February 1963.

> Top Secret.
> According to Mr Chapman Walker Mr Profumo is alleged to have met this tortuous girl 'Kolania' through Lord Astor at Cliveden, while they chased her naked round the bathing pool.
> According to Mr Chapman Walker is it also alleged that:
> 'Kolania' got him this company through the agency of a Mr Ward, who Mr Chapman Walker described as a 'psychopathic [we must presume he meant osteopathic] specialist' of Wimpole Street.
> Mr Profumo, visiting 'Kolania' in Mr Ward's house, passed in the passage the Russian Naval Attaché on his way out from 'Kolania'.
> 'Kolania' has two letters on War Office paper signed 'J' – although it is not suggested that these letters are anything more than ones of assignation.

Harold Macmillan saw that memo a few days later when he returned to London from economic talks in Rome. He, apparently, ignored it – or took no acknowledged action. We do not have access to three 'Stephen Ward' files (which remain classified), which include the correspondence between MI5 and the Prime Minister about the events before, during and after the Profumo Affair.

At the same time, MI5's Director-General Roger Hollis and the Deputy DG Graham Mitchell agreed to stay out of the Profumo-Keeler-Ivanov equation: they saw no security risk and it was not their job to be sex spies. They issued a directive: 'Until further notice, no approach should be made to anyone in the Ward galere, or to any other outside contact in respect of it. If we are approached, we listen only.'

But Tim Bligh, Macmillan's principal private secretary, and a most astute character, contacted MI5 with the information of Wyndham's memo. The spooks played ping-pong with that and then announced Profumo was 'a political matter' and they wanted nothing to do with it. But Fleet Street did: that first Sunday of February 1963, the *News of the World* displayed Christine in a glorious swimsuit as 'a witness in the Johnny Edgecombe case'.

It was a reminder that, unlike MI5, they were in pursuit.

CHAPTER SEVENTEEN

DOCTOR UNDER THREAT

'ONCE IS HAPPENSTANCE. TWICE IS COINCIDENCE.
THREE TIMES IS ENEMY ACTION.'

Auric Goldfinger, *Goldfinger*, 1959

Stephen Ward, like Harold Macmillan and the Conservative Cabinet, was in a panic. His was a trembling one; the endless cups of coffee and bursts of nicotine were showing at the edges. Ivanov had gone, without even saying goodbye, and this had devastated him. Ward had believed they were the best of friends but he gave the Russian the benefit of the doubt; possibly he had been 'rushed back to Moscow'. He was concerned about what Christine was saying for already the publicity around the Edgecombe shooting was, he felt, harming his osteopathic work. Also, he was never quite certain whether his new patients had bad backs or a deadline to meet.

He tried contacting everyone he knew of influence – Bill Astor and Sir Godfrey Nicholson among them – to get some reassurance of everyone's belief that they were all in it together. He did meet John Profumo at The Dorchester to discuss how to control what Christine might say in her memoirs, or in court. Dr Ward warned Profumo that unless they acted there would be a headline, 'Christine Keeler's Affair with Minister'.

Profumo tapped his forehead with a finger and replied: 'Christine Keeler, who's she?'

Ward hit back, furious: 'Go and ask MI5 who she is! They can tell you; they can tell you when you visited my flat and saw her there.'

They came to no conclusion as to how to act and agreed only that the chief concern was what would be said at the Old Bailey when Edgecombe went on trial. Christine was to be one of the chief witnesses. She was not happy with Ward: among other things, he had cost her £800 from the *Sunday Pictorial*. And he was the man who had brought Lucky Gordon into her life, and what a trail of horror that had been. Ward, who so desired to be inside the loop, was outside.

Despite that, there were many happy to speak with him, especially Harold Wilson's witchfinder, George Wigg. The Labour Opposition were keen, without looking like monsters, to tear apart the Tory Government by taking to pieces their Secretary of State for War, John Profumo, whom many disliked for his 'airs and graces'. It was politics but it was also deeply personal at a time of 'them' and 'us', instantly identifiable by manner and speech. Though not always: man-of-the-people Wilson puffed his pipe on camera, smoked cigars off.

Ward understood that the old guard would rally round Profumo – as they would, of course, around him.

Adding days of stress, Johnny Edgecombe's trial had been delayed because of the illness of taxi driver Joe Winton and was scheduled to begin on 14 March 1963. Before it did, and through a series of juggling deadlines and chance, a Parliamentary broadsheet, *Westminster Confidential*, a political weekly much read by MPs, spilled the Profumo–Keeler story. Andrew Roth, through Parliamentary Profile Service, Ltd., put out in the 8 March 1963 issue a story that MPs were anxious to confirm rumours 'which had run like wildfire through Parliament'.

The piece reported that 'two call-girls came into the limelight as a result of the efforts of a negro to kill them' and went on: 'This notoriety having made their calling difficult, the two girls started selling their stories to the Sunday newspapers, the *Sunday Pictorial* and *The People* in particular. One of the choicest bits in their stories was a letter apparently signed "Jack" on the stationery of the Secretary of State for War.'

No one sued. *Westminster Confidential* was too small a publication, ruled the Attorney General. Any action would simply bring on more questions, he thought. There were quite enough already.

Colonel Wigg added this to his file and confided to his Labour colleagues that he was about to pounce. Some, like the unhappy Chairman of the Labour Party, Richard Crossman, counselled caution. Harold Wilson, a political Pontius Pilate, advised the same but quietly told Wigg that he 'must follow his conscience'. Wigg treated his Special Branch friends to a Hungarian dinner at the Gay Hussar in Greek Street, Soho, and several bottles of heavyweight Bull's Blood wine.

On Thursday, 14 March 1963, Johnny Edgecombe appeared in the dock of the Old Bailey. Christine Keeler, the chief witness against him, was not present. Eight days earlier, the day after Profumo and Ward had met at The Dorchester, she had driven to Spain with Ward's friend Paul Mann and Stork Club camera-girl Kim Proctor. There was a huge sigh of deflation in the Press box where all had hoped for an in-court, and privileged, witness-box confirmation of her affair with John Profumo.

Prosecuting counsel Alastair Morton said the leading Crown witness had disappeared. 'Missing Witness' headlines made it across the evening newspapers. Also absent was taxi driver Joe Winton, still too ill with a stomach ulcer to testify, but it was decided to go ahead with the trial. Someone wanted it over in a hurry; it was.

The two principal charges against Edgecombe – shooting with intent to kill and shooting with intent to cause grievous bodily harm – were dropped.

The next morning, the *Daily Express* ran one of its glory days' front pages: the streamer top of the page shouted: 'PROFUMO: He asks to resign for personal reasons and Macmillan asks him to stay on'. The splash headline: 'WAR MINISTER SHOCK'.

One half of the front page was a double-column picture of Profumo and his wife Valerie Hobson with their political editor Ian Aitken's report on the offer of resignation in the third column. Across the page was a good, three-column photograph of Christine Keeler branded 'Vanished'. There was more to see of Christine in swimsuit poses across the inside pages.

Edgecombe was found guilty of the third charge, possessing a firearm with intent to endanger life. He was jailed for seven years, a long time, and he said it was because 'the British people wouldn't wear a situation where a Government Minister was sleeping with the same chick as a black guy'. His anger was understandable, his seven years a convenient sentence.

Strangely, while the jury were out considering their verdict on the firearms charges, at 3.45pm on a London Friday afternoon, the judge began hearing another charge against Edgecombe: the knife attack on Lucky Gordon. Christine, again the main witness, wasn't present. Edgecombe was acquitted in what looked like a race to get everything closed down before the weekend, or before Christine materialised.

The world was treated to Stephen Ward's story in the *Sunday Pictorial* on 17 March. Headlined 'My Friendship With Christine', it was a tame piece, more to appease than inform: 'To attractive young girls like Christine Keeler London is a battlefield'. He called Christine 'a dear, lost girl', and wrote of his friendship with Ivanov and how he had introduced him to Christine and had been questioned by MI5. There was no reference whatsoever to John Profumo. The article ended with a clearly heartfelt sentiment: 'Friendship can be a dirty word and compassion a crime, the world is becoming more difficult and complex for friendships to survive.'

That weekend, on the Saturday, had also seen a ghosted Mandy Rice-Davies break into print in the *Daily Sketch*. She, like Christine, could become a celebrity. Her heavily legalled article (Profumo's name was excised, he became 'a well-known man'), was run-of-the-mill life-at-the-top stuff but one significant advance was made. Ivanov, now gone, was mentioned by name, the first time he was in the frame publicly. Mandy was ghosted, saying: 'Of course Christine and I thought Eugene may have been a spy, but we would never have told him anything even if we had any information.'

The *Daily Sketch* didn't realise what a breakthrough that was.

Colonel Wigg already did. After several conversations with Harold Wilson, he had refreshed his dossier to reflect the security dangers of the Profumo-Keeler-Ivanov triangle. Wilson and his chums were leaking the Profumo story ('off the record, in confidence, I must say') all over Westminster and the City, and Fleet Street. Wigg was determined that his nemesis John Profumo would not survive. On 21 March, he fired his rockets across the Commons.

MPs were worrying themselves in debate over the rumours surrounding the Vassall Tribunal. 'Rumours' – Wigg liked that word. Late in the evening, just after 11pm, he began speaking about the gossip that had surrounded and disrupted the Vassall case, and rubbing his left elbow in a little nervous tic. He went on: 'Here was a set of rumours that gained and gained in strength, consumed men's reputations – might, in fact, have destroyed them – and which here infringed on the security of the State. But are we quite sure that the same thing is not happening again? There is not an Honourable Member in the House, nor a journalist in the Press Gallery, nor do I believe there is a person in the Public Gallery who, in the last few days, has not heard rumour upon rumour involving a member of the Government Front Bench. The Press has got as near as it could – it has shown itself willing to wound but afraid to strike. This all comes about because of the

Vassall Tribunal. In actual fact, these great Press Lords, these men who control great instruments of public opinion and power, do not have the guts to discharge the duty that they are now claiming for themselves. That being the case, I rightly use the Privilege of the House of Commons – that is what it is given to me for – to ask the Home Secretary, who is the senior member of the Government on the Treasury Bench now, to go to the Dispatch Box – he knows the rumour to which I refer relates to Miss Christine Keeler and Miss Davies and a shooting by a West Indian – and, on behalf of the Government, categorically deny the truth of these rumours. On the other hand, if there is anything in them, I urge him to ask the Prime Minister to do what was not done in the Vassall case – set up a Select Committee so that these things can be dissipated, and the honour of the Minister concerned freed from the imputations and innuendoes that are being spread at the present time.'

Emphasising his concern over 'security matters', Wigg was given support by the previously hesitant Richard Crossman (Coventry East) and the redheaded firebrand Barbara Castle (Blackburn), who also launched in. Before she did so, Northampton Labour MP Reginald Paget provided helpful comic relief for the Government Front Bench: 'What do these rumours amount to? They amount to the fact that a Minister is said to be acquainted with an extremely pretty girl. As far as I am concerned, I should have thought that that was a matter for congratulation rather than inquiry.'

If the just-in-the-job Home Secretary Henry Brooke thought that would settle matters down, he was wrong. Mrs Castle was having none of that: 'It would suit the book of many people, no doubt, to deplore the avidity with which the Press is at this moment pursuing the question of where Miss Christine Keeler has gone – the missing "call girl". If accusations are made that there are people in high places who do know and who are not informing the police, is it not a matter of public interest?'

Without evidence, she had branded Christine a 'call girl'. It was the place of the Home Secretary to reply across the chamber. He seemed to have something caught in his throat, or maybe it was a stiff neck from craning at the benches behind him. Mr Brooke said: 'I do not propose to comment on rumours which have been raised under the cloak of Privilege and safe from any action at law. The Honourable Member for Dudley and the Honourable Member for Blackburn should seek other means of making these insinuations if they are prepared to substantiate them.'

While all this was going on, John Profumo, the boulevardier, was out to dinner. He stopped at the Commons on his way home and spoke with Martin Redmayne, the Chief Whip. Now, Profumo had met with Stephen Ward at The Dorchester to talk tactics about keeping his liaisons with Christine a secret. He had been quizzed by his Government colleagues and was told of Colonel Wigg's questions and remarks. Redmayne added: 'You might have to make a statement.'

Was it arrogance or stupidity? A measure of both, perhaps. The old story, the dog-eared version, goes that Profumo went home and took a sleeping pill. He didn't want to have his wits about him when his house of cards was folding. His career, his marriage, his reputation, his future, his life was on the line – and he took a sleeping pill? Easier to sleep with a clear conscience.

The sleeping pill, of course, was blamed for the great mistake he was about to make but he'd been lying through his teeth for weeks. It is difficult to trust any explanation from Profumo, whose wife, a highly intelligent woman of the world, at this point apparently knew none of it, about why he then behaved as he did. What surely did happen was that the Tory law chiefs and the Chief Whip decided that Profumo must make a Commons statement that Friday morning at 11am and, in so doing, cut out this particular 'cancer of lies' surrounding their Minister of War.

Macmillan was contacted, he was at Pratt's, and agreed the

form of Profumo's personal statement. His Praetorian Guard was ready for action at 1.30am. The Chief Whip's messenger served them whiskies.

Profumo, supposedly sleepy and groggy, was telephoned and told to get to the Commons, where he arrived at 2.50am. Arriving separately was his lawyer, a somewhat grumpy and genuinely sleepy Derek Clogg.

Mr Clogg provided the grave, fed-up face for all those in the private room at the Palace of Westminster at the twilight hour of 3am. There, with Attorney General Hobson and Solicitor General Rawlinson and the bewildering Martin Redmayne, were Iain Macleod, Thursday Club member and Leader of the House, and William Deedes, the toothy Minister Without Portfolio who, in reality, was Macmillan's PR man. They compiled an extraordinary statement, in which almost all was true, and it was typed out by Bill Deedes, who like Hobson had been at Harrow with Profumo, in his own office with Peter Rawlinson at his shoulder.

There are many versions of what happened that evening, many assumptions. The most convincing is that the Government team were not there to act as an inquisition on Profumo but to create a statement that, if they did not stop the gossip, would end the threat of harming the Government. They had unquestioningly accepted Profumo's word that he had not slept with Christine. Survival of all was key. Iain Macleod was an exception in the soft treatment of Profumo, buttonholing him with what everyone really wanted to know: 'Look, Jack, the basic question is: did you fuck her?'

Profumo: 'No, Iain, no.'

What other questions there were of Profumo were aimed with the intention of drafting his personal statement. Yes, he had written the letter to Christine. 'Darling' was a common term of greeting in the theatrical world, where he and his wife often mixed. These men, accustomed to slipping off for the weekend on a Thursday evening, simply wanted to get the statement written and approved.

There were only a couple of moments of pause. Profumo did not like the sentence 'Miss Keeler and I were on friendly terms', telling his colleagues: 'It sounds so awful!' What they made of that is not recorded anywhere. But he had been adamant: anyone repeating the allegations would be covered in writs; his word was that of a gentleman and a Member of the House of Commons. An MP, for goodness sake!

Simple souls, or conspirators? When William Deedes had gone from 'Dear Bill' in *Private Eye* to Lord Deedes and himself a 'darling' in the *Daily Telegraph*, I talked to him about appearing in a television documentary on the Profumo business. He was affability in the extreme until the question of Profumo's statement, the one he had typed, came up. 'It's a very sexy story, old boy, good luck,' he said, cutting the conversation off.

Earlier, in his 1997 autobiography, he had dismissed as 'rubbish' the suggestion by the eminent scholar and historian Richard Lamb that he and the others had 'blithely accepted Profumo's improbable denial as gospel truth'.

Once the statement, a masterpiece whatever its veracity, was complete, Solicitor General Sir Peter Rawlinson officially warned Profumo: 'You must realise that you are making a statement that there is no truth whatever in any of these allegations. Supposing that there is, for the rest of your life, you will be submitting yourself to blackmail.'

Profumo stared him in the face: 'I quite realise that, but, as it is all true, I have nothing to fear.'

What was quaint was that no one thought to question Christine Keeler, or Lord Astor or anyone else, about the relationship: they had the means of Scotland Yard, Special Branch, MI5 and all the other alphabet-adorned departments the public are not meant to know anything about. And how had Christine been able to describe to detectives the interior make-up of Profumo's home?

Harold Macmillan was given the personal statement at 9.30am on 22 March, only five hours after it had been signed off, 90 minutes before the immaculately tailored Profumo, pale-faced against his dark suit, rose to deliver it in the Commons. He looked to Macmillan, sitting supportively beside him on the Front Bench, and then to the Speaker, Sir Harry Hylton-Foster:

With permission, Sir, I wish to make a personal statement.

I understand that in the debate on the Consolidated Fund Bill last night, under protection of Parliamentary privilege, the Hon. Gentlemen the Members for Dudley and for Coventry East and the Hon. Lady the Member for Blackburn, opposite, spoke of rumours connecting a Minister with a Miss Keeler and a recent trial at the Central Criminal Court. It was alleged that people in high places might have been responsible for concealing information concerning the disappearance of a witness and the perversion of justice. I understand that my name has been connected with the rumours about the disappearance of Miss Keeler. I would like to take this opportunity of making a personal statement about these matters. I last saw Miss Keeler in December 1961, and I have not seen her since. I have no idea where she is now. Any suggestion that I was in any way connected with or responsible for her absence from the trial at the Old Bailey is wholly and completely untrue.

My wife and I first met Miss Keeler at a house party in July 1961, at Cliveden. Among a number of people there was Dr Stephen Ward, whom we already knew slightly, and a Mr Ivanov, who was an attaché at the Russian Embassy. The only other occasion that my wife and I met Mr Ivanov was for a moment at the official reception for Major Gagarin at the Soviet Embassy. My wife and I had a standing invitation to visit Dr Ward.

Between July and December 1961, I met Miss Keeler on about half a dozen occasions at Dr Ward's flat, when I called to see him and his friends. Miss Keeler and I were on friendly terms.

There was no impropriety whatsoever in my acquaintance-ship with Miss Keeler.

Mr Speaker, I have made this personal statement because of what was said in the House last evening by the three Hon. Members, and which, of course, was protected by privilege. I shall not hesitate to issue writs for libel and slander if scandalous allegations are made or repeated outside the House.

As he sat down, Macmillan confidently clapped him on the shoulder. He smiled through, presumably, clenched teeth. If MI5 hadn't told him the details of true facts, he had been given the information, via the CIA, from American Ambassador David Bruce. There was no clue as to the thoughts of Valerie Hobson, who was watching and listening from the Distinguished Strangers' Gallery. If this was a steeplechase, Profumo had cleared all the hurdles. That afternoon, he took his wife to the races and joined the Queen Mother's group at Sandown Park. He placed a bet at 10–1 on a horse called Baxter, which won the Grand Military Gold Cup. A lucky day – that's what 'Lucky' Gordon's parents thought the day they won the lottery and bad news, for many people, was born.

That evening, Mr and Mrs Profumo were applauded when they attended a fund-raiser for the Hatch End Conservative Party at Quaglino's restaurant in Mayfair. It was a champagne event.

Profumo's remarks in the Commons as a personal statement had, by tradition, not been open to debate. The matter seemed to have been nailed but the late Ian Gilmour, onetime owner of *The Spectator* and a crucially shrewd observer, a hugely intelligent man, nailed it better in reflection of that long day of 22 March 1963:

The real errors of judgment that fuelled the Profumo affair took place before and after that night. The first mistake was Macmillan's. John Vassall worked in the private office of a senior Tory MP, Tam Galbraith, who was Civil Lord of the Admiralty. The Press and the Opposition did everything they could to talk up the connection, and on the basis of a couple of handwritten notes it was suggested Galbraith was Vassall's Whitehall protector and probably his lover.

Macmillan, distracted and impatient, demanded Galbraith's resignation. Afterwards he felt he had been bullied into sacrificing an innocent man. He was determined not to make the same mistake again. When the rumours started up about Profumo, he let it be known that it was time to hold firm. His Ministers, in believing Profumo's denials, were doing what their master wanted. Macmillan was standing up to the tittle-tattles in the Press and on the Opposition benches, which is all well and good, so long as what they say doesn't happen to be true. The experience of having disbelieved an honest man persuaded the Government to put its faith in a liar.

It is a plausible theory but Macmillan had shown just how ruthless he could be in the quest to stay in power. Breeding will out and, in this political breed, it is likely he was not haunted by Galbraith but by the thought that Profumo's sex life linked in with Soviet spies would rain all over 10, Downing Street, and wash his Administration away down Westminster.

Always the Edwardian gentleman, Harold Macmillan was also an old soldier, a fighter. Archive documents now show he was willing to break the law to prevent any premature departure of his Government. And, if he'd only known that, Stephen Ward might have escaped his day in court.

CHAPTER EIGHTEEN

DOCTOR IN THE FRAME

'THE EXPRESS HAVE GOT THE MOTHER.'

1960s Fleet Street lament

The *Daily Express* found Christine Keeler and a couple of bullfighters in Spain, three days after John Profumo's denials in the Commons. The kindly, affable reporter Frank Howitt took her for a glass or ten of sangria. Frank liked the wine, Christine the idea of the £2,000 on offer for her story. They got on well. Not all Press men were as clever and easy-going as Howitt, a listener who won his exclusives through stealth rather than aggression, though.

The Fleet Street suede shoe brigade stamping all over Spain spooked Christine and her friends to plan a return to England with the money; the *Daily Express* had also roped in her mother, Julie Payne Huish, and taken her to a London hotel hideaway. Like Stephen Ward, Christine kept publicly to the party line that there had been nothing 'improper' between her and Profumo. Others, though terrified to print it, were told the truth. Ward was still trying to keep the lid on this – for his friends.

'He never for a moment thought he was at any risk,' said Bobby McKew.

Leonard Plugge, son of the onetime owner of the building that is home to Les Ambassadeurs, was still seeing Dr Ward for bridge evenings, and said in 2013: 'He was a kindly person, always wanting to help, and there was never any sign he was troubled. He was in control. He had no reason to feel under threat, he'd done nothing wrong.'

Yet, it was through his effort to help his friends that Dr Ward became further drawn into a conspiracy not of his own making. On 25 March 1963, Colonel Wigg appeared on the BBC's flagship programme *Panorama* to discuss all things Profumo. He described Ivanov as a high-spending Russian he wanted more information about, and also stated he believed Ivanov and Dr Ward (whom Profumo said he knew) were security risks.

Ward was furious: not at his being called a security risk, but at Ivanov being described as an ostentatious, big-spending Russian. The next morning, he telephoned Wigg's office and they arranged to meet at the Commons that evening. It was an intriguing encounter, a little gladiatorial, but Colonel Wigg got the lion's share. Dr Ward explained he had written to Harold Wilson about his and Ivanov's failed joint action to get Lord Home to mediate over Cuba, in an effort made through Bill Astor and Lord Arran. In the three-hour meeting, of which there is no official record, it seems Dr Ward tried to make it explicitly clear that his efforts were in Britain's, and the world's, best interests. This was no solo Soviet enterprise.

Wigg added this to his Ward/Profumo/Wigg file; the cast was growing. When Harold Wilson was shown the dossier that April, he proffered: 'It is a nauseating document taking the lid off a corner of the London underworld of vice, dope, marijuana, blackmail and counter-blackmail, violence, petty crime, together with references to Mr Profumo and the Soviet attaché.'

Crafty as ever, Wilson did not immediately send the Wigg dossier to the Prime Minister; he sent instead, months after he had received it, Dr Ward's original letter about the Cuban Missile Crisis.

Real life interfered with all the political flapping around. In May of that momentous 1963, Lucky Gordon attacked Christine outside Paula Hamilton-Marshall's flat and she was badly hurt, suffering a black eye and terrible bruising to her face and arms. Gordon was arrested and sent for trial on 5 June 1963. It was yet another reminder of the problem and Home Secretary Henry Brooke decided he knew who was to blame, who must be stricken from the scenario.

He put Dr Stephen Ward in the spotlight.

And sinister happenings began.

The timing cannot be precise but dirty tricks unfolded from the beginning of April, shortly after Henry Brooke chaired a meeting with the Metropolitan Commissioner Sir Joseph Simpson, MI5's Roger Hollis and his own Parliamentary Under-Secretary, Sir Charles Cunningham. Unusually, the presence of Evan Jones or the Assistant Commissioner (Crime), Sir Ranulph Bacon, was not requested. The Home Secretary knew that Stephen Ward was talking, and had spoken with Colonel Wigg. The Labour Opposition was informed in writing by Wigg, in a note with his dossier: 'In my opinion Profumo was never, at any time, a security risk.' That was dated 29 March 1963, but Wigg's later actions did not reflect this belief.

Whatever the security question, Home Secretary Henry Brooke was convinced the answer was to silence Stephen Ward – or ensure anything he claimed was discounted; this could perhaps be done by jailing him under the Official Secrets Act. MI5's Roger Hollis told him this was unlikely. The Met Commissioner Sir Joseph Simpson suggested there might be some merit in pursuing Ward for living on immoral earnings, yet this was also deemed difficult. Nevertheless, as documents show, the Metropolitan Police were instructed to get Stephen Ward.

Meanwhile, Henry Brooke was under pressure from all corners, not least Macmillan. The FBI were building their 'Bowtie' file and President Kennedy's Attorney General brother Robert Kennedy was concerned JFK might be dragged into the Profumo Affair; had he slept with Christine, Mandy, Mariella or anyone else? Would he know? It was important, for President Kennedy was scheduled to visit Macmillan and Britain at the end of June.

The FBI's J. Edgar Hoover was put on the case. Yet, David Bruce and the CIA operatives still following the recalled Frank Wisner's instructions were on location with events in London. The CIA knew more than most through the efforts of Wisner. And others. Douglas Fairbanks Junior had fed them lots of dubious information implicating most of Westminster (though not himself) in sex parties. Bruce's man Tom Corbally was great friends with Irishman Johnny Francis, who after falling out with the Kray Twins had moved to America, where he had been 'adopted' by Angelo Bruno, one of the most powerful Mafia dons of the day. In the spring of 1963, Bruno was quietly in London on business. That Francis connection gave the CIA inside information on prostitution, pornography and all related sex businesses being operated in the UK by the Mob. Some intriguing names were involved, some with priceless pornography collections, and there was grave concern that names would be made public. David Bruce was also clued in.

But it was from the solicitor Michael Eddowes, self-appointed guardian of the nation, that Henry Brooke would get the fantasies to feed his already paranoiac appetite. Eddowes was barking mad with his mania… It didn't seem to matter to Brooke. Eddowes was a solicitor, for goodness sake! And he had talked to Christine Keeler; he was in the know. And Brooke was the Home Secretary.

Michael Eddowes' hysterical claims that there was a KGB worldwide conspiracy, Stephen Ward and Peter Rachman were running an espionage call-girl ring in London and New York, Rachman was an Italian Mafia Don and involved in the secret disappearance of the world's first nuclear submarine would, one might have thought, have had Brooke reaching for the salt cellar. Instead, he told his aides that Eddowes 'knows a lot about Stephen Ward'.

So, that was all that mattered.

And, in consequence, Profumo too was finished.

On 23 April 1963, Mandy Rice-Davies was on her way to Palma, Majorca, to marry the son of a Spanish Duke, Don Jose Francisco Conrado de Villalonga, but, before her flight left, she was arrested. At West London Magistrates' Court, she kicked her white heels for almost five hours before being taken to spend the night in Holloway Prison. In the morning, the court heard the charge that she had 'a document so closely resembling a driving licence as to be calculated to deceive'. Mandy was then served with a summons saying she had made a false statement to get car insurance. The police asked for her to be remanded in custody – there were other offences to be considered. Magistrate Seymour Collins fixed bail at the enormous £2,000 (for motoring offences!), which Mandy simply didn't have. She spent a week in Holloway.

On 30 April, at West London Magistrates' Court, she was fined £42 for five motoring offences. Mandy lost her fiancé and any illusions she had left. The fine, tiny compared to the bail amount, reflected the sledgehammer approach of the Metropolitan Police – acting, of course, under instruction. But, when you run into the china shop, there's no telling what might break.

While in Holloway, Mandy had been visited by Detective Chief Inspector Samuel Herbert of Scotland Yard's Vice Squad, who, with his sidekick Detective Sergeant John Burrows, was looking into the affairs of a certain Stephen Ward. Two other detectives, Sergeants Arthur Eustace and Mike Glasse, were 'tailing' Dr Ward and his known associates.

At that point with the motoring charges hanging over her, Burrows had Mandy in a corner. She was told that Christine Keeler had also been quizzed in this sudden tortuous exercise to find something 'to get Stephen Ward'. Christine, obviously, was the first contact. Burrows had rattled her cage by saying they were looking into spying and she might be jailed under the Official

Secrets Act. This prompted her to say on the record that it was Dr Ward who had asked her to get information from Profumo about nuclear warheads for West Germany. Although she was wary, estranged from Stephen Ward, this questioning made Christine contact him. He knew she had said things that might compromise him but let it go; the police did not. At Marylebone police station, Burrows and Herbert did the 'good cop, bad cop' act with Christine, where she was endlessly questioned by them, turned in circles, made to sign off on names of men she had met, men she'd had sex with, talk of Dr Ward and Lord Astor, and everyone else she had met: of Profumo and Ivanov and Michael Eddowes, of Mandy and Peter Rachman and Paula Hamilton-Marshall; of Kim Proctor, Nina Gadd and Paul Mann. In his tweed jacket, Herbert was the unsettling one.

Christine was in a chorus line of confusion. And that's when you get the high kicks and the detectives knew it. They said Lucky Gordon wouldn't be in custody forever; they gave her a warm glass of water, an uncomfortable chair and a view of a blank off-white wall. For two days, the questions went on, and at some point she said that Dr Ward had brought home 'Charles', whom she liked and had sex with. Also, that she had gone round to see Charles (she didn't identify him as the property tycoon Charles Clore) to borrow some money at Ward's suggestion.

It was with this background that the intrepid detectives questioned Mandy. She reported: 'I was ready to kick the system any way I could but ten days of being locked up alters the perspective. Anger was replaced by fear. I was ready to do anything to get out.'

Herbert told her: 'Mandy, you don't like it in here very much, do you? So you help us, and we'll help you.'

Mandy kept her side of the bargain. She said: 'Although I was certain nothing I could say about Stephen could damage him in any way – he was peculiar, certainly, but that doesn't mean criminally so – I felt I was being coerced into something, being pointed in a predetermined direction. The prospect of perhaps having to spend a further spell in Holloway over the motoring offence was enough to convince me to keep on the right side of the police. I felt like a cornered animal. I told them all they wanted to know.'

Another stroke by the investigating officers was that, after Mandy walked away from her car charges, they stopped her again and charged her with the theft of an £82 rental television. They also confiscated her passport: she could remain free but had to report at a later date. In the weeks that followed, Christine was formally interviewed 26 times, and detectives questioned more than 130 people in their desperate search for evidence – to bring any charge they could against Stephen Ward. One person interviewed was a prostitute called Vickie Barrett, a young, sad girl. She'd been charged with soliciting and the police said Dr Ward's phone number had been found in her diary. Yes, he was a regular customer and she'd had sex with him at his flat and sometimes whipped him. She was pressured to say in statements she'd serviced other men at Wimpole Mews. As was another street girl, Ronna Ricardo, who was intimidated into believing that her baby and younger sister would be taken away from her by the Social Services.

Meanwhile, Stephen Ward was receiving constant messages that friends like Beecher Moore and his patients were being interviewed by the police. He went straight to the top and telephoned Harold Macmillan's office. The Prime Minister thought it wise to listen – and had his private secretary Tim Bligh do so. The details (revealed in a verbatim transcript only decades later) make a mockery of contemporary accounts of the meeting and the claim that Stephen Ward attempted to blackmail the British Government to stop the police investigations of him.

Indeed, he made no such demands. The documents still have redactions, 'of the sensitive information which Bligh revealed to

Dr Ward'. Sir Timothy's files show that Stephen Ward rang at 3.45pm on 7 May to make an appointment, and Bligh agreed to see him at 9pm. Most of what he had to say took the form of complaints about the enquiries that the police were making about him; he was plainly told this was not the concern of the Prime Minister. However, he said that John Profumo had lied to the House of Commons about his relationship with Christine Keeler. The conversation began with Ward asking Bligh: 'How many of the facts do you actually know of the situation as it really exists?'

Bligh said he had seen the newspapers.

Ward offered to tell him the true facts. He made it clear that he did not wish to talk about security matters – 'You see the facts as presented probably in Parliament were not strictly speaking just like that, I fear. I fear a change may be forced in the situation. It's very difficult for me to say – you can see the only way in which I can save the situation, I don't know, I came to you in considerable distress with this enormous pressure being put on me all round, enormous pressure. I don't know if you know the extent of the sacrifice I did make for him, or have any idea of it. And the consequence is that I am being absolutely driven into the ground, and wondered if there was any possible thing you could do to prevent this happening?'

Ward said all his friends were being hassled about security. 'If you don't know the true story, it's impossible to understand exactly how this situation has come about, and I'm not sure if I should tell you or not… I'm quite prepared to tell you.'

Quite suddenly, he then blurted out that his lawyers had been in contact with Mr Profumo – 'He wrote Miss Keeler a series of letters. The attachment was a much deeper one than…'

Just as suddenly, Bligh paused Ward, and said he would start taking notes as he went on: 'He wrote, I think five letters in all [to Keeler]. Two I was able to destroy – I just found them lying around. There's no reason on earth why… she attached no value to them at all. And I didn't read them – I don't know what they were at all. One was destroyed by somebody called Lambton [Christine Keeler's friend Michael Lambton]. And one I haven't been able to track down – it doesn't seem to be in existence. And one was sold to the *Sunday Pictorial*. Did you know about this?'

'Well, no, I didn't know anything about this case at all.'

Ward then said he had made his 'sacrifice' for Profumo, in allowing the paper to publish an article purporting to be by him in exchange for the letter. But by then the letter had been seen by the Labour MP George Wigg and others, and the rumour of the affair spread in Fleet Street. Bligh said he was not clear how he could help. Ward told him he was interested in clearing his name; he wanted to stop the Fleet Street rumours. He asked if Ivanov was a security risk. (The reply has been censored and remains so more than half a century on.) Ward said: 'I personally was very fond of the Russian. I hope he wasn't a spy or anything dreadful.'

They continued to discuss Ivanov's role for two pages of text (all of Bligh's side of the discussion has been removed). Then they returned to considering how Bligh might help clear Ward's name. Ward suggested 'a statement in the House, something of that sort'. Bligh said: 'Lots of people ring up and say can they come and see me, but they don't always bring the problems I can help with. It's just one of those… with the best will in the world, I don't see that there is anything…'

Ward then made the nearest he comes to a threat: 'What you are really saying is there's no possible statement or anything that would allow me to drop my libel actions, which would obviously be embarrassing or anything like this.'

Bligh: 'No. I think that one must proceed with the normal remedies that are open to a citizen of this country. That's all you can do.'

Dr Ward: 'Well, I'm sorry. I didn't come here to make any demands. I just sort of hoped, but obviously I'm not in a position to, but anyway I'm sure you knew all those facts, you must have done, but it is interesting to compare them with your own conclusions as to whether they fit.'

Bligh said he had to get back to the Commons.

Dr Ward ended: 'I didn't really come here with the intention of telling tales out of school... I'd prefer you did preserve confidence as far as Mr Profumo is concerned.'

Sir Timothy Bligh (whose portrait now hangs in the National Gallery, with Christine Keeler's) did his duty. He immediately sent his notes of the conversation to the Prime Minister and the Commissioner of the Metropolitan Police, Sir Joseph Simpson. The next day he sent a full transcript to Sir Roger Hollis, head of MI5. Pauses in the transcript suggest their conversation was taped. Bligh took a full note of the meeting.

With no joy from this encounter, Ward sent off letters to the Home Secretary, Mr Henry Brooke, his own Marylebone MP, Sir Wavell Wakefield, and to Harold Wilson. Still nothing, but he believed that whenever Bill Astor returned from America all would be well. Yet, his letter to the Home Secretary revealed his frustration – and his savvy that the man persecuting him was the one with whom he was corresponding: 'It has come to my attention that Marylebone police are questioning my patients and friends, in a line however tactful which is extremely damaging to me both professionally and socially. This inquiry has been going on day after day for weeks. The instruction to do this must have come from the Home Office.

'Over the past few weeks I have done what I could to shield Mr Profumo from his indiscretion, about which I complained to the Security Service at the time. When he made a statement in Parliament I backed it up although I knew it to be untrue. Possibly my efforts to conceal his past and to return to him a letter which Miss Keeler had sold to the *Sunday Pictorial* might make it appear that I have something to conceal. I have not.

'The allegations which appear to be the cause of the investigation, and which I only know through the line of questioning repeated to me, are malicious and entirely false. It is an invention of the Press that Miss Keeler knew a lot of important people. It was by accident that she met Mr Profumo and through Lord Astor that she met him again. I intend to take the blame no longer. That I was against this liaison is a matter of record in the War Office. Sir Godfrey Nicholson who has been a friend of mine for twenty-five years is in possession of most of the facts since I consulted him at an early stage. May I ask that the person who has lodged the false information against me should be prosecuted.'

Dumbfounded by no reaction whatsoever, he issued a press statement on 21 May: 'I have placed before the Home Secretary certain facts of the relationship between Miss Christine Keeler and Mr John Profumo, the War Minister, since it is obvious now that my efforts to conceal these facts in the interests of Mr Profumo and the Government made it appear that I myself have something to hide – which I have not. The result has been that I have been persecuted in a variety of ways causing damage not only to myself but to my friends and patients – a state of affairs I propose to tolerate no longer.'

Not one newspaper published anything other than the fact that Dr Ward had written to the Home Secretary. But it was all running riot. Harold Wilson was getting pressure from his MPs and Wilson was pressing Macmillan. It seemed there was nothing going except 'this bloody Profumo business'. Which for Burrows and Herbert there was not. They had talked to Bill Astor and found he'd paid a cheque to meet Christine and Mandy's rent at Comeragh Road. That meant, in their minds, that Astor was guilty of running a brothel and the girls had had sex there for money. Someone in the Met hierarchy had a quiet word with them about that line of inquiry.

Harold Macmillan was increasingly seeing Stephen Ward, not John Profumo, as the main problem. He wanted time to circle his troops, to engage in defence manoeuvres that would protect his ministers and his Government. But there was more to dismay him and lead him close to a criminal move. His concern made him summon Sir Roger Hollis, and the head of MI5 admitted all they knew, much that Macmillan and his private secretary Timothy Bligh did not.

It was a most difficult time. MI5 and MI6 were in a down period. Oleg Vladimirovich Penkovsky had finally been trapped by Moscow, following 16 months of spying for the CIA and MI6, and, after a show trial (something that could never happen in Britain?), he was shot on 16 May 1963. Businessman-spy Greville Wynne who'd been part of that courtroom circus got eight years in jail but returned to Britain a broken man after only eleven months, exchanged for Gordon Lonsdale, aka Konon Trofimovich Molody, controller of the Portland spy lovers Harry Houghton and Bunty Gee.

In the midst of all this, Labour MP James Chuter Ede tabled a question for Henry Brooke, asking for the details provided by Dr Ward. The question was up for reply on 20 June, only days before President Kennedy arrived to visit his friend Harold Macmillan.

The 69-year-old British Prime Minister was lost for words, much as he had been when he met Kennedy for the first time in Key West in March 1961. Then, during a break in nuclear arms discussion, JFK enquired: 'I wonder how it is with you, Harold? If I don't have a woman for three days, I get a terrible headache.'

Now, a little more than two years later, sex had given Macmillan a much more powerful headache.

CHAPTER NINETEEN

DOCTOR IN THE SPOTLIGHT

'IS THAT CHRISTINE KEELER?' ASKED A
SPECTATOR. 'NO,' SAID HIS NEIGHBOUR, '
ONLY ELIZABETH TAYLOR.'

Exchange at the Cassius Clay/Henry Cooper fight at
Wembley Stadium, 18 June 1963

Henry Brooke, a headache for all he encountered, became British Home Secretary after everyone else was sacked. He was possibly the worst performer in that job in the twentieth century. Unlike Profumo, he was a defender of former Prime Minister Neville Chamberlain, and landed his senior position following Macmillan's 'Night of the Long Knives' in the summer of 1962.

He got off to a bad start, messing up the security arrangements for a State visit from King Paul and Queen Frederica of Greece. That over, he got it very wrong in the case of a 22-year-old Jamaican woman called Carmen Bryan. She'd pleaded guilty at Paddington Magistrates' Court on 12 June 1963 to petty larceny, shoplifting £2 worth of food because she was hungry. The magistrates were harsh – deportation. And no bail, no appeal. Bryan was sent to Holloway Prison for six weeks to allow time for her to be formally ejected from Britain.

Brooke couldn't understand the provocative headlines and the anger of Parliament, whom he told on 19 July that year: 'I think it would be a great act of injustice if I were to stand in the way of her returning to Jamaica. I am not prepared to look at this case again.'

Someone had a word. Bryan was freed on 30 July and allowed to stay in Britain, and the law changed; deportations for misdemeanours were stopped. The late presenter David Frost on the BBC's *That Was The Week That Was* named Brooke 'the most hated man in Britain' and ended a mock profile of him with: 'If you're Home Secretary, you can get away with murder.' Brooke was the last Home Secretary to allow the death penalty to be carried out; he was not the man to let Stephen Ward off the hook.

Especially with such unprecedented Parliamentary pressure. The Commons was a scabrous hothouse. And Question Time on John Profumo was looming. As May 1963 was ending, Profumo asked to see the Prime Minister, but Macmillan had packed his plus-fours and was in Scotland, playing golf at Gleneagles. Profumo did an extraordinary, and very English, thing: he went on holiday too. It is a remarkable English trait that nothing disrupts a holiday, even calamity. The War Minister was photographed in a Venice gondola. But Profumo, with wife Valerie Hobson, abandoned his time around the Grand Canal earlier than planned. He was scheduled to have a meeting with Lord Dilhorne, who was pursuing his official inquiry, on 6 June, a Thursday. The Lord Chancellor asked if he could return to be interviewed on the Wednesday. Profumo therefore returned to London on the Bank Holiday Whit Monday.

It was always understood that he had told Hobson that weekend in Venice that he had lied in the Commons: any reasonable person would believe she knew that from early on. Someone – and it would be a guess, Dr Ward, Bill Astor, MI5, Tim Bligh, Henry Brooke or, most possibly, his friend William Deedes – had warned Profumo that Christine Keeler had told so much of the affair to the police, in recordings in preparation for a memoir, that it would be impossible to go on denying: the devil was in the detail. And she was to appear in court on 5 June to give evidence against Lucky Gordon on assault charges.

The falling-on-the-sword option appeared the only one left.

Number 10 was under repair (not from the Profumo battering) and so the Minister of War met private secretary Sir Tim Bligh and the wet Chief Whip Martin Redmayne, a man who could have prevented this very moment, at Admiralty House, where Macmillan had taken refuge. The Prime Minister was still in Perthshire when Profumo arrived to tell them he had lied to the Commons and to offer his resignation as a Minister and as an MP.

They began a draft letter of the resignation and, in it, Profumo's legal team pointed out that their client had libelled Christine Keeler. Timothy Bligh looked him over and later said: 'It was felt that worse things had happened since *King Lear*.' Together, they completed the wording and read his letter out to Macmillan in Scotland. The next day, Macmillan gave them his reply over the phone. Both letters were made public on the afternoon of 5 June at 6pm:

Dear Prime Minister,

You will recollect that on 22 March, following certain allegations made in Parliament, I made a personal statement.

At that time rumour had charged me with assisting in the disappearance of a witness and with being involved in some possible breach of security.

So serious were those charges that I allowed myself to think that my personal associations with that witness, which had also been the subject of rumour, was, by comparison, of minor importance only.

In my statement I said that there had been no impropriety in this association. To my very deep regret I have to admit that this was not true, and that I misled you, and my colleagues, and the House. I ask you to understand that I did this to protect, as I thought, my wife and family, who were equally misled, as were my professional advisers.

I have come to realise that, by this deception, I have been guilty of a grave misdemeanour and despite the fact that there is no truth whatever in the other charges, I cannot remain a member of your Administration, nor of the House of Commons.

I cannot tell you of my deep remorse for the embarrassment I have caused to you, to my colleagues in the Government, to my constituents and to the Party which I have served for the past twenty-five years.

Yours sincerely,
Jack Profumo

Macmillan's reply was brief:

Dear Profumo,

The contents of your letter of 4 June have been communicated to me, and I have heard them with deep regret. This is a great tragedy for you, your family and your friends. Nevertheless, I am sure you will understand that in the circumstances, I have no alternative but to advise the Queen to accept your resignation.

Yours very sincerely,
Harold Macmillan

The resignation letter went to Buckingham Palace at noon and Timothy Bligh ordered a police guard to be put on Profumo's house at 3, Chester Terrace, Regent's Park.

It was all too late – for them all. Harold Wilson was in America and was contacted to see what tack the Labour Opposition should take. He replied: 'No comment – in glorious Technicolor. And that's what I'm telling you; no comment on the wide screen.' Wilson wanted much discredit to fall on Macmillan but also for him to remain as Prime Minister as 'Labour's most valuable asset'. He told Richard Crossman: 'The one thing I am really frightened of is [Chancellor of the Exchequer, Reginald] Maudling.'

He also didn't like the idea of facing Iain Macleod at the General Election, which was 16 months away at most. In all of this, other players, pawns to the politicians, like Stephen Ward, were of use only as instruments towards gaining power. Labour MP Anthony Wedgwood-Benn wrote in his diary of 4–8 April 1963, during a West German conference, that he had talked at length with Crossman 'about the Profumo–Keeler scandal'. He wrote, and this is before Profumo resigned, that Crossman said: 'Dr Stephen Ward, the Harley Street osteopath procurer, ran a sort of brothel on the Astor estate at Cliveden. Profumo lied in his statement to the Commons and Wilson is putting in a note of what happened to Macmillan with a warning that it will be raised if something isn't done about Profumo. I'm not in favour of private life scandals being used politically but it certainly makes the Government look pretty hypocritical.'

The Americans thought it was all over for Macmillan. Ambassador David Bruce had held several meetings at Grosvenor Square about Profumo and Stephen Ward – both men he knew and had been entertained by – with quiet American Tom Corbally and several others, including a friend from MI5 who has never been identified in CIA, FBI or UK documents. But it is insisted there was someone unidentified at the meetings. Bruce, who had a real poker face (his facial muscles never moved), allowed nothing on that. There is a circumstantial case for it being Corbally's friend Johnny Francis.

President Kennedy had a soft spot for Macmillan – to him the gentle elder statesman. It was Ambassador Bruce's job to protect his President. He sent a 'For Your Eyes Only' cable from London to JFK on 15 June 1963, which read:

A sacrifice is increasingly demanded here, and the appointed lamb for the altar is the Prime Minister, who must already have appreciated the sad truth that no ingratitude surpasses that of a democracy.

US Attorney General Robert Kennedy was acutely aware of the problem of his brother's inability to keep his flies closed when a female was within a few hundred yards, and the thought of sex and scandals made his office break out in secret documents and inquiries. And gave J. Edgar Hoover even more control of stockpiling dirty secrets of the Kennedy family. David Bruce was a more reflective man – he'd coped with 'Wild Bill' Donovan. In his cable to JFK and his Secretary of State, Dean Rusk, he told his President that few in the British Government believed that Macmillan would have connived to avoid an almost inevitable disclosure, had he known that Profumo had lied.

David Bruce was prescient. He said that, because of the fanfare over Profumo's resignation, a superb story headlined worldwide containing even more than sex, drugs and rock'n'roll (it also had Royalty and lords and ladies and such double standards) that the British public, 'their appetite for sensations already whetted by partial revelation', would demand a sacrifice. He pinpointed a potential victim, saying in his cable:

Meanwhile, the lurid details of the involvement of degraded personalities like Dr. Ward, Miss Keeler and other nymphs fan the popular imagination, inciting both meretricious and wholesome indignation.

Throughout the power corridors of Whitehall was the ongoing fear that America would disown Britain over security matters, the vanished Kim Philby, Vassall and now Profumo, and the nation would be isolated in the espionage world. But JFK had still to make his meeting with Macmillan – the sign of a brave man, given his own sexual predilections. Macmillan instigated a judicial inquiry, with Lord (Tom) Denning being given the job on 21 June 1963, and becoming the man who would distort almost every action that happened in the short period between 8 July 1961 and the summer of 1963.

On the eve of Profumo's resignation, Stephen Ward was interviewed by Desmond Wilcox on the independent TV premier news programme *This Week*. It was yet another attempt on Ward's part to fight back: 'The key point for me to clear my name was to indicate that I had not encouraged the relationship between Miss Keeler and Mr Profumo. I was disturbed about certain parts of it and, as tactfully as possible, I had informed the Security Service. I wanted to make it absolutely clear that I hadn't encouraged it and, knowing that I had a friend in the Soviet Embassy, I think I was rightly disturbed about it.'

Desmond Wilcox: 'Some people might say that you wrote this letter to the Home Secretary in order to blackmail him to switch attention from yourself.'

Ward: 'No, this was never my purpose. I'm deeply sorry that it did result in this. For a while it seemed possible that Mr Profumo's part in this affair could have been concealed altogether. Then the Press flushed him out.'

The well-briefed Wilcox quietly enquired if Ward had been running a call-girl ring.

Ward: 'No, indeed I wasn't. This my friends know and I think the police know now. I suppose the police will continue their investigation till they are satisfied that I am in the clear. This I hope they'll do.'

It was a faint hope.

The frame-up of Stephen Ward was further pursued when Lucky Gordon went on trial accused of attacking Christine Keeler in Devonshire Street on 17 April 1963. On the second day, Gordon

SCAPEGOAT

dismissed his lawyer and said he would go it alone. When it was Sergeant John Burrows' turn to take the witness box (he had originally arrested him), Gordon asked: 'Did you say you wanted to speak to me in connection with your enquiries into Stephen Ward procuring young girls for high society? You said you wanted me to help in your enquiries.'

'That was about other matters,' Burrows replied.

Two Defence witnesses, Clarence Comacchio and Truello Fenton, had not been found by the police. Wild with rage, Gordon shouted: 'The police know where these men are!'

He was subsequently found guilty and the judge told him: 'I am sorry that under the present regulations you are not liable to be deported.'

Gordon got three years in jail for his attack on Christine.

Ward knew he was cornered. So too was Macmillan, frantically looking for time to shield the Government. What caused Dr Ward most despair was his friend Bill Astor's abandonment: he had thought all would be well when 'Bill came back from America', but, instead of waving a magic wand and making all the horror vanish, Astor simply asked for the return of the keys to Spring Cottage. Dr Ward's loyal friend Warwick Charlton visited him shortly after that and reported: 'It was obvious to all but the blind that a tempest was about to break around the luckless Stephen.' Yet, he said Ward had held out hope and told him of his belief in the friendship of Astor (who'd provided the cheque for Christine and Mandy's rent) and the Cliveden set.

'With Bill back I really thought that now all would be well. I had always believed that Bill wouldn't let me down. I thought he could do something to restore my good name. I thought he might hold a party at Cliveden, collect some notables, and have me down as a sort of gesture of solidarity. Dreams. Imagine my shock when he at once asked me to let him have a letter vacating the cottage. Oh, he was very nice about it. He suggested that it would be the best thing to do in all the circumstances. I was absolutely

278

flabbergasted. I think I then began to realise that the waves were coming aboard and I would be clinging to the mast. And all the time there was no one at all to turn to. I began to feel trapped.'

The Stephen Ward he encountered that day upset Warwick Charlton who, in a magazine interview, reported: 'I found a very different Ward. Almost shamefacedly he told me how Astor had backed down. I could tell that this was a massive blow to his self-esteem; I knew also that that was the one thing Stephen could never tolerate. I asked him what on earth he expected, for from the beginning I had warned him to expect nothing from the Establishment.

'"You were right. They are all the same. They all thought you could buy it with a cheque book."'

For three months, the Metropolitan Police had pursued some charge against Stephen Ward. They were about to arrest him but the Prime Minister still wanted a few more days.

He tried to change the course of British history.

The archives of the Prime Minister's Private Office show that on 30 May 1963 he and his law officers were told that Stephen Ward was about to be charged with living on immoral earnings. The horror was that John Profumo would be called as a witness and, if proof were required they did not believe the War Minister's denials, this was it. If Profumo had been involved with Keeler, then who else, what else, was to be revealed at the Central Criminal Court?

Macmillan asked his private secretary Timothy Bligh to speak to Joseph Simpson, Commissioner of the Metropolitan Police, and ask if Stephen Ward's arrest might be postponed by a few days.

The delaying tactic to arrange this would be to make a later meeting with the Lord Chancellor before action was taken against Ward. Sir Joseph Simpson seems to have prevented that breach of the law. Bligh's archive note reveals: 'The Director of Public Prosecutions is now prepared to proceed against Dr Ward if a certain witness [Keeler] returned to this country over the weekend. She was expected to do this and to be prepared to make a statement on Tuesday, 4 June. The Commissioner said that if the Lord Chancellor wished to see him before Tuesday he would of course be willing to go along. But he would know that I recognised the delicacy of the position.'

So it was that Bobby McKew, unwittingly, was telling Stephen Ward that day in Regent's Park about his 'any-moment-now' arrest. If ever there was an invitation to run from the authorities, this was it. Ward believed in his innocence, that right would out. He was the same with Warwick Charlton, who told him he could arrange an advance, as much as £5,000, so that he could escape Britain. Charlton reported: 'He felt that he, and he alone, was the hunted one. Every time the phone rang it was to report that friends had been questioned, had fled to safety. I decided to be blunt: "Stephen, you must accept that girls you have known have made statements to the police about you. The police still have not enough to go on. Maybe they never will have. Go abroad. Moral offences are not extraditable."'

All that mattered to Stephen Ward rose in him then: his blind faith in the system, in justice, in the snobs he'd tried to join.

'But I haven't committed any moral offences. All they have against me are lies, lies and vicious lies...'

CHAPTER TWENTY

DOCTOR IN THE DOCK

'MY OBJECT ALL SUBLIME
I SHALL ACHIEVE IN TIME –TO LET THE
PUNISHMENT FIT THE CRIME.'

W.S. Gilbert, *The Mikado*, 1885

There are policemen who will tell you that they've attended trials of villains they've arrested and after half an hour or so they want to give evidence for the Defence. Barristers bemuse, play games and legal charades, and twist 'Hello' and 'Goodbye' into Armageddon moments.

In his final days, Stephen Ward was the star of a beautifully acted and choreographed and very cleverly scripted morality play. The dialogue didn't ring true but was of no matter.

Nothing ever did about the trial of Stephen Ward. It has been healthily reported over time but it is still an illusion, a game of cards, of solitaire, where there is always one missing: you just can't get out.

The Director of Public Prosecutions was sent the Stephen Ward Dossier, noted in magenta, by the main investigators, Chief Inspector Samuel Herbert, the formal, former Army sergeant-major, and Detective-Sergeant John Burrows, who would become, in time, as comic as Laurel and Hardy. They were asked for more material and delivered. On 8 June 1963, they were presented with a warrant for the arrest of Stephen Ward.

They did the polite thing and were at his Bryanston Mews flat at 6am that Saturday morning. Ward, who had been under Metropolitan Police surveillance for the past three months, was not there. No one had told the detectives he was staying with his journalist friend Pelham Pound in Watford. On arrest, he said: 'Oh my God, how dreadful! I shall deny it. Nobody will come forward to say it is true.'

They took him away, wearing his slippers, sunglasses, white shirt and blue trousers and a look of wry amusement. You want to believe he knew they were on their way to Bryanston Mews and spoiled their morning arrest moment.

Still dressed in his Watford front-room lounging gear, he was charged that evening with eight counts under the Sexual Offences Act, 1956. He had been living on the immoral earnings of Christine Keeler, Mandy Rice-Davies and others and procuring girls for sex over a period of more than two years. I spoke to his friends about what they felt all those years ago.

'As soon as I heard that Stephen had been arrested, I thought, "This is something that won't run,"' said Kim Waterfield.

Jill Adam was equally convinced: 'Someone told lies – Stephen was not a bad man.'

Shirley Anne Field was in America, promoting her film *The War Lover* (1962), when she heard. 'I talked to Jeanne Baldwin and we made plans to be in London to see and support Stephen. It was such rubbish – he was in prison and I couldn't see him.'

Not all were so fast to support their good friend, the talented Dr Ward. While in prison, in a remand cell in Brixton, he paid half a crown (25 pence) a day to have a cell with a soft bed, carpet and an armchair. When this detail was revealed, American *Time* magazine dubbed him 'The Prince of the Ponces'. He'd need sharp public relations; those who could freely provide them did not.

As he sat in jail and Christine took a screen test for her 'life story', his friends gathered for lunch at Les Ambassadeurs. The one-armed lawyer Billy Rees-Davies, who hosted orgiastic dinner parties ('He was very, very naughty,' said Bobby McKew, whom Rees-Davies once represented in court) and enjoyed Hod Dibben's parties, where he craved being whipped, told the round-table consisting of Sir Colin Coote, Sir Godfrey Nicholson, Sir Gilbert Laithwaite and Vasco Lazzolo that it would be a risk to give evidence for Dr Ward. Their own peculiarities might be made public. Lord Astor had decided not to give evidence and best they followed that route. Eminent patients, many of whom truly regretted their decision, followed Astor's lead. McKew, not a man given to hiding his distaste, said in 2013: 'Stephen did think his rich friends would help him – Bill Astor, for instance. But Astor pissed off. He was a bit of a shit, anyway – I didn't like him. He didn't want to know and he was so friendly with Stephen. I think Stephen got a shock when not one of these names, big names, stood by him. It was his ordinary friends who stood by him.'

Vasco Lazzolo intended to do so; he just wanted to clear it with Dr Ward's painting subject, the Duke of Edinburgh. Lazzolo was painting the Duke's portrait that very June and he realised that, when he gave evidence at Ward's trial, Fleet Street might well link the two and drag in Prince Philip's name as someone who had known Dr Ward. He told the Duke what he had decided to do and explained he would understand if he wanted to cancel. The painter was told: 'Nonsense. We carry on.'

Detective Inspector Herbert was not so understanding: the police could find some pornographic material in Lazzolo's studio and prosecute him. It was an empty threat but pinned down the empowerment of the determination to convict Ward, who was freed from his Brixton cell to attend the first day of the hearing of the charges against him at Marylebone Magistrates' Court on 28 June 1963. By then, 'The Confessions of Christine' had appeared, at a cost of £23,000, in the *News of the World*, illustrated by the late

Lewis Morley's infamous portrait of Christine sitting apparently naked astride a chair.

She was the first star on the Prosecution parade that Monday at Number 2 Court. Dr Ward had elected for a jury trial, which meant the lower court had to hear the case against him – not his Defence – and then rule if it was strong enough to go to a jury. A foul system as it makes the impanelling of a completely unprejudiced jury for the ensuing trial an impossibility, especially with the unmissable publicity surrounding the trial of Stephen Ward, the 'Trial of the Century', and so on. Dr Ward's nemesis, his opponent – and that is very much the word – was Mervyn Griffith-Jones, a man as tightly rolled up as his umbrella. He will be forever famous for his remark during the 1960 obscenity trial of *Lady Chatterley's Lover*. As prosecutor, he pointed out to the jury that D.H. Lawrence had used the words 'fuck' or 'fucking' 30 times in his novel and enquired: 'Frankly, is this a book you'd want your wife or servants to read?'

His background was Eton and the Brigade of Guards. He was as in touch with the day-to-day as the Dalai Lama, but he had all the cards, and so the witnesses were gathered and tutored and rehearsed by Scotland Yard's finest.

It was a dull, wet day outside, and Stephen Ward was dragged into the grey-walled court with the Press and the 18 members of the public – whose overnight patience had won the voyeurism lottery – squeezed into the spectators' gallery. They heard the eight charges – good, quaint language – and, with that, they set to.

Immediately, there was a flavour of the way Griffith-Jones was going. He could make words like 'angel' and 'saint' sound distasteful if he tried. Think what he made of some of the words and human moving parts of which the jury was about to learn. Griffith-Jones in Dante-drive made 'sexual intercourse' seem like 'the Apocalypse' – his words as precise, sharp and chiselled as his looks. He began with a fusillade of foaming disgust: 'The story, which is a somewhat sordid story, covers in all a period from some time in 1958 until Ward was arrested in June of this year...'

He elaborated on the charges, brought in Cliveden, Mariella Novotny and most of all the sex-for-cash activities of Christine Keeler and Mandy Rice-Davies, procurement of girls under 21 and arranging abortions.

Christine, who arrived in a Rolls-Royce, looked stunning, her dark hair spilling innocently over a demure oatmeal dress.

Griffith-Jones spoiled the moment: 'Had you by this time started to have intercourse with Ward?'

'No, never,' said Christine.

She denied Dr Ward had made any suggestion to her about her future at that time and said it was then that she met Peter Rachman, who owned the Bryanston Mews flat, and she broke off with Ward. She continued to see him, however, and later went to live with him at Orme Court. There, she said, she used to meet his friends but did not have intercourse with any of them. She moved to Comeragh Road with Mandy and, at the beginning of June 1961, stayed with Dr Ward at 17, Wimpole Mews.

Griffith-Jones continued: 'While you were at Comeragh Road were you – and Davies – making sufficient money to pay the rent of the flat?'

'Yes.'

Griffith-Jones: 'Did you receive money from anyone else to go towards paying the rent?'

'Yes.'

'One or two people?'

'One.'

'Who handed you that money?'

'Well, nobody handed me the money. It was paid through the landlord.'

'Did you see that done?'

'No, I did not. Dr Ward told me that this was done.'

'Who did he say actually handed the money to the landlord?'

'Lord Astor.'

Griffith-Jones enquired why she introduced Dr Ward to girls at Wimpole Mews.

'Well, because he liked girls.'

Sometimes girls used to stay the night, she added.

Griffith-Jones: 'What was the position between Ward and yourself?'

'We were like brother and sister.'

After asking if she had intercourse with anyone while living at Ward's flat, the Prosecutor warned, 'I do not want names.'

Christine said she had a boyfriend, one boyfriend at a time.

There was some laughter from the public gallery, only a moment of light relief.

Keeler admitted having intercourse with Eugene Ivanov 'on one occasion' and with Mr Profumo, and having met a 'gentleman from India or Pakistan'. She said she'd had sex at Wimpole Mews with Jim Eynan, who'd given her money and she'd received one or two presents, small ones, from another man. Pressed for detail, she said: 'One of these men who gave me presents did give me money but not for myself, it was for my mother.'

When asked who the man was, she said: 'It was Mr Profumo.' She said she gave the money Profumo gave her to her mother, and of the money she received from Mr Eynan she kept some for herself and gave some to Dr Ward. Eynan, she insisted, was purely a friend. He used to give her about £20, she said, and, when Griffith-Jones asked what proportion of this she gave to Ward, she replied: 'I was not paying the rent at the time and I used to give him more than half.'

Once when she was broke, said Keeler, Ward suggested that she should go to see a man. She had intercourse with this man and he paid her about £50. 'I really don't know what I did with the money – I most probably paid back money I owed to people. I owed Dr Ward money and paid him what I owed him. I used to borrow money from Dr Ward as spending money.'

She denied that Ward had ever been in the flat while she had had intercourse with another man and told of an Indian doctor who had wanted to rent a room at Wimpole Mews: 'The object of the man's coming once a week was to make love. Stephen suggested I should be the girlfriend this man was to have.' She said she did not go to bed with the Indian doctor, although she met him later at the flat. Keeler was in the flat while Miss Rice-Davies and the Indian went to the bedroom and she added that Ward had told her not to tell anyone about this or mention it to the police. She spoke of going to auditions for models and bringing back girls whom she met at these auditions for Dr Ward, about five or six in all. Sometimes, Ward discussed the girls with her afterwards, saying who was 'good, wonderful or bad'.

Christine's trial co-star, Mandy Rice-Davies, perky as ever, slipped neatly into the witness box. No surprise, it was the same day that Inspector Burrows had set for her to be present on the television theft charge.

She was wearing a black coat and a shocking-pink hat – bright and petalled, keen to attract attention, just like Mandy. Using her white gloves as props, she said she was introduced to Dr Ward by Christine Keeler and had gone with him to the cottage at Cliveden, where she had had sexual intercourse with him. She also admitted having intercourse with one of the men whom Ward had brought to the flat at Comeragh Road.

Ward mentioned marriage to her, she said, but he did not say why or how they were to live. 'He always said he didn't have any money and he just said he had lots of friends. We have always got Bill, who can help us,' said Mandy.'

Griffith-Jones dug on: 'Were other men mentioned? I am not particularly anxious to drag men's names out; I want to avoid it.'

The only two men he mentioned, said Mandy, were Lord Astor and Douglas Fairbanks Junior. That woke them up at the back of the court. Mandy went on to say that she did not agree to marry Ward: 'When he suggested marriage, he said that his friends and Bill would help us. After I had married him, it would not have been an arrangement where he would have minded. I mean, having love affairs with other men.'

About the Indian doctor (the astonishingly never named in court Savundra), who had wanted to rent a room to bring girls to, she said Dr Ward had said to her: 'Why let outsiders get in?'

Mandy said she had sex with the Indian about four times at the flat and that he had left £15, £20 or £25 each time. Whenever she had the money, Dr Ward used to ask if she could give him some money for the rent and would ask to borrow some. She gave or lent 'two or three pounds at a time' to Ward, she said. She then dropped in something unexpected: 'While I was living at the flat, I had intercourse with Lord Astor.'

Griffith-Jones became angry. His face went a rainbow of vivid colours, from pink to white, like a multiple-flavoured ice ceram. He did not want names mentioned! Mandy then gave evidence about an abortion that was carried out at the Wimpole Mews flat.

It was Dr Ward's lawyer James Burge's chance to enquire of Mandy. She told him: 'I've enough jewellery and mink to keep me over the next years. I have no malice against Ward anymore – I didn't want to come here any more than anyone else.'

Burge said that she had dragged in the names of Lord Astor and Douglas Fairbanks Junior and suggested that she had, in fact, never met Fairbanks.

'Yes, I did.'

'Except in connection with a film test?'

'No. Twice I had a meeting with him. Not in connection with films and twice with Christine Keeler.'

'Is it quite untrue for you to suggest that you have had relations with Lord Astor?'

'Of course it is not untrue. I am not going to perjure myself in court.'

Burge then asked if she knew that Lord Astor had made a statement to the police saying her allegations were absolutely untrue.

Mandy giggled. 'He would, wouldn't he?'

She said the theft charge over the television 'was cooked up anyway' but denied the suggestion that she'd been told, if she gave evidence against Dr Ward, the charge would go away.

Burge persisted: 'After the evidence given by you yesterday, were you told the charge would not be proceeded with?'

'I phoned a man from the TV company at lunchtime and asked him to come here at 4.30. I cleared it up and I told the police and then they said there would be no charge against me.'

Several unnamed female witnesses gave evidence about Dr Ward helping them get abortions; another woman about being invited by him to 'perform' behind a two-way mirror. Ronna Ricardo was asked by Griffith-Jones to say how she met men in Ward's Bryanston Mews flat. Reluctantly, she explained that she earned money by visiting men and being paid by them. She said she had never given Ward any money.

Burge then turned over Inspector Herbert about the pressure put on Mandy.

The policeman replied: 'I would not say under the pressure of a possible criminal charge. No. She knew that would be dealt with on 28 June.'

Which, of course, was after she testified for the Prosecution.

When the preliminary hearing concluded, there were seven charges going with Stephen Ward to the Old Bailey for his trial proper starting on 22 July 1963.

The police objected to bail but it was granted at £2,000, half paid for by Pelham Pound, the other half by his friend and supporter Dominick Elwes. Ward had spent 26 days in prison; he had lost weight, much of the colour from his face, but, surprisingly, apparently none of his spirit. He went to stay with Noel Howard-Jones at his Chelsea flat, saying: 'Sleep, sleep – that is what I want.'

Howard-Jones told me how parts of the case against his friend had been built: 'Police were posted outside his surgery and would be asking his patients as they came out whether they'd slipped him an extra few pounds to get them a girl.

'And most of these people, being people who had reputations to consider, didn't come back. And within the space of a couple of months they had ruined the man. Scotland Yard deployed policemen to interview hundreds of witnesses. It was unlike any other criminal investigation, not sparked off by some crime and trying to find out whodunit, but a witch hunt into one man and trying to find out something that he'd done.

'I was questioned in my office. My first job – I'd been there a couple of weeks – when two detectives from Scotland Yard arrived to see me. It did wonders for my reputation with my employers. The thrust of their questions was clearly to determine whether I could tell them anything which would indicate that Christine was a prostitute and that Stephen was her ponce. And I was naive enough to tell them, I was a penniless law student and she was my girlfriend. No way! And I thought that was the end of the matter.

'Stephen was getting almost to the level of paranoia at the end but who says paranoiacs don't have enemies? Before his arrest, I'd say: "Look, Stephen, this is England, don't worry. Whatever they're up to, it's going to blow up in their faces because you've done nothing. And they've ruined you." They threw the book at him to start with. They accused him among other things of procuring abortions, which was something to which he was violently opposed. And the purpose of doing that was that that was an offence which would enable them to fix a trial in the Old Bailey.

'I saw less and less of Christine and, after she started talking to the Press, I just didn't want to see her at all. Stephen felt, if it hadn't been for him, Profumo and Christine would never have met and so he felt, for some reason, which seems incomprehensible to me now and even did then, obliged to go to bat for Profumo. And, when he found that sticking his head above the trench threshold even for that purpose just seemed to accentuate this persecution that was going on, he tried to go the other way and sent the signal: "Guys, if you won't get off my back, two can play at that game" – and that was fatal.'

CHAPTER TWENTY-ONE

DOCTOR ON TRIAL

'THE CROWDS ROUND THE COURTS WERE
UNCOMMONLY NASTY. THE WITNESSES HAD TO WALK
THROUGH A VAST LEER, A HUGE CONCUPISCENT
EXPOSURE OF CHEAP DENTURES.'

The Meaning of Treason, Rebecca West, 1965

When the Stephen Ward morality play moved to its larger stage, Court Number One at the Central Criminal Court – all marble and ancient, with Wren's great work in the background as a symbol of freedom from oppression, survival of whatever a Blitz can bring – was surrounded by people who hadn't been to church, never mind St Paul's, in a long time. The distinguished writer Rebecca West noted them 'leering', and film footage also suggests a French revolutionary flavour, all very anti-toff. Yet, Ward hadn't belonged, although he had wanted to. They were ten-deep round the Old Bailey, eager to see Christine and Mandy, who had their hair done at Vidal Sassoon and bought new outfits for the trial.

In the dock, Ward looked ragged, his hands heavily stained with nicotine, nails a little unkempt. There were now five charges against him on that opening trial day of 22 July 1963. The first three of living on the earnings of prostitution, of Christine Keeler at Wimpole Mews during a 15-month period between June 1961 and August 1962; of Mandy Rice-Davies at Wimpole Mews during a four-month period between September and December 1962; and of Ronna Ricardo and Vickie Barrett at Bryanston Mews during a five-month period between January and June 1963. The two other counts were that Ward incited Keeler to procure a girl under 21 to have intercourse with him. Two other charges of procuring abortions were to be heard separately.

Also in the legal system was Lucky Gordon, who had been given leave to appeal his jail term for attacking Christine.

Lord Denning loomed over the trial. He was taking evidence for his Inquiry and had spoken with Profumo and others.

But in charge was Sir Archie Pellow Marshall, 64, a fusspot and a swirl of scarlet and black in his judicial gowns, who did not have much in common with the Defendant or indeed many others in his courtroom. For Griffith-Jones, it was the real thing after his dress rehearsal at Marylebone. Pulling up his thespian socks, he gave it all it was worth in an opening speech, which suggested Ward had been running Sodom and Gomorrah: 'The Defendant is 50 years old,' he boomed. 'It is not perhaps without significance that he is a man years older than the girls – young women, not to exaggerate the matter – with whom this case is connected.

'It has been impossible from the records we have found to ascertain what his actual income was. Not only are his accounts not perhaps complete, but also he was earning some money from his drawings because he appears to be a talented artist. Whatever the extent of his earnings for this period might have been, they were quite obviously not sufficient for what he was spending.

'Prostitution, as a matter of law and for the purpose of this case, is where a woman offers her body for sexual intercourse, that is normal sexual intercourse, or for any acts of lewdness for money.

'It does appear that Christine Keeler and the Defendant, though they have lived together, never had sexual intercourse with one another. It was apparently a brother and sister relationship. The Prosecution allege the position to be as from June 1961 until August or September 1962 that Christine Keeler was completely dominated – in some curious way you may think, dominated – and under the influence of Ward and being used by him not only to make a little cash from intercourse she was having from time to time with men who visited the flat, but also to procure girls for his own satisfaction.

'This case is not an ordinary one of a boy trying to take up a girl; perhaps hoping she would go to bed with him. You may think that there are matters far more sinister.

'We have the evidence of the living on the earnings of prostitution at Bryanston Mews for the last period from January to June.

'There are two persons involved. Neither Keeler nor Davies was there. They seemed to have dropped out of the picture but there are two more who enter, one a Miss Ricardo and another Miss Vickie Barrett.'

It was the first ever mention in court of Vickie Barrett, 22: it was said that she was picked up in January 1963 by Ward; driving a white Jaguar in Oxford Street (he had driven her to Bryanston Mews for a party). Griffith-Jones was finding his voice: 'She was told he would get her clients and would look after her interests, take the money for her and keep it for her so she would then save a little and be able to buy new clothes and a more luxurious apartment and therefore charge higher fees. For two and a half months, two or three times a week she would be brought to the flat and there would be a man in bed waiting for her; that, in ordinary language, is just brothel keeping. This sort of thing happened 30 times with Miss Barrett. She then left but she never received a penny of the money which she had earned and which had been paid to the Defendant for him to save for her.'

Keeler was then run through her previous performance with added drama. Griffith-Jones asked how she came to have intercourse with Charles Clore – 'Dr Ward suggested, if I went to him, he would give me money.'

Griffith-Jones then pushed his luck: 'Can you tell the jury, roughly speaking, what proportion of the money you received from men you gave to the Defendant while you were at Wimpole Mews.'

'Well, I usually owed him more than I ever made. I only gave him half of that.'

Burge then got his chance to ask some questions of Christine about the evidence she gave at the trial of Lucky Gordon. She insisted she had told the truth and, when Burge said that Gordon had said her injuries were not caused by him, Keeler replied: 'The man is mad. Of course they were.' She denied that Comacchio and Fenton had been present at the time of the incident involving Gordon or having ever lived with Gordon. The judge then asked if she had ever had intercourse with Gordon, and Keeler admitted that she had, at his home.

'Did you say all your injuries were caused by him?'

'Yes, I did and may I say that everyone connected with this has tried to blackmail me.'

During the trial, there was an exhibition of Stephen Ward's sketches and paintings at Museum Street Galleries. He attended and talked to potential buyers. The catalogued value of the drawings was £19,000, with sketches of the Royal Family for 500 guineas and one of Ivanov at 150 guineas. Although art critics were unenthusiastic, all the work of the Royal Family sold (Ward needed the money for his legal costs) and the buyer was Anthony Blunt, the Cambridge spy and Keeper of the Queen's Pictures; he didn't want any scandal.

The triumphant hypocrisy of the trial was in the pale face of Ronna Ricardo, who told the court she had lied at the Marylebone Magistrates' hearing.

Judge Marshall looked up abruptly: 'Are you telling the jury that you deliberately went into the witness box then and said things that were completely untrue?'

She nodded and whispered agreement.

Griffith-Jones demanded an explanation for her false testimony and was told by the tearful Ricardo: 'Because I was scared, just scared to back out of my statements to the police.'

He read out various statements she had made to the police about being introduced to a man by Stephen Ward. Ricardo said these statements were not true. The judge asked: 'Are you suggesting that the police put these words into your mouth?'

'Yes.'

Griffith-Jones: 'You must realise that to have these words put into your mouth and have this written down as yours is a very wicked thing to do. Did you never complain?'

'Who could I complain to? I did not want to sign the statement, I did not want to have anything to do with it.'

'Why did you sign it?'

'I wanted the police to leave me alone.'

Ricardo said she was told that she would not have to give evidence and that she was kept so long at the police station she was ready to sign anything; there was a threat that her brother would be 'nicked'.

She agreed that she had gone to Dr Ward's flat with her boyfriend and a girlfriend; she and the man and Dr Ward and the girl all had sex in the same room.

'All four of you together?' gasped Griffith-Jones, as the judge helped his case even further by jumping in: 'I want to know what happened in that room, all four of you together. Was there anything beyond sexual intercourse?'

Ricardo simply shook her head.

Ward got some benefit from the honesty of Ronna Ricardo but Vickie Barrett was the bad news of the day. A convicted prostitute, she wore a nylon raincoat tightly wrapped around her tiny body, and described how she was picked up by Ward in his white Jaguar.

'He got out and came up to me and asked me if I would like to go to a party – he had just got a few friends with their wives and girlfriends and he wanted a girl to have conversation with. As we were driving up to his flat he said he had a man in the flat who wanted to go with a girl; he said the man would give him the money. He gave me a contraceptive and told me to go into the bedroom and strip. He said he would make coffee while I was in the bedroom.'

She said she went into the bedroom and found the naked man. Afterwards, Dr Ward gave her coffee. She asked him about the money and Ward said he had received it and she agreed to his keeping it for her. The jury were shown Ward's black and white sketch of Barrett, with bright-red lips. She said the same happened the following week and later she had visited Dr Ward's flat and beaten elderly and middle-aged men with a cane and a horsewhip at their request.

Griffith-Jones: 'With your knowledge of the trade, rather profession, what would be the normal payment for services such as you rendered? How much a time?'

'Five pounds in the flat.'

Griffith-Jones: 'And for the whipping, what is the market price?'

'A pound a stroke.'

It was Burge's job to deflect all that. He made a strong opening statement: 'It would be sheer hypocrisy for any of us to pretend this was a normal criminal case. In a normal case the man who sits in the dock is presumed to be innocent; the jury know nothing before they hear the evidence in the case as to either the allegation against him or what is alleged to support it. In this case one cannot shut one's eyes to the fact that each one of you must have come to the jury box with a background of knowledge of various matters which arise by reason of a public scandal. It is very easy to exhort you, as the Prosecution has done, to dismiss that from your minds but rather hard to do so in practice. You, and only you, preserve the balance between a man who is charged with a series of revolting offences and a prosecution which is based more largely, you might think, upon prejudice than upon actual evidence.

'For months on end, following the declaration in the House of Commons on 22 March, the police have combed the country in a frenzy in order to find evidence implicating the Accused.

'Although public opinion has obviously been horrified by the scandal that was raised through no fault of this man, and therefore demands expiation, some speedy sacrifice so that the matter can be established and disposed of and forgotten, that is not a consideration that will affect you in deciding issues here.

'It was quite clear that something had to be done. Obviously the highest authorities were concerned with this investigation.

'It was a situation in which officers can either make their names or sink into oblivion. It is obviously a matter which they could go into with the knowledge of what was behind it and the knowledge that they have to do their very best to provide a case.

'A man would clearly not be human if he were not influenced in the enthusiasm of his inquiry by these considerations. They have allowed their enthusiasm and possibly the fears of the possibilities of failure to spur on their investigation of the various witnesses and to colour their evidence in the interpretation of facts.'

He called his first witness, Stephen Ward.

Dr Ward gave an admirable account of himself. His voice was clear and succinct; he countered all the points and made some good ones about the difficulties of running a call-girl business while being watched by MI5 – after telling them about Christine and Profumo – and said that Vickie Barrett would have been seen by the teams of reporters outside his flat.

And, possibly, his house guest Sylvia Parker (who flew in from Italy to confirm she had never seen Barrett). Burge asked about Mandy's rent. Dr Ward said that her room was worth considerably more than the £6 a week that she paid; she was also very extravagant on the telephone (the bill came to £54). Her total contribution towards the expenses of the flat, including the time her father and mother stayed there while she was in hospital recovering from the suicide attempt she made after Rachman's death, was £24, plus £5 or £6 towards the phone bill.

On the question of procuring girls, he answered: 'It is ridiculous – I am perfectly capable of finding the girls for myself. I have, I suppose, said to Miss Keeler that, if she met anyone who was interesting to draw, I should like to do this. She did not get hold of any girls for me.'

On Vickie Barrett: 'Her whole evidence was a tissue of disgusting lies from beginning to end.'

Miss Ricardo, he said, had on one occasion come to his flat. He knew she was a prostitute and he had sketched her on several occasions.

Burge told the jury his client was a man who in one respect had the secret of eternal youth, and he liked young women but the jury must remember, 'Was he conducting a business, living as a parasite on the earnings of prostitution? It is a very, very wide gap between a man with an artistic temperament and obviously with high sexual proclivities leading a dissolute life and saying he has committed the offence here of living on the earnings of prostitution. On a fair and impartial view, I will ask you to say these charges have not been made out and find him "Not Guilty".'

It was good, but it wasn't over. As he began to leave the witness box, Judge Marshall quizzed Dr Ward on his definition of a prostitute. With that ringing in the ears, the jury were then overwhelmed by Mr Mervyn Griffith-Jones pointing out those who had said it was his divine calling to see that Dr Ward was convicted: 'I do hope that you will not put that against any responsible member of the Bar who happens to be instructed on behalf of the State to place before a jury the evidence of a man's alleged offences.

'You may find a great deal of the evidence isn't true. It is no good approaching a case like this with one's eyes shut to reality. What is this doctor, so called, of 48 doing when he happens to mention these girls to Lord Astor one day? I do not know. Two penniless, promiscuous girls who are performing in a nightclub and this man happens to mention the matter to Lord Astor one day, who immediately "coughs up" a hundred pounds to pay the rent? I do not know. What is the inference? Is it mere friendliness? Is this really brotherly concern about these two girls who are broke? Or do you think, with any knowledge of human life, and the ways of a thoroughly immoral man, the inference is that there was something far more sinister than that? And that is the picture upon which all else builds up in this case: this West End osteopath, Dr Stephen Ward, trotting round there with his middle-aged men friends; Astor and Fairbanks and certainly two others.

'Then we have Mr Profumo giving Miss Keeler money – for her mother, she said. On the question of whether she was a prostitute, it makes no difference whether it was for her mother or not. One wonders whether Mr Profumo would have given the money if she had said "No" to the sex.'

The barrister pointed at Ward, who sat upright in the dock, a wry look on his face, sketching on a block of white paper: 'He, of any of the people we have heard in this case, has reason enough to lie. Because this man may be said to be a filthy fellow, it doesn't necessarily follow that he is guilty of the offence with which he is charged.

'I don't for one moment say that the fact that he is a filthy fellow is wholly irrelevant from the case. You may think it highly relevant on a number of points. The evil of this – and it is evil, you may think – goes very deep.'

The jury was left with that till the next day. Ward gave James Burge a sketch he'd done of him making his final remarks. It was most dignified and relaxed, a cool and brave performance.

The following morning, one of the swiftest appeals in criminal history happened; in nine minutes, Lucky Gordon's three-year jail term and conviction were dismissed because of evidence that should have been presented at his trial. Strangely, a transcript of the judgment was immediately sent off to the Old Bailey, where Stephen Ward continued sketching.

Griffith-Jones did the talking. When Dr Ward did say something, the judge snarled: 'You must keep quiet.'

Dr Ward replied: 'I am sorry, my Lord. It is a great strain.'

His persecutor was fast. Griffith-Jones smiled at the jury: 'No doubt it is a great strain for a guilty man when the truth emerges. It often happens that one has to wait until almost the end before the true picture suddenly blossoms.'

He got round to the awkward matter of Keeler and Lucky Gordon's successful appeal. For if Christine lied at one trial, why not another? 'Gordon's appeal has been allowed. That does not mean to say that the Court of Criminal Appeal have found that Miss Keeler is lying. They have allowed the appeal simply and solely because these two witnesses were not there.'

He returned to his favoured subject: 'We have come from the very depths of lechery and depravity in this case – prostitution, promiscuity, perversion and getting girls to go out and borrow money by giving their bodies for it.

'You will not convict the Defendant just because he was at the centre of all this depravity and just because his homes at Wimpole Mews or Bryanston Mews were the pivot upon which all this turned. But that in fact he was taking money from these various women, money earned by prostitution. That he was a thoroughly immoral man.

'If you think that is proved, members of the jury, you may think it is in the *highest public interest* to do your duty and return a verdict of Guilty on this indictment.'

It was a bravura performance by the man James Burge complained could make the word 'honeymoon' sound obscene. Ward looked shaky, like the scaffold, but it was being held up by the skill of the articulate Griffith-Jones.

Now Mr Justice Marshall closed the deal for the jury, summing up: 'We are now reaching the last stages of a trial that has probably achieved greater notoriety than any trial in recent years. One would have thought that this country has become a sort of sink of iniquity.'

The judge elaborated and disingenuously but precisely pierced the heart of Stephen Ward's downfall, his despair: 'The persons involved here, on his story, were his friends. It is a factor the importance of which you must assess to yourselves when you consider the case.

'There may be many reasons why he has been abandoned in his extremity. You must not guess at them but this thing is clear.

'If Stephen Ward was telling the truth in the witness box, there are in this city many witnesses of high estate and low who could have come and testified in support of his evidence.'

With that, he adjourned proceedings until the following day. Smiling at the jury, he said: 'I have no doubt that will be the last day.'

At the end of the seventh day of his trial, Stephen Ward, his skin almost translucent, left the Old Bailey in a black cab and returned to Noel Howard-Jones' flat in Vale Court, Mallord Street, Chelsea.

It was a sombre evening and Ward spent most of it writing letters. With him were Howard-Jones and, of course, a young female companion, 22-year-old Julie Gulliver. He asked Howard-Jones to send the letters, 'only if I am convicted and sent to prison'.

At 9pm, he went to the kitchen and made a meal for himself and Gulliver. Before midnight, he drove her home to Bayswater and she wished him good night with: 'Good luck for tomorrow, darling.'

CHAPTER TWENTY-TWO

DEATH OF THE DOCTOR

'TO SEE THAT THINGS ARE HOPELESS
BUT STILL BE ABLE TO THINK YOU CAN DO
SOMETHING ABOUT IT.'

F. Scott Fitzgerald's definition of madness from 'The Crack-Up', 1936

Stephen Ward said he was going to take the drophead white Jaguar for a spin along Park Lane from Bayswater before driving back to Chelsea.

Noel Howard-Jones said he thought he heard Dr Ward arrive back at his home around 1am, but went quickly back to sleep.

That elusive time, probably about an hour, has been a puzzle for more than half a century. There have been accounts that Ward met a newspaper photographer from whom MI5 had stolen photographs in the 60 minutes plus. The cameraman was quoted as saying that Ward, appearing pressured, insisted on meeting again at 7.30am to go to the Home Office.

Which doesn't sound like a man about to kill himself. Which is what he supposedly did on his return that night: on official evidence.

There is no dispute that there was a large dose of Nembutal sleeping medication – the equivalent of between 12 and 20 pills, 20 being dangerous though not deadly – in his system. Throughout the trial, Dr Ward was taking Nembutal on prescription.

That evening, as usual, he got a tall glass of water from Howard-Jones' kitchen and apparently swallowed many more than his usual number of tablets. He had set two mattresses on the floor of the front room, but, first, he sat at the table and wrote another letter, his fourteenth, this time to his host, the young man who had provided so much kindness.

He fell asleep and did not complete the letter:

Dear Noel,

I am sorry I had to do this here! It is really more than I can stand – the horror, day after day at the court and in the streets. It is not only fear; it is a wish not to let them get me. I would rather get myself. I do hope I have not let people down too much. I tried to do my stuff but after Marshall's summing-up, I've given up all hope. The car needs oil in the gear-box, by the way. Be happy in it. Incidentally, it was surprisingly easy and required no guts.

I am sorry to disappoint the vultures. I only hope this has done the job. Delay resuscitation as long as possible.

At 8.30am, Howard-Jones heard the telephone ring. It was in the lounge close to Stephen Ward. Half asleep, he expected Dr Ward to answer it. When the phone rang on, he came through from the bedroom. He told me: 'I looked at Stephen and I thought he was dead; his face was blue. I shouted his name and slapped his face hard. But he didn't stir and I thought I was too late. Then he breathed and I knew there was a chance, dialled 999 and waited for the ambulance.

'I tried artificial respiration – I'd had enough first aid knowledge. He had in the letter said to delay resuscitation so I had some hesitation, particularly in view of the depth of the coma and his respiration rate. I felt that he'd probably have incurred severe brain damage already and that bringing him back to life would be as a vegetable. I rang 999 for an ambulance.'

DEATH OF THE DOCTOR

It arrived, with Fleet Street close behind. Which is why there is a photograph of Dr Ward being lifted on a stretcher from the flat. A red hospital blanket is over him; his head hangs limply to one side. It's a strange image, all wrong – like a newspaper wet in the street with the headlines running into a mix of grey and black nonsense. Which this was; it didn't make sense.

The ambulance took the unconscious Dr Ward to St Stephen's Hospital on the Fulham Road, less than a mile away. He'd lost his reputation and his reason for living; the doctors were working to retrieve his life. When they got him into Ward 3D, he remained in a coma but the staff believed he had a chance. He was surrounded by all manner of medical equipment and a prison guard, in case he tried to escape.

Later that day, at the Old Bailey, an unsympathetic Sir Archie Marshall ruled the show must go on: 'The responsibility is mine. From everybody's point of view it would be better for the summing-up to be continued and the verdict to be taken.' A pause, then he observed on the still-innocent man absent from the dock: 'I also want it to be understood that Ward shall be immediately put under surveillance.

'Bail is withdrawn from now and the normal steps will be taken to secure greater security.'

And he got on with the summing-up, which in total took more than five hours. The jury took four and a half hours to reach a verdict. As the dock remained empty, it was announced.

They found Stephen Ward guilty of two of the five charges against him: living on immoral earnings, which involved Christine Keeler and Mandy Rice-Davies. On the other three charges, the one involving Vickie Barrett and the two relating to procuring, they returned a verdict of not guilty. Mr Justice Marshall said he would postpone sentence until Ward was well enough to return to the Old Bailey.

That never happened.

After 79 hours in a coma, Stephen Ward died in St Stephen's Hospital on the afternoon of Saturday, 3 August, never having recovered consciousness. Officially, he never knew the verdict. Deep down, he must have known for quite some time.

It is easy to say that this prompted him to kill himself. Entertainer Michael Bentine told the authors of *Honeytrap* in 1987 that he believed his friend was murdered, 'assisted in dying' by Special Branch. Also, they reported an MI6 man telling them that an MI5 freelance agent was present with Dr Ward on that last night and induced him to take more sleeping pills when he was already dozy on medication. The man was named as Stanley Rytter of the Polish circle surrounding Peter Rachman. That theory was supported by Christine Keeler's onetime lover Serge Paplinski, who told the authors: 'Stanley was there with Ward on the last night – he always said he was poisoned.'

Bobby McKew retorts: 'Paplinski was a police informer. Charlie Richardson [the 1960s gangster] and I were going to a funeral and I asked if another friend was coming and Charlie said: "Best not, if he comes and Paplinski's there then there'll be two people in the hole [grave]." You couldn't trust him at all.'

But Norbert Rondel could; his loyalty once given was never taken away. He'd offered to act as a bodyguard for Dr Ward during the Old Bailey endurance and, when that was turned down, said he would 'keep an eye on him'. His true mission was to enable the theft of unknown photographs and letters from the flat at Bryanston Mews that night. As such, he had paced up and down the King's Road before watching Dr Ward's white Jaguar take a right turn into Old Church Street and a left into Mallord Street. Rondel watched Dr Ward get out of the car – with another man. He told some associates the other man had his back to him but 'was a gent, wore a pinstriped suit'.

Who seems to have been, and remains, a ghost. Was there another doctor in the house, with a soothing hypodermic needle?

Noel Howard-Jones told me decades later: 'I still have a

conscience about Stephen's last night. He was depressed, almost obsessional, and I maybe wasn't as good an audience as I should have been. Anyway, he decided to go out. Where he went, I don't know.'

Around this time, Harold Wilson received a letter saying in 1938 John Profumo had been intimate with a woman under MI5 surveillance, who had fled England just before the war began. In a letter only seen years later, Wilson replied: 'It is only now that we are learning something of the men chosen to rule over us.' It was not long before Wilson himself was wildly rumoured to be one of the Kremlin's top men. Those were eclectic times but there was no place for Stephen Ward, whom society could not pigeonhole – and that frightened them.

Noel Howard-Jones was there: 'This was a very special kind of time at the beginning of the 1960s. It was a time when all of a sudden being smart and being successful didn't necessarily involve having a posh accent.

'There were the rising stars of society, pop singers and hairdressers and people who were good at sports and so on. And at the same time there was this extraordinary liberalisation of sexual freedom. Society was changing very rapidly and for a lot of people this was very disconcerting. Anything to suggest that the upper classes indulged in the kind of behaviour that Profumo and Ward did had to be rigidly suppressed.

'The ultimate effort to put a lid on this was Denning. Lord Denning never contacted me or asked for my opinion on anything. I spoke to a few people who he did talk to, and all of them said that Denning's mind had clearly been made up before he started.

'They said his eyes would go all glazed when something was said that didn't fit in with his rather Dickensian view of the whole thing: that Stephen was an evil man; that these were poor innocent girls; that Profumo was even more innocent, if not poorer, and had been seduced by an innocent girl who had been corrupted by Stephen Ward. The only people he was interested in talking to were those who would say things which he wanted to hear. It was like the house that Jack built – everything went back to Stephen Ward.

'And he had to pay the price that a villain such as he should have paid: end of story. I couldn't have contributed anything to that sort of junk. *The Denning Report* is a load of rubbish but about what you could expect from a man who's been charged with investigating a series of events which include a gross miscarriage of justice. It blows my mind that the Stephen Ward trial papers are being suppressed until 2046. I thought there was a slogan that justice has not only to be done but to be seen to be done. Surely that should apply to injustice in an even greater measure?

'That's why I left Britain. In England, I couldn't see a policeman in the street without it always coming back to me. Every time I do think about it, I have regrets about it because the man was innocent. And there aren't degrees of innocence.

'He was hounded to death in a way which was more reminiscent of Kafka than something one would expect in England.

'I'd been at boarding school since the age of six. And in the Royal Marines for two years. At school and so on, Britain was the best country in the world. Our policemen were wonderful; judges were pillars of wisdom and integrity, and of course now we all know better. And this particular scandal was instrumental in changing that.

'They all closed ranks. He had a lot of friends and they ran for cover. He seemed to try to find a lot of excuses for Christine but he was pretty disappointed; everybody was behaving disappointingly as far as he was concerned. Mandy Rice-Davies had a wider audience after the trial. Mandy was an intelligent, sometimes funny, little gold-digger. Christine took it much more badly, but let's not forget that Christine had taken her pieces of silver for telling her story. And it was, without pushing the comparison too far, Stephen that was being crucified.

'I think the fact that he was nice to her afterwards, didn't send her packing, just heaped coals of fire on her head. I don't think Christine was a bad person. And I think she realised she'd played a part in something terrible. I'm not sure that Mandy would have cared one way or another.

'I find it hard to make my heart bleed for Profumo – it's not even as though you can say that a brilliant political career was destroyed because he wasn't the cleverest War Minister that we ever had.

'Bill Astor was affable and had no conversation at all. His one skill that he claimed was that of castrating horses. Pleasant! Not a memorable character really. He was polite, well educated in the sense of knowing how to hold a knife and fork. Christine? If Profumo had never happened, she might have met somebody, got married, led a reasonably conventional life. I think Christine had regrets about it, but I'm perfectly certain Mandy had none at all. Stephen's dead. He would have been by now anyway, but he lost a number of active years of what was a very full life and spent the last months of his life in utter misery.

'Yes, Stephen was the victim.'

CHAPTER TWENTY-THREE

DOCTOR'S INQUEST

'I DON'T WANT REALISM. I WANT MAGIC! YES,
YES, MAGIC! I TRY TO GIVE THAT TO PEOPLE.'

Blanche DuBois, *A Streetcar Named Desire*, Tennessee Williams

'The story must start with Stephen Ward,' reported *The Denning Report*, an instant best-seller on publication in September 1963.

It did not end with his life.

With Stephen Ward, until now, there has been more epilogue than prologue. Which began with Lord Denning, a puritan with tabloid instincts. In America, his findings were titled *The Profumo–Christine Keeler Affair* and marketed as a penny dreadful. 'Reads like a combination detective thriller and a sex novel,' said *The New York Times*.

Indeed, 'novel' was a key word for the work, with chapter headings like 'Christine Tells Her Story', 'The Meeting of the Five Ministers', 'The Slashing and the Shooting' and 'The Man in the Mask', in which Denning made unsubstantiated allegations against Dr Ward.

More honest would have been a Zola-style 'J'accuse' about deception, hypocrisy, ambiguity and betrayal of justice and standards. Instead, Denning ignored relevant Defence evidence, the intimidation of the Defendant and witnesses. He flirted with the untested: 'Ward admired the Soviet regime, sympathised with the Communists, was ready to arrange for whipping and other sadistic performances'.

What he wrote brings anguish even more than half a century later to Stephen Ward's nephew, Michael Ward, who in the summer of 2013 noted: 'It has always been clear that my uncle never lived off Miss Keeler's or anyone else's immoral earnings. Witnesses in his trial were put under appalling pressure to lie by the police at the instigation of Conservative politicians, primarily the Home Secretary. The police told Ward's friends that, if they gave evidence in his favour, life would be made difficult. Most disgracefully, this stitch-up of my uncle was completed by the highest judiciary in the land. It was a sad business. *The Denning Report* did little credit to the great jurist, an essentially unworldly but prurient old man.'

With the tide slowly going out, the facts and inferences and panics that got lost in the space of time inevitably reveal the shape of things as they really were. There's little doubt that Stephen Ward, like the army officer Alfred Dreyfus falsely accused of treason 70 years earlier in France, was harassed out of the way for political reasons. With the connivance of moral censure. To save face, embarrassment, political reputations and lives, all packaged up as for the national interest, for 'security concerns'. It was at a time when the spook agencies were turning mountains of hearsay and speculation into moles. Everyone was frightened of their own shadow, hence 'spooks'.

Who swiftly began to edit out their contributions. Of one thing Michael Ward is certain: 'Stephen Ward never had any dealings with the Foreign Office. His were confined to MI5, advising one of its officers of Ivanov's conduct. MI5's silence at his trial is perhaps not surprising as it is essentially a secret service.'

The 'security' over Ward goes on. Documents remain censored and will be for another generation or two. You can get files but some vital material is redacted. This attitude is emphasised by a note written by Home Secretary Henry Brooke on a Government initiative regarding what should happen to materials gathered around the Stephen Ward case: 'The sooner this evidence (given under pledge of secrecy) is destroyed the better. It is signed H.B and dated 29 September 1963.

Those still alive talk of the man described as 'the most evil I have ever met' by Lord Denning as a kindly, never-hurt-a-fly person. Yet, there was clearly devilment, often a juvenility, in Stephen Ward and his pursuit of teenaged girls would raise eyebrows and concern in the twenty-first century. He was a seeker of dubious, not-for-profit pleasures, but in the post-war era this was not unusual. He lived in a time when older men were what was available and were regarded as a good investment, a security. The war had wiped out many young men, many romantic opportunities. We can imagine Stephen Ward as one of those carefree movie characters – Cary Grant, say, in *North By Northwest* – who get caught up in a conspiracy they know or care little about and still insist they can save the day, the girl and themselves. And, of course they do, for that's how Hollywood pens the script: that's fantasy and happy endings.

Stephen Ward had different scriptwriters: he was in a disaster movie. He drowned in a cruel tide of Establishment hysteria.

COVERING POCKET   Sir C. Cunningham

E.R.

Mr. Otton

The records of the Denning Inquiry have been held by the Lord Chancellor (with whom the Law Officers agree) to be public records and they must therefore be dealt with in accordance with Public Records Act. This means that we must first decide whether they are to be preserved or whether they fall into a category which can be destroyed. There is clearly room for argument here. On the one hand, they are the records of a major Inquiry of great public interest; on the other, they are in the main records of evidence of which a great deal was plainly unreliable and irrelevant and which in the long future could give a very distorted picture of current society.

If it is decided that the records must be preserved, the ordinary rule would mean that after 30 years they would go to the Public Record Office, and after 50 years they would be open to inspection. It is possible, however, with the Lord Chancellor's agreement, to retain them in the Department to which they belong for a longer period than 30 years, or, if they are then transferred to the Public Record Office, to prohibit their disclosure.

Arrangements are being made to continue the inter-departmental discussions, which began some time ago, of all these extremely difficult questions. In the meantime, there is, of course, no question of the records being disclosed. The decision about their treatment will eventually have to be taken by Ministers.

[signature]

29th November, 1963

Thank you.
The sooner this evidence
(given under pledge of secrecy)
is destroyed the better.

HB.
29/11

The note, signed by Henry Brooke, calling for the secret destruction of the Denning materials.

314

DOCTOR ON STAGE

'IT'S ALL BECAUSE OF OUR FUCKING SURNAME.'

Valerie Hobson, wife of Jack Profumo on an upset following
the resurrection of the scandal, 1987

Stephen Ward was a West End musical in 2014. It opened in London days before Christmas 2013, in a production hailed by Andrew Lloyd Webber as a 'revelatory tale of a travesty of justice'. The composer, whose work includes *Evita* and *Phantom of the Opera*, has taken billions of dollars at the box office and said of his latest title character: 'The police were instructed to get something on this man Ward to turn him into an apology for what went on.'

So, even more, the story that was supposed to be suppressed goes on. It always has. In his enormously influential and multimillion-selling book *Milestones*, Islamic campaigner Sayyid Qutb talks of how 'the scandal of Christine Keeler and the British minister Profumo was not considered serious to British society because of its sexual aspect', citing it as an example of the way non-Islamic societies limit morality to economic affairs while ignoring the sexual.

From East to West, millions know the list of names whom Stephen Ward knew: John Profumo spent his post-scandal life as a volunteer at Toynbee Hall, a charity in London's East End. He died, aged 91, in 2006. His wife, Valerie Hobson, who stood by him, dedicated her life to charity until her death in 1998.

Eugene Ivanov died, aged 68, in 1994. He returned to Moscow a hero but was shunted aside by the authorities and his wife, who divorced him. He spent years alone with his vodka.

Mariella Novotny, 42, choked to death on her own vomit in 1983; her death was ruled accidental but suspicion of dirty tricks remains. Hod Dibben survived her, remarried, had two children, and died in the early 1990s, aged around 88.

Colonel George Wigg died, aged 82, in 1983. He was arrested and charged with kerb-crawling for prostitutes in 1976 but claimed he was 'only trying to get an early edition of the *Daily Express'*. Wigg was found not guilty, the case against him he said was an Establishment plot.

Christine Keeler, 72 in 2014, lives quietly in London, where she writes and works for an animal charity.

Mandy Rice-Davies was 69 in 2014. Married for the third time, she acted as an adviser to Andrew Lloyd Webber's production of *Stephen Ward*.

Many say they already know the story of Stephen Ward but few do. I have talked to many who were on good and close terms with the man. He seemed to present the same personality to most. What none of them can understand is that he killed himself. Many do not believe it and think it was an accidental overdose or something far more sinister – like his trial. The tall and enjoyable Barry Stonehill, a man who has seen much of the world and most things in it, invited me to lunch at his club in Chelsea in September 2013. As we sat over coffee, he laid his palms on his knees and leaned towards me: 'I can, I truly can, see Stephen sitting here in front of me. There is no way on God's earth he would have killed himself. I knew him too well to believe that – he was murdered.' With that, he leaned back and shouted, alerting much of the room: 'He was *murdered*!'

'By whom?' I asked.

He smiled and said: 'Everyone.'

ACKNOWLEDGEMENTS

This is the only place – and page – where it pays to have debts. I have many to those generous enough to share their time and memories of Stephen Ward and the society in which he lived, thrived and died. It was invaluable to understand the background of the story in which all that happened could happen. This book is dedicated to Bobby McKew simply because it could never have existed in such detailed form without him. He talked himself into speaking of things he'd held back for half a century and more, and also convinced previously reluctant eye-witnesses to speak with me. I thank all of them who appear in the book but especially Shirley Anne Field, who took hours away from her always busy schedule, and Kim Waterfield, who has an envious recall of times, places and conversations.

I have drawn, as all must, on the work of the late Warwick Charlton, who has provided history in the form of a series of interviews with Stephen Ward, which were published in *Today* magazine in 1963. In them, it is generally a troubled Dr Ward who talks – not the gadabout and sexual cavalier who is presented by those who knew him before the events that haunted him on that hot July day at Cliveden. Noel Howard-Jones remains so enraged by the treatment of Stephen Ward that he flew from his home in Belgium to London just for the day to put the case for his friend. Afterwards, he couldn't get back to Heathrow fast enough.

The National Archives library at Kew Gardens, Richmond, was the source of thousands of documents, which revealed much – but not all – of how the Macmillan Government dealt with the errant John Profumo and the man who became the scapegoat, Dr Stephen Ward. A library, and more, of books provided further wisdom. The reporting of Fleet Street's finest and law reports helped with reportage of Stephen Ward's committal hearing and trial. Publisher John Blake and his team, especially editor Chris Mitchell, were constantly supportive. I found it fascinating while working on Stephen Ward's story to follow the 2013 debate and bedlam over freedom of the Press in Britain. It is something that must never be forsaken. The Cold War spies, the death of Buster Crabb, the elegant spy John Vassall: great efforts were made to conceal the truth about them and much more. Stephen Ward was sacrificed to save Establishment embarrassment. Yet, the truth, lurking in memories and hidden documents, will reveal itself. No matter how determined officialdom and self-interest is to lock it away.

Douglas Thompson, Suffolk, November 2013.
www.dougiethompson.com

BIBLIOGRAHY

'STEPHEN WARD WAS THE HISTORIC VICTIM
OF AN HISTORIC INJUSTICE.'

Lord Goodman, 1963

Aldrich, Richard J., *The Hidden Hand* (The Overlook Press, 2002).

Allsop, Kenneth, *The Angry Decade* (John Goodchild Publishers, 1958).

Andrew, Christopher, *The Defence of the Realm: The Authorised History of MI5* (Allen Lane, 2009).

Baker, Carlos, *Ernest Hemingway* (Scribner, 1969).

Bartlett, Donald, Steele, James B., *Empire: The Life, Legend and Madness of Howard Hughes* (Norton, 1979).

Benn, Tony, *Out of the Wilderness, Diaries, 1963–67* (Arrow Books, 1988).

Beschloss, Michael R., *Kennedy and Khrushchev, 1960–1963* (HarperCollins, 1991).

Birtley, Jack, *Freddie Mills* (New English Library, 1977).

Bloch, Michael, *The Duke of Windsor's War* (Weidenfeld & Nicolson, 1982).

Block, Alan A., *Masters of Paradise, Organized Crime and the Internal Revenue Service in The Bahamas* (Transaction, 1991).

Blond, Anthony, *Jew Made in England* (Timewell Press, 2004).

Boyle, Andrew, *The Fourth Man* (The Dial Press, 1979).

Breslin, Jimmy, *Damon Runyon* (Ticknor and Fields, 1991).

— *The Good Rat* (Mainstream, 2008).

Burke, Carolyn, *No Regrets: The Life of Edith Piaf* (Bloomsbury, 2011).

Cable Street Group, *The Battle of Cable Street 1936* (Cable Street, Whitechapel, 1995).

Cantor, Bert, *The Bernie Cornfeld Story* (Lyle Stuart, 1970).

Caro, Robert A., *Lyndon Johnson: The Passage of Power, Volume 4* (The Bodley Head, 2012).

Carter, Miranda, *Anthony Blunt* (Farrar, Straus and Giroux, 2001).

Catterall, Peter, *The Macmillan Diaries (1950–1957)*, (Macmillan, 2003).

— *The Macmillan Diaries Vol II: Prime Minister and After: 1957–1966* (Macmillan, 2011).

Charlton, Warwick, *Stephen Ward Speaks* (*Today Magazine*, 1963).

Cirules, Enrique, *The Mafia In Havana* (Ocean Press, 2004).

Clark, Alan, *Diaries* (Weidenfeld & Nicolson, 1993).

Cockburn, Alexander, St. Clair, Jeffrey, *Whiteout: The CIA, Drugs and the Press* (Verso, 1998).

Collins, Dr Martin, *Osteopathy in Britain: The First Hundred Years* (Book Surges, 2005).

Conrad, Harold, *Dear Muffo: 35 Years in the Fast Lane* (Stein and Day, 1982).

Cooper, Pamela, *A Cloud of Forgetting* (Quartet Books, 1993).

Dale Scott, Peter, *Deep Politics and the Death of JFK* (University of California Press, 1996).

— *Crime and Cover-Up: The CIA, the Mafia, and the Dallas–Watergate Connection* (Open Archive Press, 1977).

Dallek, Robert, *Nixon and Kissinger* (HarperCollins, 2007).

Davis, John H., *The Kennedy Clan, Dynasty and Disaster, 1848–1984* (Sidgwick & Jackson, 1995).

Denning, Lord, *The Denning Report* (Popular Library Edition, New York, 1963).

BIBLIOGRAPHY

Deedes, W.F., *Dear Bill* (Macmillan, 1997).

Dorril, Stephen, *Black Shirt: Sir Oswald Mosley and British Fascism* (Penguin, 2007).

Drage, Charles, *Two-Gun Cohen* (Jonathan Cape, 1954).

Edgecombe, Johnny, *Black Scandal* (Westworld International, 2002).

Edwards, Robert, *Goodbye Fleet Street* (Jonathan Cape, 1988).

Eisenberg, Dennis, Uri, Dan, Landau, Eli, *Meyer Lansky: Mogul of the Mob* (Paddington Press, 1979).

Evans, Sir Harold, *Downing Street Diary: The Macmillan Years, 1957 to 1963* (Hodder & Stoughton, 1981).

Exner, Judith Campbell, with Demaris, Ovid, *My Story* (Grove, 1977).

Fabian, Robert, *Fabian of the Yard* (The Naldrett Press Ltd., 1950).

— *After Dark* (The Naldrett Press, 1954).

Fallon, Ivan, *Billionaire: The Life and Times of Sir James Goldsmith* (Hutchinson, 1991).

Farr, Tommy, *Thus Farr* (Optomen Press, 1989).

Farrell, Nicholas, *Mussolini* (Weidenfeld & Nicolson, 2003).

Field, Shirley Anne, *A Time for Love* (Bantam Press, 1991).

Fitzgerald, F. Scott, *The Great Gatsby* (Charles Scriber's Sons, 1925).

Fleming, Ian, *Casino Royale* (Jonathan Cape, 1953).

Fox, James, *The Langhorne Sisters* (Granta Books, 1998).

Fraser-Cavassoni, Natasha, *Sam Spiegel: The Biography of a Hollywood Legend* (Little, Brown, 2003).

Freeman, Iris, *Lord Denning* (Hutchison, 1993).

Gardner, Ava, *Ava: My Story* (Bantam Books, 1990).

Gibson, Ian, *The Shameful Life of Salvador Dalí* (Faber and Faber, 1997).

Goldsmith, Lady Annabel, *Annabel: An Unconventional Life* (Weidenfeld & Nicolson, 2004).

Green, Shirley, *Rachman* (Michael Joseph, 1979).

Hayward, James, *Agent Snow: The True Story of Arthur Owens, Hitler's Chief Spy in England* (Simon & Schuster, 2013).

Hennessy, Peter, *Having it So Good: Britain in the Fifties* (Penguin Books/Allen Lane, 2006).

— *Secret State, Preparing for the Worst, 1945–2010* (Penguin Books, 2010).

Hersh, Seymour, *The Price of Power* (Summit Books, 1983).

— *The Dark Side of Camelot* (Little, Brown, 1997).

Hill, Billy, *Boss of Britain's Underworld* (The Naldrett Press, 1955).

Irving, Clive, Hall, Ton, Wallington, Jeremy, *Scandal '63* (Heinemann, 1963).

Israel, Lee, *Dorothy Kilgallen* (Delacore Press, 1979).

Ivanov, Eugene, with Sokolov, Gennady, *The Naked Spy* (John Blake, 1992).

Jameson, Derek, *Touched by Angels* (Ebury Press, 1988).

Kahn, Roger, *A Flame of Pure Fire: Jack Dempsey and the Roaring '20s* (Harcourt, 1999).

Keeler, Christine, with Thompson, Douglas, *The Truth at Last* (Sidgwick & Jackson, 2001), republished as *Secrets and Lies* (John Blake, 2012).

Kennedy, Ludovic, *The Trial of Stephen Ward* (Victor Gollancz, 1964).

Kessler, Ronald, *The Richest Man in the World: The Story of Adnan Khashoggi* (Warner Books, 1986).

Knightley, Phillip, *The Master Spy* (Alfred A. Knopf, 1989).

Knightley, Phillip, Kennedy, Caroline, *An Affair of State* (Jonathan Cape, 1987).

Khrushchev, Sergeevich, *Khrushchev Remembers* (Little, Brown, 1970).

Kynaston, David, *Austerity Britain: 1945–1951* (Bloomsbury, 2007).

— *Modernity Britain: Opening the Box, 1957–1959* (Bloomsbury, 2013).

Lacey, Robert, *Little Man* (Little, Brown, 1991).

Lamb, Richard, *The Macmillan Years (1957–1963)* (John Murray, 1995).

BIBLIOGRAPHY

Leasor, James, *Who Killed Sir Harry Oakes?* (Heinemann, 1983).

Lee, Carol Ann, *A Fine Day for A Hanging: The Real Ruth Ellis Story* (Mainstream, 2012).

Lewis, Norman, *The Honoured Society* (Eland Books, 1984).

Mackenzie, Gordon, *Marylebone: Great City North of Oxford Street* (Macmillan, 1972).

Margaret, Duchess of Argyll, *Forget Not* (W.H. Allen, 1975).

Mailer, Norman, *Oswald's Tale: An American Mystery* (Random House, 1995).

Manchester, William, *The Death of a President* (Michael Joseph, 1967).

Marks, Laurence, *Ruth Ellis: A Case of Diminished Responsibility?* (Harmondsworth: Penguin, 1990).

Mass, Peter, *The Valachi Papers* (Putnam's, 1968).

McDougal, Dennis, *The Last Mogul: Lew Wasserman, MCA, and the Hidden History of Hollywood* (Crown, 1998).

Moldea, Dan E., *Dark Victory: Ronald Reagan, MCA, and the Mob* (Viking Penguin, 1986).

Norwich, John Julius, *The Duff Cooper Diaries* (Weidenfeld & Nicolson, 2005).

Oglesby, Carl, *The JFK Assassination* (Signet Books, 1992).

Owen, Frank, *The Eddie Chapman Story* (Allan Wingate Ltd., 1953).

Owen, James, *A Serpent in Eden* (Abacus, 2005).

Philby, Kim, *My Silent War: The Autobiography of a Spy* (Arrow Books, 2003).

Piaf, Edith, Cerdan, Marcel, *Moi Pour Toi: Lettres D'Amour* (Ud-Union Distribution, 2004).

Pincher, Chapman, *Treachery, Betrayal, Blunders and Cover-Ups: Six Decades of Espionage* (Mainstream, 2011).

Profumo, David, *Bringing The House Down: A Family Memoir* (John Murray, 2006).

Qutb, Sayyid, *Milestones* (Islamic Book Service, 2001).

Raab, Selwyn, *Five Families: America's Most Powerful Mafia*

Empires (Thomas Dunne Books, St Martin's Press, 2005).

Read, Leonard, with Morton, James, *Nipper Read: The Man Who Nicked the Krays* (Futura Paperbacks, 1992).

Rees, Goronway, *A Chapter of Accidents* (Chatto and Windus, 1972).

Reid, Ed, Demaris, Ovid, *The Green Felt Jungle* (Trident Press, 1963).

Reynolds, Bruce, *The Autobiography of a Thief* (Bantam Press, 1995).

Richardson, Charlie, with Long, Bob, *My Manor* (Sidgwick & Jackson, 1991).

Rimington, Stella, *Open Secret* (Hutchinson, 2001).

Sandbrook, Dominic, *Never Had It So Good: A History of Britain from Suez to the Beatles* (Little, Brown, 2005).

— *White Heat: A History of Britain in the Swinging Sixties, 1964 to 1970* (Little, Brown, 2006).

Scott, Jeremy, *Fast and Louche* (Profile Books, 2002).

Sebag Montefiore, Simon, *Stalin: The Court of the Red Tsar* (Weidenfeld & Nicolson, 2003).

Shellard, Dominic, *British Theatre Since the War* (Yale University Press, 1999).

Sherry, Norman, *The Life of Graham Greene, Volume Two: 1939–1955* (Random House, 1994).

Stanford, Peter, *Bronwen Astor: Her Life and Times* (HarperCollins, 1999).

— *Suez to the Beatles* (Little, Brown, 2005).

Summers, Anthony, *The Kennedy Conspiracy* (Warner Books, 1992).

— and Dorril, Stephen, *Honeytrap* (Coronet, 1988).

— *The Arrogance of Power: The Secret World of Richard Nixon* (Phoenix Press, 2001).

— and Swan, Robyn, *Sinatra: The Life* (Corgi, 2006).

Sutherland, Alasdair Scott, *The Spaghetti Tree: Mario and Franco and the Trattoria Revolution* (Foreword by Len Deighton) (Primavera Books, 2009).

BIBLIOGRAPHY

Tate, Barbara, *West End Girls* (Orion Books, 2010).

Thomas, Donald, *An Underworld At War* (John Murray, 2003).

— *Villains' Paradise: Britain's Underworld from the Spivs to the Krays* (John Murray, 2005).

Thompson, Douglas, *The Hustlers* (Sidgwick & Jackson, 2007).

Tosches, Nick, *The Devil and Sonny Liston* (Little, Brown, 2000).

— *Dino: Living High in the Dirty Business of Dreams* (Doubleday, 1992).

Turkus, Burton B., Feder, Sid, *Murder Inc.* (Da Capo Press, 1992; reproduction of 1951 edition).

United States Treasury Department, *Mafia: The Government's Secret File on Organized Crime* (2007).

Unsworth, Cathi, *Bad Penny Blues* (Serpent's Tail, 2009).

Vaill, Amanda, *Everybody Was So Young* (Little, Brown, 1998).

Van den Bergh, Tony, *Who Killed Freddie Mills?* (Penguin, 1991).

Von Tunzelmann, Alex, *Red Heat: Conspiracy, Murder and the Cold War in the Caribbean* (Simon & Schuster, 2011).

Waldron, Lamar, with Thom Hartmann, *Legacy and Secrecy: The Long Shadow of the JFK Assassination* (Counterpoint, 2008).

— with Thom Hartmann, *Ultimate Sacrifice: John and Robert Kennedy, The Plan for a Coup in Cuba and the Murder of JFK* (Constable, 2005).

Webb, Duncan, *Crime Reporter* (Fleetway Colourbacks, 1963).

Weiner, Tim, *Legacy of Ashes: The History of the CIA* (Penguin, 2007).

West, Nigel, *A Matter of Trust, MI5: 1945–1972* (Weidenfeld & Nicolson, 1982).

West, Rebecca, *The Meaning of Treason* (Virago, 1982; *Esquire Magazine*, 1963).

Wilson, Derek, *Rothschild: A Story of Wealth and Power* (Mandarin, 1994).

Wilson, Harold, *The Labour Government 1964–1970: A Personal Record* (Weidenfeld & Nicolson and Michael Joseph, 1971).

Wright, Peter, *Spycatcher* (Viking Penguin, 1987).

Young, Wayland, *The Profumo Affair: Aspects of Conservatism* (Penguin, 1963).

Ziegler, Philip, *King Edward VIII* (Collins, 1990).— *Wilson: The Authorised Life* (HarperCollins, 1995).

INDEX

INDEX

INDEX

INDEX

INDEX

HIM